An Uncommon Love

The Early Life of Sudha and Narayana Murthy

Chitra Banerjee Divakaruni

JUGGERNAUT BOOKS
C-I-128, First Floor, Sangam Vihar, Near Holi Chowk,
New Delhi 110080, India

First published by Juggernaut Books 2023

Copyright © Chitra Banerjee Divakaruni 2023

10 9 8 7 6 5 4 3 2 1

P-ISBN: 9789353456443
E-ISBN: 9789353457686

The views and opinions expressed in this book are the author's own. The facts contained herein were reported to be true as on the date of publication by the author to the publishers of the book, and the publishers are not in any way liable for their accuracy or veracity.

All rights reserved. No part of this publication may be reproduced, transmitted, or stored in a retrieval system in any form or by any means without the written permission of the publisher.

Typeset in Adobe Caslon Pro by R. Ajith Kumar, Noida

Printed at Manipal Technologies Limited, Manipal

Character is destiny.

> *– Heraclitus*

And ninety-nine are with dreams content,
　　But the hope of a world made new
Is the hundredth man who is grimly bent
　　On making the dream come true.

> *– Ted Olson, 'Dreamer and Doer'*

Contents

Part 1: Dreaming the Same Dreams	1
Part 2: 'I'll Be Your Safety Net'	175
Part 3: Service and Joy	269
Epilogue	331
A Note on Infosys	340
A Note on Narayana Murthy	341
A Note on Sudha Murty	342
A Note on the Infosys Foundation	343
Author's Note	344

Part 1

Dreaming the Same Dreams

Part 1

Dreaming the Same Dreams

1

On a pleasant October evening in 1974, a slender young woman hurried along a narrow residential street in Pune, her short, bobbed hair curling around her vivacious face. Though she usually favoured light cotton saris in the office, or jeans and T-shirts when not at work, today for some reason – she was not sure why – she had chosen to dress more formally and was wearing a khadi sari in white, her favourite colour. She was headed for the flat of her co-worker Prasanna, a young man with whom she had become friends because they rode the TELCO (Tata Engineering and Locomotive Company) bus together to work each day and because they both came from Karnataka.

This, she recognized, was an unusual excursion for her. She felt a tiny shiver along her spine: a frisson of anticipation and excitement.

The young woman liked Prasanna because, like her, he was a voracious reader. Each day on the bus, he would have a different book with him. She would glance over at what he was reading and feel pleasantly surprised because usually it was something she had read already, like *The Discovery of India* or *My Experiments with Truth*. Sometimes they would talk about the book and she would dive in eagerly into their discussion with forthright opinions. But recently Prasanna had surprised her. He had been engrossed in a writer she had never heard of: George Mikes. The titles of Mikes's books were unusual, too: *How to Be an Alien*, *How to Tango: A Solo across South America* and *How to Unite Nations*. And on the flyleaf of each book was written, with a confident flourish, a name and a place. The places were unexpected, exotic: Paris, Rome, Munich, Istanbul and Kabul.

The young woman couldn't resist asking, 'How is it you have all these books? And who is this man, anyway? A global bus conductor?'

Prasanna had laughed. 'He's my friend – and now my flatmate. I stay in the front room of a flat he shares with a colleague called Shashi Sharma and his parents. He has certainly travelled to many countries and had many adventures! Why don't you come over sometime and meet him? He's a most interesting man, full of stories. Also, he's a Kannadiga like us. You'll love his collection of books. They've taken over most of our living room. In fact, I'd say that books are the only things he cares to own.'

The woman had hesitated. She had never visited a male friend in his flat. As the first woman employed by TELCO, living alone in a city far from her more traditional home town of Hubli, she knew there were many eyes on her. Thus, she was ultra-careful about her behaviour, about establishing boundaries. When she went on a company business trip with male colleagues and was required to share a company guest house, she kept strictly to herself. When she went out with male friends for dinner, she made sure to pay for herself so there would be no confusion about their relationship. 'Paying my share allows me to keep them at the right distance,' she explained to her women friends.

But this time, on the verge of saying no, she hesitated. It was too tempting, the thought of an entire room filled with exotic foreign writers she had not read and might never come across elsewhere, shelves and shelves of books she could perhaps borrow. And the owner of the books – she admitted to herself that she was quite curious about him. What would he look like? In her mind, she imagined this intrepid world traveller to be suave and debonair, tall and broad-shouldered. Maybe, she thought, because she loved Hindi movies, he would look like Rajesh Khanna, sporting sideburns and boots.

'All right,' she had finally said. 'I'll stop by tomorrow, just for a little while.'

When she walked into Prasanna's flat, though, she was surprised by the man her co-worker introduced her to. He was thin and slight, with thick glasses and a small scar on his forehead – a far cry from a movie star. He had on a checked coat that was nothing like the fashionable leather jackets the heroes of Hindi movies favoured. He was quiet – almost shy, she thought – until they started discussing books. Then he shed his reticence and sparkled with intelligence and an eloquence that startled her. She discovered that they shared a passion for Kannada writers: Kuvempu, Shivarama Karanth, Triveni and S.L. Bhyrappa. But more exciting was the fact that his bookshelves – as crowded as she had imagined – sported many new and fascinating writers. There were also more books by Mikes. She read out the titles excitedly: *Little Cabbages*, *The Prophet Motive*, *The Land of the Rising Yen*, *How to Scrape Skies* and *Shakespeare and Myself*.

'It's *Meekesh*,' he said gently, correcting her pronunciation of the Hungarian writer's name.

While the young woman could be prickly when told she was wrong, she found that, for some strange reason, this time she did not mind. Her visit stretched longer than she had intended as she listened to him talk about his favourite writers and describe how he had discovered them while living in Europe. At the end of the evening, before she could ask, he offered to loan her as many books as she wanted. He filled a shopping bag – the simple kind a housewife might take to the market to buy vegetables – with the volumes she chose.

At the door, as she was about to say goodbye, he took a deep breath. 'May I invite you to have dinner with me tomorrow night – maybe at a restaurant?'

It was not her habit to go somewhere with a man she had just met. But to her surprise, she heard herself agreeing. Was it because their conversation, at once frank and deep, had made her feel she knew this man better than she did most of her colleagues, even people she had worked with for months? Was it the way his eyes shone with intelligence behind his glasses? She pulled herself together and said, 'But Prasanna must come with us, too.' In a stern voice, she added, 'And I will pay for my dinner.' She chose the venue: Poona Coffee House, which was inexpensive and unpretentious and served tasty meals and was therefore popular with young people. It was the kind of restaurant where one went with friendship – not romance – in mind.

He agreed to everything, bowing gallantly – like a Parisian might, she thought. Later, he would say, 'Do you know, you lit up the room when you walked into our flat. I'd travelled all over the world, but I'd never met a woman so fully interested in life. I couldn't stop thinking about you after you left.'

The next night, he showed up outside Poona Coffee House half an hour early. Despite what she had said, he tried to pay for her dinner. But she found herself unable to get angry with him. She could already tell that he wasn't like other men, who might presume there might be a romance brewing if they bought dinner for a woman. There was a straightforwardness in him that, as a straightforward woman herself, resonated with her.

That is how Sudha Kulkarni, twenty-four, and Narayana Murthy, twenty-eight, began a relationship that would open the doors of aspiration for many young people who came from similar middle-class backgrounds and ultimately change the face of entrepreneurship and philanthropy in India.

———

In a little while, Prasanna, having completed his training at TELCO, moved to Mumbai with a new job. Murthy, in the meantime, was spending most of his free time with Sudha and was barely in the flat. It was a convivial set-up: Shashi was a friendly young man who played tennis, rode a motorbike and listened to lively music on his turntable. Murthy worked with him at a think tank called Systems Research Institute (SRI), set up by his mentor, Professor Krishnayya from the Indian Institute of Management Ahmedabad (IIMA). The two had almost nothing in common though they became good friends, and before meeting Sudha, Murthy would often share his meals with him and his family. While Sudha and Murthy had common friends, most evenings it was just the two of them. They discovered, to their delight, that they had many similarities. They both loved eating out, and they preferred the same kind of restaurant – the inexpensive, unpretentious cafes favoured by university students and TELCO trainees where one could order a rice plate for Rs 2.50, such as Vaishali, Rupali, Darshan, Cafe Good Luck, and of course, Poona Coffee House, for which they had a special soft spot. They agreed that enjoyment depends on attitude and not the amount of money one spends.

Murthy would hurry up and finish his work so he could meet Sudha as she got off the TELCO bus. They would then walk over to Darshan, a fruit juice joint, where the waiters – many of them students – were friendly and easy-going and let them hang around for as long as they liked, even after they finished their drinks: always a queen-sized orange juice for Sudha and a king-sized banana milkshake for Murthy. Later they would have dinner at a simple eatery. On special occasions such as a birthday, they walked all the way to the cantonment, to one of their favoured restaurants, Chung Fa, because they both loved Chinese food. They would order fried rice and spring rolls for Rs 9, sit at a rickety wooden table in a corner and spend the evening vigorously debating various issues.

They were both well read and interested in world events; they both held strong opinions and were not shy about voicing them. Sometimes, they would get into good-natured arguments.

One night, Murthy, a staunch socialist who had been influenced as a teenager by his father's ideas as well as Jawaharlal Nehru's open admiration of the USSR, announced, 'Russian is the language of the future. That's why I've been studying Russian and collecting Russian books for the last two years.'

Sudha shook her head determinedly. 'I'm positive that English is going to remain the language of the world. That's why I make it a point to read as many English books as I can, even though I went to a Kannada-medium school and enjoy reading Kannada more.'

Murthy stubbornly held on to his Russian books even after he changed his life philosophy to compassionate capitalism. After their marriage, it would take Sudha many years of cajoling before he would allow her to dispose of them!

When Murthy waxed eloquent about the rights of the common labourer, she held fast to her own opinion. 'You're speaking theoretically. You'd think differently if you were on a factory floor like me, forced to deal with the difficulty of getting workers to negotiate collectively.'

Though they argued vociferously, they were willing to listen to each other's point of view. Neither of them convinced the other, but perhaps that was never their intention!

In their more traditional native state of Karnataka, such meetings would not have been possible for Sudha and Murthy. Luckily, Pune in the mid-1970s was a progressive and cosmopolitan city. A large percentage of its young workers had come from other states and even from other countries such as Mauritius, Iran and different areas of Africa, and mingled freely with each other. Having lived in France and travelled across Europe, Murthy was already comfortable with conversing with the opposite sex, and Sudha had, for a long time, been used to talking to her male classmates. All these circumstances smiled upon the young Sudha and Murthy, allowing them to hold intellectual conversations, appreciate each other's unique philosophies, become friends – and eventually fall in love.

On some evenings, Murthy and Sudha were joined by friends. Vinay Kaul, a tall and lanky young man who had been a TELCO trainee at the same time as Sudha, was close to them both. One day, he told Murthy why he had chosen to make friends with Sudha. He had noticed her from the first, as she was the only woman on the shop floor, and he – like most of the other men – had heard the amazing story of how she had been hired. He knew her to be efficient and polite, but she maintained her distance, so he had done the same thing, interpreting her caution as standoffishness. Then he witnessed something that made him realize how wrong he had been.

Vinay told Murthy, 'Around this time, TELCO had hired several blind people to do some simple jobs at the plant. One day, one of the women had grown confused while leaving the plant. She was wandering across the shop floor in the wrong direction and was about to bump into some machines. No one was paying much attention to this, but Sudha noticed. She interrupted her own work and ran over to the woman before a supervisor could shout at her. She took the woman by the hand and guided her all the way to her bus. Along the way, she chatted casually with the woman to make her feel comfortable.

'I was really impressed by Sudha's kindness. She was so busy, but still she took the time to help someone who could never do anything for her in return. So I made a special effort to get to know this unusual woman!'

The two of them soon became fast friends, and Sudha even adopted Vinay as her brother, laughingly insisting on collecting a gift from him each time after tying his rakhi. This friendship turned out to be a very good thing, as Vinay would come to her aid in a moment of difficulty, when her relationship with Murthy was in jeopardy.

Vinay's parents, who lived in the area, were very kind and hospitable, and Sudha and Murthy spent many enjoyable evenings in their home. The relaxed home environment was the perfect place to spend time together and learn more about one another. Sudha discovered that Murthy was an excellent debater and a deep thinker, committed to the altruistic ideals of socialism. Though polite and reticent by nature, when it came to discussing the finer points of socialism, Murthy could get quite passionate. He would often have heated arguments with Vinay's father, who shared some – but not all – of Murthy's convictions. Vinay, too, jumped into these discussions. At one time, the two young men seriously discussed formally joining the Communist Party together, which caused Sudha significant concern. Fortunately for her, this never happened.

While Sudha was more interested in humour, fiction and human drama, Murthy was particularly fond of books with political or philosophical themes. But occasionally their tastes would converge, as they had done with George Mikes. Vinay once gifted Murthy a book that they both liked a great deal – *Chance and Necessity* by the Nobel Prize winner Jacques Monod which argued that life was the result of 'pure chance'. Inside the book, Vinay inscribed a line that Sudha would later recognize as surprisingly prophetic: 'To one who leaves nothing to chance.'

Murthy, on the other hand, observed how emotionally intelligent and empathetic Sudha was. She asked Mr and Mrs Kaul many incisive questions about their family's history and the home they had left behind in Kashmir. Her lighter side appealed to him as well. She loved to sing and tell jokes, dissolving into laughter herself as she got to the punchline. She soon grew close to Vinay's mother and sister, and Murthy suspected that Sudha's bubbly charm was the real reason they were invited to the Kaul residence so often to enjoy the lavish dinners cooked by Mrs Kaul and to stay over at night. Both Sudha and Murthy were easy, informal guests, happy to sleep in makeshift beds on the floor, Murthy in Vinay's room, and Sudha with Vinay's sister.

One of Sudha's best-loved activities was going to the movies. Soon after they met, she admitted to Murthy unashamedly, 'I'm a "first day, first show" kind of girl.' Once she made a bet with the women in Mahila Niwas, the ladies' hostel where she stayed, that she would watch a different movie each day for 365 days.

'If you can really do that,' her friends said, 'we'll give you Rs 100 and the title of Miss Cinema.'

'Done!' said Sudha, who was never afraid to take on a challenge. She became a regular at all the Pune theatres, such as Nilayam, Natraj, Lakshmi-Narayan and Deccan. She did not discriminate between Hindi, Marathi, Kannada and English films. Where cinema was concerned, she was an omnivore! By the end of the year, she had won the bet and had become an expert commentator on all kinds of movies. Her friends applauded her and cheerfully handed over her prize.

Murthy liked movies, too, but money for entertainment had been in short supply during his childhood and teenage years. He saw only a few movies, mostly when he went to visit his favourite uncle, Kittu Mava, in Sidlaghatta, a small town in Karnataka.

'But there is one movie experience that happened when I was around sixteen years old,' he told Sudha. 'And it has stayed with me all my life! We were living in Mysore at that time. I was in the first year of my engineering studies. One day my closest friend, B.N. Murali, came to me and said, "Alfred Hitchcock's *Psycho* is showing at Gayatri Talkies. Our group of friends is planning to go, and I want you to come, too." I said I would join them, but then a family responsibility came up and I couldn't do it. After seeing the movie, Murali could not stop talking about what an amazing film it was, a once-in-a-lifetime experience. He kept urging me to go and see it before it left the theatres. Finally, I promised him, but due to circumstances I could not manage it. After some time, Murali stopped asking me if I had seen the movie.

'Finally, the theatre announced it was the last day for *Psycho*. It struck me that if I didn't go to see it that day, I would have broken my promise. The cheapest tickets were for the night show, so I decided to go at that time. I figured I would be able to get a ticket easily as most people in our area, being working folks, did not like going to the movies so late.

'I was certainly right about that! When I entered the movie hall, I found that I was the only person there! That made this terrifying movie even scarier. I closed my eyes during all the frightening scenes, and I put my fingers in my ear, but that made things worse because I kept imagining that someone was creeping up behind me. I wanted to walk out, but I had promised Murali I would watch the movie.

'At long last, the movie got over. I've never been happier to see credits rolling on the screen! I rushed out and started on my way home. It was around 12.30 a.m., and the road was completely empty. The night was foggy, which I thought was eerie and unnatural, though perhaps it was just that I was never outside at such a late hour. I was certain I heard footsteps following me. When I hurried up, those footsteps seemed to hurry up, too! In spite of the cool weather, I broke out in a sweat. I was so thankful when I finally reached home and stumbled into our courtyard. The lights had been turned off to save electricity, and I knocked on the door for a long time before one of my brothers heard me and let me in. I went straight to bed and, even though I shared the room with my brothers, for the next several nights I covered myself head to toe when I slept. I don't know why I thought that would protect me!'

Murthy laughed, recollecting his youthful folly, and Sudha laughed with him.

Murthy and Sudha spent many evenings watching the latest releases together. Amitabh Bachchan and Jaya Bhaduri were two of her favourite actors. And of course, she had a soft spot for the dreamy-eyed Rajesh Khanna. But she enjoyed older movies, too, starring Dilip Kumar, Guru Dutt, Madhubala and Vyjayanthimala. Murthy, who went to the movies mostly so that he could spend more time in her company, was quite happy to let Sudha choose the films they would see. In the cinema hall, he spent as much time watching emotions flit across Sudha's expressive face as he did observing the actors. He was impressed that Sudha could learn a movie song after hearing it only once or twice, and he loved it whenever she sang a current hit for him.

Murthy and Sudha's preferred time to go to the movies was late at night. The last show was when Natraj Theatre was the least crowded, so they did not have to put up with smart-aleck comments or whistles and catcalls during the more romantic scenes. There was just one problem. Mahila Niwas had a strict 10 p.m. curfew, after which a guard manned the gate. So as soon as the show was over, the two of them would have to rush back to the hostel, often being forced to hire an autorickshaw even though it was not too far away.

One night, though, despite all their efforts, they arrived too late. A guard stood at attention at the gate, which was pulled shut. Sudha's heart sank. She knew that, if she asked him to let her in, he would write down her name and she would get in trouble with the management.

It was the very proper and law-abiding Murthy who came up with a plan to save her. They hurried to the side street that bordered the building, where Sudha counted the windows and figured out which one belonged to one of her good friends. She and Murthy lobbed pebbles over the wall at the window until her friend, waking, peered out to see what was going on. When Sudha explained her situation, whispering so that the guard would not hear her, her friend agreed to help. She went to the doorway of the hostel and called to the guard, telling him she had heard some strange noises in the back of the building.

Once the man left his post to investigate, Sudha slipped in through the gate. It was quite the adventure, and she and her friends had a good laugh over it the next day.

Despite her best efforts, Sudha continued to miss curfew once in a while. But thanks to Murthy, she now had a strategy. And it worked every time.

While Murthy was willing to bend some rules for Sudha's sake, where his deeper values were concerned, he refused to budge, no matter what the cost. This became clear when he accompanied his employer and mentor, Krishnayya, on a business trip to Kolkata around this time.

After the all-day meetings, the clients invited them to a business dinner at a restaurant located in a five-star hotel. Murthy was very hungry and looking forward to a good meal, but as they arrived at the hotel, he noticed several beggars on the pavement. Emaciated and clad in rags, they stretched their palms towards him. In addition to his socialist leanings, Murthy had been brought up by a mother who believed in sharing what little she had with the poor. Deeply pained by their condition, he gave them some money, but he still felt uncomfortable. He told the clients, 'I'm sorry, I cannot eat at such a lavish and expensive place while people are starving just outside its doors.'

This statement caused considerable awkwardness with the clients as they had made a special effort to plan a celebratory dinner for their out-of-town guests. They, along with Krishnayya, tried to change Murthy's mind, but he was adamant and refused to enter the restaurant. It was an embarrassing situation for Krishnayya as he tried to mediate between his clients and his headstrong mentee. He was also concerned because Murthy's extreme idealism could have jeopardized their deal. Ultimately, Murthy went without food that night.

On their way back by train from Kolkata, another such incident occurred. Murthy saw an old woman sitting uncomfortably on the edge of a bench at night. He gave her his own reserved berth to sleep in and spent the night perched on the bench.

Krishnayya admired Murthy's principles, but he felt obliged to point out that going to such extremes to follow them would lead to a lot of difficulties in his young protégé's life. Murthy listened politely, but Krishnayya could see that he was not going to change his mind!

When Murthy told Sudha what he had done, though, her eyes shone with admiration and empathy, and she told him he had done the right thing. She, too, could be obstinate when it came to her principles. She, too, believed in generosity and helping the less fortunate, and was willing to put up with discomfort and disagreements if necessary for this. Both Sudha and Murthy were profoundly idealistic young people, deeply influenced by their parents and their values. It's often the case that such people are drawn to each other, each finding a mirror in the other. In this way, the bond between these two began to strengthen.

As they got more comfortable, Sudha and Murthy began to slowly share their pasts with each other. They spoke frankly about the family members who had taught them important values, and the challenging – even painful – events that had shaped their characters. Especially in Murthy's case, some of these incidents were hurtful secrets that he had held inside for many years.

Sudha loved telling Murthy about her grandparents on both sides. As a girl, she spent many of her vacations with her mother's parents in the village of Shiggaon in north Karnataka. She loved the rural environment. To a city girl, it was quite exotic, with its thatched huts, groves of coconut trees, ponds where people bathed and washed clothes, and numerous farm animals that she could see up close. But most of all she enjoyed spending time with her grandfather, H.R. Kadim Diwan, whom she greatly admired. He was a teacher – as was her mother before she got married – and Sudha noticed that, even after his retirement, he was shown a great deal of respect by the entire village. People often stopped by his home to ask his opinion on village matters.

Sudha's love for books was nurtured by her grandfather. Not only would he usually be found with a book in his hand, but he would also take her every evening to their little village library. Soon Sudha, a rapid reader, had finished reading all the books there.

One day she told her grandfather, 'I want you to take me to another village.'

'Why?' her grandfather asked. 'Is there someone you want to meet or something you want to see?'

'No,' Sudha said. 'I want to get some new books from a different library.'

Impressed by her enthusiasm, her grandfather agreed. As grandfather and granddaughter went on their expedition, hunting for new books for the bright, curious young girl, Kadim Diwan said, 'If life is good to you, Sudha, and if you have more money than you need when you grow up, promise me that you will buy books for at least one library.'

Sudha heard the deep emotion in her grandfather's voice. 'I will,' she said solemnly. She never forgot that promise.

'Let me tell you a story,' Sudha said one day to Murthy, 'a story about rice.'

In her grandparents' home in the village, there were two granaries. The one in the front of the house was used for storing the more expensive white rice; the one in the back stored thick red rice, considered to be of lower quality. The doors to the granaries were small, making it difficult for adults to bend and enter, so if beggars or holy men came by, singing songs and asking for alms, Sudha would be dispatched to fill a bucket with rice from the granary in front. She was instructed to give the mendicants as much white rice as they needed. But at night, when her grandmother cooked for the family, Sudha would be told to go to the granary in the back and fetch red rice for the family's needs. This was a mystery to young Sudha, who never understood why they had to eat the less tasty red rice while the better-quality rice was given away as alms.

Being a curious and outspoken girl, one day she asked her grandparents, 'Why do we always eat the red rice that is not so good and give the white rice to the poor?'

Unlike elders in many traditional families, her grandparents encouraged Sudha to think for herself. So they took her question seriously. Her maternal grandmother, Krishna, whom Sudha fondly called Avva – mother – said, 'When we give something to others, we should always give the best. God is not in temples or churches or mosques. He's with the people. If you serve them, you serve God.'

Her grandfather quoted a verse from an Upanishad and added, 'Our scriptures teach us to donate with kind words, happiness and sincerity. Donate without expectations because it is a duty. And always donate without caring about caste, creed or religion.'

As she ate her dinner of red rice, Sudha pondered what her grandparents had said. Their words stayed with her and began to shape her character in important ways.

The story from Sudha's childhood that Murthy found most touching involved her maternal grandmother, Avva. Avva was an extremely intelligent woman. Though never formally educated, she was able to mentally calculate the answers to complex mathematical problems. For instance, one day the children's mathematics teacher was quizzing them on their understanding of algebra. He asked, 'A gambler goes out of his house with Rs x. He goes to the first gambling den, loses half his money, doubles it at the second and loses one-third at the third place. How much is he left with now?' Avva astonished them all by calling out the right answer from the kitchen, stating that the gambler had returned with two-thirds of the original amount! She also had an amazing memory. She could recall, in perfect detail, what people wore for a certain wedding years ago. Sudha would inherit this ability to remember details.

Avva loved stories, just as Sudha did, and one of their treasured activities was reading together the serialized Kannada novels of Triveni (a popular contemporary writer), which appeared in the Kannada weekly magazine *Karmaveera*. Rather, Sudha would read, and her grandmother, who was illiterate, would listen avidly. They were in the middle of reading the novel *Kashi Yatre* when Sudha went away for a few days to attend a wedding.

When she returned, she found Avva in tears. When the distressed Sudha asked her what the matter was, Avva said that the new issue of the magazine had arrived, but she hadn't been able to read it even though she longed to learn how the characters in *Kashi Yatre* were faring.

'You have no idea how stupid and dependent it made me feel,' she told Sudha. 'When I was young, I wanted to go to school, but no one thought that it was important to give me an education. They used to laugh at me – or they would get annoyed. "You're a girl," they would say. "Your job is to have children and take care of your family – there is no need to fill your head with big ideas."'

Her grandmother's sorrow lodged deep in the twelve-year-old Sudha's heart. Until then, she had taken her education for granted and even complained about studies. Now she realized how privileged she was. She made herself a promise: she would teach her sixty-two-year-old grandmother to read, no matter how hard it might be. They struggled at it, sitting together and practising every day during Sudha's vacations.

By the time of the Dussehra festival, her grandmother had achieved her goal! On Saraswati Puja day, she surprised Sudha by touching her granddaughter's feet, showing respect to her as her teacher. Sudha in turn gifted her with a copy of the just-published novel, *Kashi Yatre*, and when her grandmother read the title and the publisher's name aloud, Sudha felt a unique thrill go through her: the thrill of transforming someone's life through teaching.

'But the grandparent who had the deepest influence on me,' Sudha told Murthy, 'was my paternal grandmother, Amba, whom I called Ajji. Ajji was widowed early in life. She looked like any other traditional widow of the time, with a white sari that covered her shaven head. I will always remember the sadness in her voice when she told me what had happened to her once her husband died. "No one asked my permission before chopping off all my beautiful hair." Until then, I'd never thought about the sad plight of widows. Ajji opened my eyes to that – and to many other things.'

Ajji's spirit was undaunted by the hand fate had dealt her. She decided to become a midwife, taught herself the necessary skills, and delivered over a hundred babies. She helped women of all castes and religions. She never turned down someone who needed her help; whether they were rich or poor did not matter to her. Day or night, she was ready to respond to whoever came knocking at her door.

Endowed with practical intelligence, Ajji had developed a series of processes to ensure the safety and success of her 'patients'. People could not visit the mother unless they were healthy and freshly bathed. Everything that came in contact with the mother was cleaned with turmeric. She made the new mother drink water that had been boiled with an iron rod in it to replace iron lost through bleeding.

Ajji treated the entire childbirth process as normal and discussed it frankly with her granddaughters. Sudha even accompanied her to a midnight delivery once – an adventure that left a deep mark on her. It was no coincidence that both Sudha's father, Dr R.H. Kulkarni, and her elder sister Sunanda decided to become gynaecologists. When Sudha herself opted for engineering, a field of study that was considered inappropriate for women, she remembered what Ajii had demonstrated through her lifestyle and stood firm against all the relatives who tried to change her mind.

Ajji also said to Sudha, 'A woman can do a man's job. But a man cannot do a woman's job.' It was a statement that Sudha would think of at a crucial moment in her life.

The values that Ajji stood for and her out-of-the-box thinking were to have a strong influence on Sudha. Her grandmother was a rebel disguised as a traditionalist – a canny strategy that Sudha recognized as very effective. She herself would employ it at the right time in her life.

Sudha's upbringing was quite exceptional for a young Indian woman of that time because she was given the freedom to read what she liked, to go outside the house just like her brother Shrinivas, and to travel alone in buses when she was as young as eight years old. Later, when she decided to cut her hair short and wear pants, no one stopped her. Her father discussed menstruation – considered an 'unclean state' in conservative families – frankly and openly with her and her sisters when it was the right time, pointing out that it was just a biological condition and nothing to be ashamed of. As a result, from a young age, Sudha developed confidence, a strong will, and an ability to think analytically and independently. She was also very courageous. One foggy morning, when she was walking to school by herself, a man tried to snatch her gold earrings. Instead of being afraid, Sudha yelled fiercely, berating him, and smacked him hard with her umbrella. The startled thief ran away as fast as he could.

Murthy, thinking about how strictly his own sisters had been brought up with the dual 'virtues' of obedience and docility, and with a suitable marriage as their only goal, said to Sudha, 'Do you realize how lucky you are to come from a family where you were never held back because you were a girl? Where you were actually encouraged to study and to stand up for yourself?'

'I do,' Sudha said, suddenly serious. 'It was a true gift. That's why I must make the most of it.'

Growing up, Sudha had a close relationship with her siblings, and they rarely quarrelled. She looked up to her older sister Sunanda. While her younger siblings, Jaishree and Shrinivas, were enrolled in an English-medium school after the family moved to Hubli, Sunanda and Sudha went to a Kannada-medium school in Hubli because that was what they were used to.

But from a fairly young age, Sudha sensed the importance of learning English. Every weekend, she would go to the public library with her brother Shri, who was her favourite sibling. Sudha and Shri shared a deep passion for reading. They would pack their lunches and spend the whole day at the library, reading books in English. Often, Sudha would ask Shri, who was very bright and precocious for his age, the meanings of English words she did not know, and he would tell her. How dearly she loved him was clear from early in her life when, as a four-year-old, he cut up her dolls with a pair of illicit scissors he had procured from somewhere. Anyone else would have thrown a fit – and perhaps beaten him up. But Sudha, though upset, ultimately forgave him and even protected him from the anger of their parents.

Sudha was not particularly skilled – or interested in – 'girlish' pastimes. While Sunanda and Jaishree occupied themselves with embroidery, knitting and artwork, she would want to play outside or read. But when it was necessary, she rose to the occasion. When Sunanda went off to college, Sudha took over the daily task of braiding Jaishree's hair before school. She was not particularly good at this – and Jaishree was quite fussy – so Sudha often had to redo her braids. But she was always patient with her younger sister. They grew particularly close because after Sunanda left for college the two shared a room. When Jaishree was about to depart for Canada after her marriage, Sudha gave her a pillow that she had slowly and painstakingly embroidered with her sister's name. Jaishree loved this pillow, and she would often hug it during the freezing Canadian winters when she was homesick.

⸻

Not all of Sudha's childhood escapades were admirable, but she enjoyed sharing even these misadventures with Murthy because she loved to make him laugh. One of these occurred when she was eight years old. One fine morning, Sudha told her mother, Vimala, who had been a schoolteacher, that she was done with education. 'I don't want to go to school any more,' she explained. 'I can read, write, multiply and divide. That is enough for life.'

This was a shock to her mother. She had never come across something like this in her family. Aghast, she asked Sudha what she would do instead.

'I'll read the newspaper in the morning,' Sudha said. 'And in the afternoon, I'll read magazines and library books.' At first, her mother thought it was just a passing phase, but it turned out that Sudha was serious about this. No one could get her to go to school. She was spanked for her stubbornness, and when that didn't work, her mother turned to the elders in the family to talk some sense into her. Her grandmother pleaded with her to at least study until she graduated from school, but Sudha refused. Other relatives said, 'Somehow get her through Class 10. This girl is clearly lazy and not too bright. You had better get her married off as soon as you can.'

None of this had any effect on Sudha. In the following weeks, she would get up in the morning, have breakfast with her siblings, and see them off to school before settling down to read magazines like *Chandamama*. Her mother was so furious that she refused to speak to her. But soon, Sudha herself got bored. She discovered the *Chandamama* stories were repetitive, regurgitating the same plots and jokes. She missed her friends and siblings. Most of all, she missed the intellectual stimulation of school, trying to answer the teachers' questions, learning new things. After two months, she announced she was ready to return to school. From then on, she dived hungrily into her studies and loved every subject she came across.

Murthy was both amused and amazed by this story. In his home, he told Sudha, such stubbornness would have resulted in severe punishments from his father. In fact, neither his siblings nor he had ever dared to stand up against their father, even if he insisted on something that was not right.

'What an exceptional upbringing you had!' he said to Sudha.

Murthy's family background was similar to Sudha's in several ways. They were both Kannadigas; they were middle children; and they came from families that valued education highly. Like Sudha's grandfather, Murthy's father was a schoolteacher – and later, an inspector of government schools. However, the atmosphere and culture of his home life couldn't have been more different. Money was often short in Murthy's household, and his father was a very strict man. He had to work very hard to take care of a large family, on a government teaching job, and was not as close to his children as he would have liked. He focused instead on teaching them about literature (introducing them to Shakespeare and Wordsworth), politics and Western classical music. He was an admired teacher, extremely good in English, mathematics and physics, and often rated as the best in these subjects in his school. His children, including Murthy, respected him deeply and were in awe of him, although they were somewhat distant from him.

Sudha's father, Dr R.H. Kulkarni, was an affectionate, even indulgent parent, willing to discuss all her important life decisions with her. She idolized him and, at the same time, thought of him as her dearest friend, someone in whom she could confide. Murthy's father, Rama Rao, in contrast, was a reserved man who had faced many disappointments in his life. Though he had received a scholarship to study abroad, his mother, who was very traditional and believed that crossing the ocean (the kala pani) would make him lose his religion, had refused to allow him to go. Despite the fact that he had never visited London, he could draw a map of the city and explain to his children where the Houses of Parliament and the Imperial College (to which he had been admitted to) were. Rama Rao finally took up a teaching job and later became an inspector of schools, but he always felt that life had been unfair to him. These feelings were compounded by the fact that his first wife had died, leaving him with children to look after. This shaped his personality: he was strict yet affectionate, a disciplinarian, extremely upright, idealistic and honest but had a temper. His problem was that he was never satisfied with whatever he or his children achieved. He always wanted them to aim higher and would constantly lecture them at mealtimes on issues and philosophies, telling them to put the interests of society ahead of themselves. Even when he took them on a rare Sunday outing to the Maidan, it would be so that they could listen to political speeches (sometimes by Nehru). Everything, for him, was a lesson that he needed to impart.

While Murthy did not particularly enjoy these daily harangues, he was young at this time and thus very impressionable. His father's speeches on the glories of socialism, coloured by Nehruvian philosophy, and the importance of contributing to nation-building went deep into him. These ideas would guide him in his twenties and make him an admirer of socialism. Even after he decided to become a compassionate capitalist and entrepreneur, they would shape the way in which he envisioned his dream company. On the other hand, having learnt of the negative effects of his traditional family on his father, who had been robbed of a chance to study in London, and seeing the persecution of the lower castes in the villages and small towns where he lived, Murthy became extremely averse to such behaviour. He particularly detested the fact that lower-caste men were hired to clean toilets in upper-caste homes. He vowed that such a custom would never be followed in his own home. Once he moved into his own place, he always cleaned his toilet himself. Another custom that Murthy disliked was the fact that some Brahmins proudly flaunted their caste superiority, expecting better treatment at temples or during festivals. Once he became an adult, Murthy refused to wear anything that indicated his caste.

While Murthy learnt many positive values from the lectures Rama Rao routinely dispensed to his captive audience, he also sometimes had to face his temper. One Sunday afternoon, seven-year-old Murthy was playing at home with a friend from the neighbourhood. His father was sleeping, and Murthy's mother, Padmavathamma, warned them not to disturb his father's holiday nap. But the boys were immersed in their game and did not listen. In their excitement, they became quite loud. The next thing Murthy knew was that he was flying across the room. He heard a thud and felt a sharp pain in his head. Shocked, he realized that blood was pouring over his face. His mother later told him that his father had awakened due to the children's racket, stormed out, slapped Murthy's friend, and kicked Murthy so hard that his head hit the sharp edge of a steel trunk. Despite his mother's frantic efforts, Murthy lost a good deal of blood. And the scars from that day, both physical and mental, remained with him.

It was a story he had never told anyone before. To the aghast Sudha, Murthy said, 'I never forgot that incident. It affected my relationship with my father and distanced me from him. But I learnt an important lesson that day.'

Sudha was afraid to probe further, but finally she could not remain silent. Touching his scar gently, she asked, 'What lesson was that?'

The answer revealed to her something crucial about the man sitting in front of her and perhaps made her fall a little deeper in love.

'I learnt never to be violent with children,' Murthy said sombrely.

~

Fortunately, like Sudha, Murthy had an affectionate extended family. He spent many of his holidays with his grandparents or with his maternal uncle, Krishnamurthy Rao (his dear Kittu Mava) in Sidlaghatta. He told Sudha these were some of his happiest memories. While not rich, his uncle was generous-hearted and made sure he sent Murthy home with at least one or two sets of new clothes. Perhaps he knew that money was in short supply in Murthy's household, and new clothes were often considered an extravagance.

'I especially remember watching Telugu films like *Devdas*, *Pelli Chesi Choodu* and *Mayabazar* with friends and family, and memorizing and singing popular songs, such as "Vivaha Bhojanambu". My friends often asked me to sing for them.'

That is how Sudha learnt that Murthy, too, had a good singing voice! After this, she would sometimes ask him to sing for her, and he would shyly oblige her.

Murthy told Sudha, 'My closest friends there were the son of a dosa maker in a small restaurant near my uncle's place and the son of a grocery shop attendant. Our dreams were small. Our pleasures were inexpensive. They taught me to enjoy small things.' It was a habit that would remain with him all his life.

~

When Murthy was young, Rama Rao was transferred often – from Tumkur to Srinivasapur to Mandya to Madhugiri and finally, when Murthy was in Class 10, to Mysore – and as a result Murthy had to learn to make new friends in each new place. Often, he did this by causing mischief in school and clowning around to make his classmates laugh. When, in 1954, his father was sent to Mandya, a middle-sized town in Karnataka, the eight-year-old Murthy developed the habit of sitting in the last row in class. He was particularly naughty in geography class, which was taught by a man who was lame in one leg. Every time the teacher noticed that Murthy was up to some mischief in the back of the class, he would physically drag him from the last row to the first and resume his teaching. But as soon as he turned his back to write on the board, Murthy would run back to the last row, and the poor teacher had to repeat the process.

'It would be accurate to say that more dragging than teaching happened in that class!' Murthy told Sudha ruefully.

Sometime later, this teacher passed away and there was a memorial for him in the school. Perhaps regretting his pranks, Murthy composed a song in his honour. Knowing that he was a good singer, his classmates urged him to perform it at the memorial, in front of all the teachers and the headmaster. The song went like this in Kannada: '*Kodiyalada kunta kanmarayadano; Ganita shatradali jaana / Sangeetadali nipuna / Boogoladali praveena / Charitryali prachanda.*' It commemorated his teacher for being very bright in arithmetic, a maestro in music, an expert in geography, and unbeatable in history. Unfortunately, the song began with a description of the teacher's lameness.

Murthy was singing his composition enthusiastically, his eyes closed, when he was shocked by a hard slap to his head. It was his English teacher, yelling at him for making fun of his dead colleague – though that had not been Murthy's intention at all.

'This incident put a damper on my public performance plans for quite some time!' Murthy told Sudha.

Like Sudha, Murthy also went to Kannada-medium schools. It was only after he went to Mysore that he learnt the importance of learning English – and that, too, from a most unusual source.

'We had a grocery shop opposite our house,' Murthy told Sudha. 'I was often dispatched there to buy items we had run out of. Many times when I got to the store, I would see the old shopkeeper deeply absorbed in reading the *Deccan Herald*. He told me it was the best English newspaper in Karnataka at that time.

'For some inexplicable reason, this shopkeeper took an interest in my education. Often, he would quiz me on international news, including political events, sports and science. I would invariably fail. One day, he gave me a long lecture on why English was important for my career and asked me to read the English newspaper every day. When I told him that we did not get one at home, and that my father would never agree to the extra expense of buying one, he offered me the first use of his English paper. From that day on, I would be eagerly waiting for his shop to open every morning at 7 a.m. I would immediately run there and read the paper for half an hour before going to school. This is when I got into the habit of reading English.'

While Sudha and Murthy had many things in common because of their shared Kannada background and their love for reading, their very different childhoods shaped them in unique ways. The warm, encouraging attitude of Sudha's parents, along with the affection of both her grandparents, made her into a sweet-natured, bubbly and confident person who laughed and befriended others easily. It is possible that several of the young men who knew her were in love with her!

On the other hand, all the young Murthy could hope for – especially from his father – was a gentle exhortation to do even better. As a result, Murthy grew into a young man who was bright, intense and, like his parents, principled – sometimes to an extreme degree – but never satisfied with what he had achieved and always aiming higher, solitary by nature, and unwilling to compromise. Paradoxically, it was their differences, more than their similarities, that drew Sudha and Murthy to each other. Together, they completed each other, like a yin–yang circle. But differences can also lead to severe challenges, especially under stressful circumstances. Though they had no inkling of this at the time, many such challenges awaited them.

One such challenge was the template of marriage that Murthy carried in his subconscious, based on what he had seen of his parents' marriage. (He would only become aware of it and the assumptions that rose from it, and the challenges that it created for him and Sudha, much later.) Murthy's parents' relationship was a traditional one of that period: affectionate yet also formal. While his parents co-existed in the same house – his father earned and his mother provided her husband with all the daily necessities such as food and clean clothes, and looked after the children, including those from his first marriage – they rarely sat down to chat. Murthy's mother was Rama Rao's second wife. Unlike him, she had had only a few years of schooling and although the two would speak openly about matters to do with their children and family issues, it was not a modern companionship where they exchanged ideas and listened to each other. Rama Rao was caring and dutiful towards his wife and offspring. He would, for instance, nurse the children when they were sick and take his wife to the cinema but would rarely show any outward signs of affection towards her.

This marital model left a strong impression on the young Murthy. Although his relationship with Sudha was very unlike this, especially in the early years, and they spent much time discussing important issues and advising each other, as things got very busy and stressful with Infosys, Murthy would find himself reverting to this old template where he took care of the 'outside world' and expected Sudha to handle 'home issues'. And like his father, he would have little time for companionship. Instead, he kept whatever worries and fears he had – and the loneliness they engendered – largely to himself because as a child he had learnt that that was what a man was supposed to do.

2

Sudha had a much more liberal childhood than Murthy's – but she, too, had come through significant challenges. Hers occurred when she went to college – no, even earlier, when she announced that she wanted to study engineering. This was an unusual choice for that time and place, and almost everyone in the family opposed her.

'It was as if I had dropped a bomb inside our house!' Sudha told Murthy, laughing. 'Even Avva, whose favourite grandchild I was, was certain that if I went into this male-dominated field, no man in all of north Karnataka, where we came from, would marry me! My aunts prophesied that I would end up marrying outside the community (to them, this was the epitome of disaster). In that case, they warned me, none of them would attend my wedding. Not that I cared about that! My mother tried to persuade me to study mathematics, as she had done. My maternal grandfather wanted me to study history, which was his subject. Even medicine, they felt, would be a better choice. After all, there were a good number of lady doctors around. My older sister, Sunanda, had already followed in our father's footsteps and was studying medicine.

'But I was not interested in medicine – an early frog dissection at school had made that amply clear to me! I wanted to strike out on my own, and I wanted to go into a field where I could bring about change and affect lives in a positive manner. I already liked what I knew of applied science, and I felt engineering best suited my goal.

'Only my father stood by me. He told me, "I trust you. And I will support you." But he, too, warned there might not be another girl in my class. "What if you have to spend four years without a real friend to talk to?" he asked. Always a straight-shooter, he also pointed out that my decision would have long-lasting consequences. "Think carefully," he warned me. "A career and a husband are not choices you can change easily, like a sari."'

Time would prove him right. There would be no other women in Sudha's class of 150 in B.V.B. College of Engineering in Hubli – and the 149 male students there would do their best to make her life a misery.

But Sudha told him she did not care about these problems. A lover of history, she had recently been reading Hiuen Tsang's travelogue, *Si-Yu-Ki*, where he describes how everyone discouraged him from embarking on the dangerous journey to India. But it was that journey, which encompassed seventeen challenging years, that led him to write his masterpiece. Gathering inspiration from Tsang, she said, 'I'm ready to face the consequences of my choice.'

Sudha had no trouble gaining admission to B.V.B. College of Engineering – her exam marks were excellent. But the staff of the college, and even the principal, were unhappy and nervous at the thought of having to teach a girl. The principal met with her father and told him that they were bound to have problems because of her presence on campus. 'We don't have a ladies' room for her to relax or even a women's toilet. And young men of that age – with their raging hormones – are bound to trouble her in all kinds of ways. I can foresee that she will have a terrible time. Please make her change her mind.'

Sudha's father, no matter what his inner reservations, staunchly supported his daughter. 'She isn't doing anything wrong,' he declared. 'How can I, in all conscience, stop her?'

The principal then requested three things of Sudha: that she should always wear a sari, that she should not chat with the boys, and that she should not spend time in the college canteen, where the young men congregated. She agreed to all of them.

On her very first day of college, Sudha walked into the classroom and discovered that some of her classmates had purposely poured ink all over the first-row bench assigned to her. In spite of her father's warnings, this deep level of hostility shocked her. She had never come across such unkindness in her entire life. She pressed her lips together, blinked away her tears, and wiped the bench clean with a piece of newspaper. *Perhaps*, she thought, *things will get better once the male students see me behaving professionally. After all, I'd been good at making friends in school.* But her classmates refused to even acknowledge her – except to harass her.

'For the first six months, no one said a word directly to me, even during teamwork,' Sudha told Murthy. 'But they had plenty to say indirectly!'

The boys – they were too immature to be called men – in her classes aimed paper airplanes at her back with messages scrawled on them, such as 'Women belong in the kitchen'. They surreptitiously stuck flowers in her hair and taunted her, calling her Miss Flowerpot. Even the professors said things like 'Engineering is a man's domain. Girls are not intelligent. She won't pass.' A yearly ritual at the college had students leaving anonymous chits by the campus 'fish pond', to be read out loud in front of a crowd on the annual college day. Most of the comments that first year were targeted at Sudha.

There were derogatory Kannada limericks aimed at her habit of wearing a white sari, such as *'Avva avva genasa/Kari seeri udisa/Gandana manege kalisa* (Mother, mother, here is a sweet potato. Give me a black sari and send me to my husband's home. Because I'm always wearing a white sari). There would also be songs adapted from popular Hindi movies, such as *'Sajan re jhooth mat bolo/Sudha ke paas jaana hain/Na haathi hain na ghoda hain/Vahan paidal jaana hain* (Dear, please don't lie. I have to go to Sudha's house, but I have neither elephant nor horse, so I will go walking to her).

Sudha was deeply upset by such crude and cruel behaviour. Never in her life had she been a target like this, especially when she had done nothing to deserve it. But though she wept in her bed at night, in college she did not show any reaction to all this crass teasing. Nor did she complain to the administration – or even her parents. She knew what they would say: *This is exactly what we were afraid of.* They would tell her to quit – and she refused to give in like that. She focused all her energy instead on the reason she was in college: her studies. She became the top student of her class, acing her exams every year.

Soon, sheepishly, the boys began to ask for her help with assignments and grew dependent on her for surveys and drawings. Most people would have refused, after facing this kind of harassment. But Sudha graciously helped her classmates whenever they requested. She was large-hearted enough to hold no grudges, and by the time she graduated, she had made several good friendships that would last through the years.

Murthy was astonished to learn this, and angry on her behalf. 'How could you be so forgiving when they had caused you so much grief?' he asked.

'I understood that they didn't know any better,' Sudha said. 'They had never faced this kind of situation, and they probably felt threatened.' Never one to dwell on the negative, she added, 'Maybe, because of their behaviour, I grew more determined and studied harder than I would have otherwise!'

Of the many details of college life that Sudha shared with Murthy, one struck him especially hard. The entire time that she was a student at B.V.B. College, the facility did not have a single women's restroom. Sudha used to complete her morning classes and then walk to her home, which took her forty-five minutes each way. She would eat her lunch, use the restroom, and then rush back to college so that she would not be late for her afternoon classes. No matter how uncomfortable or tiring this was, she had no other option. It was the kind of problem that, as a man, he had never had to face. Now it was etched into his mind.

Murthy, too faced bullying and teasing but at school not at college. Through his youth, he had moved from one government school to another. He did well in his studies, was respected, and enjoyed the attention and affection of his teachers. While his family's financial status was weak, it did not seem to matter much in the classroom. But after his father moved to Mysore when he was twelve, things changed.

Because there were no top-ranked government schools in

Mysore, his father was forced to put him in a private school called Sharada Vilas High School. Here the economic disparity between him and the majority of the students was immediately and starkly apparent. They were better dressed and better tutored, and they made fun of the new 'mofussil' kid with the unfashionable clothes. Worse, Murthy had developed a squint, and his classmates teased him cruelly by imitating this squint. They would corner him in between classes, squint at him, laugh uproariously and run off. This constant teasing wore Murthy down.

Murthy knew it would be no use to appeal to his father, who believed that his children should fight their own battles, or even to his older brother Sridhar, who was too docile to be his champion. Finally, he went to his mother, who was his confidante in such matters, with tears in his eyes. He told her he could not bear this torture and did not want to attend this school any longer.

Though she had only studied up to Class 8 in her village high school, Murthy's mother was a thoughtful and compassionate woman who was very charitable. A conventional woman in most regards, who spent her time in the kitchen or looking after the children, it was she who gave Murthy the affection and love he needed as a child. The advice she gave Murthy remained with him all his life. She told him that the way a discriminated person could fight and succeed against the discriminators was by demonstrating that he was better than them in an area they were weak in, but which they cared about. That to her was the only solution in an environment of bigotry and bias. Murthy took his mother's words to heart. He focused all his energies on his studies, sitting on the first bench and ignoring his tormentors.

Murthy told Sudha, 'If my mother had not given me the recipe to build my self-confidence, I'm not sure where I would have ended. But because of her advice and encouragement, by the end of Class 10 I topped the class. Our headmaster, K.V. Narayan (KVN), called me to his office, congratulated me and wrote on my report card that I must aim high.'

KVN was to become a significant influence in Murthy's life. He taught chemistry and often conducted experiments in class to demonstrate chemical reactions. Once when performing an experiment using common salt, he was measuring out a small quantity of salt carefully with a teaspoon. Watching this, one of the students snickered. KVN stopped the experiment and asked him what was so funny. The student said that KVN's stinginess with common salt seemed somewhat ridiculous.

'Young man,' KVN said sternly, 'this salt is the property of the school, and so it has to be handled carefully. Please come to my house after class. I will give you a jar full of common salt for free. That is my personal property. So I can be generous with it.'

This habit of treating public property with better care than one's own personal property was instilled in the young Murthy that day, becoming a deeply held value for life.

Murthy did very well in his Secondary School Leaving Certificate examination, ranking fourth in the state of Mysore out of 1 lakh students. He received a national scholarship of Rs 100 a month, for nine months per year, for his pre-university course – money that would help pay his older brother's fees. However, when he hurried home excitedly to share the good news with his father, Rama Rao simply asked, 'What happened to the first three ranks?'

Murthy went on to stand third in the state of Mysore for his pre-university examinations. This time he did not even bother to share the news of his success with his father. Nor did he tell him that he was going with his friend Chandru to take the Joint Entrance Examination for admission to the prestigious Indian Institutes of Technology (IITs).

While gaining admission into an IIT in 1962 was not as difficult then as it is today, it was still very challenging. However, Murthy had no problems with the examination. He did extremely well and was selected, as was Chandru. Both of them received appointments where they would be counselled about the branch they would be offered. An excited Murthy decided he would like to study electronics at either IIT Kanpur (IITK) or IIT Madras, which he was most likely to have got, given his performance in the admission exams.

Filled with elation, he went to discuss his plans with his father as soon as the latter came home. 'You will not have to pay anything,' he ended. 'My national scholarship will cover my hostel costs.'

Rama Rao was very happy and proud of his son's performance but shocked him by refusing him permission to go. He reminded Murthy, sadly, of his financial situation. The scholarship at IIT used to arrive only at the end of the year in those days. Rama Rao would have had to take a loan of about Rs 700 in the first year, which he could not do with his monthly salary of Rs 180 and eight children. He consoled Murthy by saying that he would do well wherever he went, including at the local National Institute of Engineering college in Mysore.

Murthy's dreams were crushed. He felt it was completely unfair that after being selected and awarded a national scholarship he could not pursue the education he wanted. But who could he appeal to?

'The circumstances of my birth were my fate,' he would tell his son, Rohan, many years later. 'I felt devastated by them but helpless in their grip.'

That evening, Murthy went over to Chandru's house and explained to him that he would not be going for the IIT counselling. When the heartbroken Murthy started crying, Chandru consoled him. They had planned to go together to Chennai and have fun looking around the city for a few days since Murthy's interview was four days ahead of Chandru's. It was to have been a great adventure for the two friends. Now Chandru went to Chennai by himself and was allotted the metallurgy stream at IIT Madras. On his return, he described the campus in detail, with Murthy listening hungrily.

When Chandru left to join IIT Madras in July, Murthy went with him to the railway station to bid him farewell. Chandru could see his dear friend's disappointment, and even amid his excitement, it saddened him.

'Once again, I could not stop the tears from rising to my eyes,' Murthy confessed to Sudha. 'That was a sad day for me. I told Chandru to keep me up to date on his life as a student at IIT Madras, and he promised. As the train rolled out of the station, I could see my dreams of IIT dissolving into thin air. Chandru kept his word. The most exciting and painful part of my week during the ensuing year was receiving a weekly letter from Chandru where he described vividly his hostel life, his room, his classes, his teachers, his classmates, how his subjects were taught, the cafeteria and the food that seemed exotic and delicious to him, the weekly open-air theatre movies, the moving mountains (the campus buses) and the still rivers (hostels). After reading his letters, I would be depressed for some time and bitter about this wonderful opportunity that fate had so casually snatched from me. For years, I could not bear to talk to anyone about it.'

His efforts to make Infosys wholly meritocratic, irrespective of an employee's financial background, arose partly from this blow.

Even though Murthy did very well at the National Institute of Engineering (NIE) and received a major scholarship that covered all his expenses and more, the unfulfilled longing for IIT would lodge like a thorn in his heart and remain there all his life.

Murthy would hand over his scholarship money, which was Rs 900, to his mother at the end of each year, to use according to the family's needs. Once she gave him back Rs 50 to get a pair of trousers and a shirt stitched. Murthy was delighted because this was a rare treat. He gathered his friends, and they made an excursion to the bazaar, all of them highly excited. After much discussion, Murthy chose the material and had a pair of brown terylene pants and a cream-coloured bush shirt stitched for himself. Terylene was a new material, still quite rare except in major cities, and Murthy felt that for once he fitted in with the 'cool' crowd. He loved his new clothes and folded them away carefully on the shelf that was allotted to him at home, planning to save the outfit for a special occasion.

Meanwhile, his older brother Vasu had obtained a job as an economics lecturer at Poornaprajna College in Udupi, but he did not have proper clothes to wear to work. Their mother managed to get him one pair of trousers and a white shirt, but this was clearly not enough. She then called upon Murthy.

'Give your new clothes to Vasu,' she told him. 'He needs them more than you do.'

Though he loved his mother dearly, Murthy was upset at what he considered to be a most unfair demand. Once again, he was being asked to make sacrifices for the benefit of a sibling. Understandably, he did not agree to it. It was one of the few times he went against his mother's wishes.

The night before Vasu was to leave for Udupi, Murthy's mother called Murthy to a quiet corner of the house and reminded him of an all-night play they had recently watched together, titled *Daanashoora Karna*. In it, Karna, the great philanthropist-warrior, gave lavish gifts to any poor person who asked him for alms. When Indra, disguised as a beggar, asked for the gift of his magical armour, his kavach and kundal that kept him safe in battle, Karna did not hesitate even though he suspected Indra's treachery.

'Did you learn nothing from the play?' his mother admonished him in her gentle way. 'Did you not see that the greatest joy lies in giving and not in receiving?'

Murthy's mother rarely rebuked him, so her quiet disapproval lodged deep in his heart. Mortified, he gave his treasured outfit to Vasu. Her admonition must have left a deep mark on him because later in Pune, he would literally give the clothes off his back to poor people who did not have enough.

~

Fortunately for Murthy, graduate school would provide him with another opportunity to study at an IIT. He had started off at the Indian Institute of Science (IISc) in Bangalore, but he was dissatisfied with the focus on rote learning by some of the older professors who taught there in 1967. (By the time Sudha enrolled there in 1972, IISc had revamped the curriculum and teaching methods and introduced more flexible courses.) Wanting a greater challenge, and remembering his earlier dream, Murthy applied to IITK for his master's degree. Here he received a scholarship of Rs 250 a month. Frugal by nature, he even managed to send part of the money home to his mother.

Murthy found the educational experience at IITK to be unconventional and exciting. Because the institute had a collaboration with eight American universities, there were several American and US-educated faculty members in each department. This kind of intermingling was a rarity in Indian universities at that time. These professors were very different from the stolid and serious teachers at the NIE. They were in their twenties and thirties, full of energy, interested in experimental teaching methods and new fields of study, and willing to hold long discussions about their passions with their students.

Another thing unusual about this campus was that it had three computers that had been sent over from US universities, a rare occurrence at the time. Murthy was excited to learn this as he had never seen a computer up close – and his classmates sometimes took advantage of his naivete.

He told Sudha ruefully, 'One of my hostel mates, Sadasivan, a worldly-wise young man from Mumbai, was quite mischievous. Soon after I joined IIT, he took me to the computer centre and led me to a large, noisy machine. "Here, check out this computer," he told me. "It's our biggest one!"

'I was mesmerized by how the machine was chewing up cards from one side and spewing out paper from the other end. For a long time, I stood there gawking at it. When I returned to the hostel, I bragged to everyone that I'd seen the biggest computer on the campus. But all my classmates burst into laughter, informing me that Sadasivan had pranked me. What I'd seen was only a printer!'

Soon after that, Murthy did come across the real computers. From the first, he was fascinated by them. He sensed that they were powerful and filled with potential. *I will learn as much as I can about them*, he vowed.

One day, serendipitously, at lunchtime in the mess hall, Murthy happened to sit next to a professor from the US. The conversation turned to computers, and the professor declared, with evangelical zeal, that he was positive that the computer was one of the most important inventions of the time. 'It's going to change the world,' he told Murthy and recommended some papers for him to read. Those papers opened up a whole new world for Murthy and convinced him that computers were the way of the future. Never a man for half measures, he obtained permission from his department and changed his major from control theory to computer science – an action that would ultimately have an enormous impact on his life.

Murthy soon discovered that he had an innate understanding of computers; he became fluent in computer languages, from the powerful string processing language LISP to the formula-oriented FORTRAN. Thus began a lifelong love affair.

At IIT, Murthy came into his own. He was diligent and interested and paid close attention to the lectures. He was pleased and a trifle surprised to discover that he did not have to work very hard to perform reasonably well. Though IIT was known for its cut-throat culture, Murthy did not subscribe to this. Like Sudha, he was willing to help classmates if they needed assistance, something that was uncommon at this competitive campus. As a result of this, he was well liked by his classmates.

For Murthy, this was a happy, carefree time, his first experience of living away from home, with some money of his own to spend on simple treats. In the mess, he learnt to appreciate (though it took some time!) north Indian food, particularly aloo parathas with dahi. He went out with friends to the inexpensive Chinese restaurants that were popular with students and tried out and enjoyed many dishes that he had never imagined eating. He had more freedom than ever before and enjoyed the company of a close-knit group of friends who felt they could discuss life issues quite frankly with each other. They were busy with studies during the week, but every Friday evening they relaxed together, playing games of rummy and teen patti until 2 a.m. They also enjoyed sleeping in over the weekend and going for late breakfasts. Murthy's room was often the gathering spot for his friends.

One day, after a long, lazy weekend breakfast when everyone was replete and relaxed, the talk turned to what kind of woman each of them would like to marry. One of the young men announced, 'I want someone beautiful – like Hema Malini!' Another said, 'I want a rich man's daughter. That way, I'll get enough dowry to start my own business.'

At first, Murthy did not say anything, but when his friends insisted, he spoke in his simple way. 'I would like a woman who speaks my mother tongue, Kannada. That way, we would have deeper and more meaningful conversations.' Perhaps because in this northern city he was missing South Indian cuisine, he added, 'I also want her to be able to cook traditional Kannada dishes – the kind my mother makes.'

Fate would make his wishes come true, but with a twist. Sudha was a Kannadiga, but she openly admitted, early in their relationship, that she was not fond of cooking. She was quite happy to outsource that responsibility to Murthy when possible. And when she did cook, Murthy discovered that, because she came from the region north of the Tungabhadra river, her dishes were heavily influenced by Maharashtrian cuisine. Her bisi bele bath, south Karnataka's most popular dish, for instance, tasted quite unlike his mother's!

One of the memorable incidents of Murthy's stay at IITK was the visit of Sri Mahesh Yogi. Mahesh Yogi had just become famous, thanks to the visit of the Beatles to his ashram at Rishikesh. He came to IITK in 1968 for a lecture on transcendental meditation. Lecture Hall 7, where the talk was held, was full, though Murthy felt it was a lot of mumbo-jumbo. At the end of the lecture, Mahesh Yogi decided to visit and initiate students into transcendental meditation at just one residence hall the next morning, which was a Sunday. A lottery was held to decide the hall of residence for his visit. Hall V – Murthy's hall – was chosen.

On Saturday night, Murthy and his friends stayed up chatting and playing cards till 6 a.m. and then went into the hall where Mahesh Yogi was ready to initiate students into transcendental meditation. Mahesh Yogi gave a short lecture, called each student, and whispered something into his ear. When Murthy's turn came, Mahesh Yogi asked him who his best-loved god was. Murthy flippantly said that he did not play favourites with God!

Maharishi was a little upset but suggested Ram as Murthy's favourite god. Then he asked the assembly to close their eyes and chant the chosen name of God. After about ten minutes, Mahesh Yogi asked the students to describe what they felt. Most were effusive and described feelings of ecstasy and bliss. When it was Murthy's turn, he told the truth – that he felt sleepy. He was surprised to hear Mahesh Yogi announce that he was the only student who had learnt transcendental meditation among the audience. He said Murthy was eligible for the advanced course at Rishikesh and would receive a huge discount! He even invited him to join him full-time!

Murthy and his friends had a huge laugh over this.

Murthy's friend Sadasivan loved to brag, and one of the things he bragged about was that he knew several Bollywood actresses. Murthy and his other friends from the then-backwater town of Mysore listened with fascination as Sadasivan spoke of Sharmila Tagore and Zeenat Aman as if they were his close friends. After a while, Sadasivan's friends, including Murthy, pleaded with him to take them to Mumbai on the next holiday. 'We want to meet some actresses as well,' they said.

'I'll take you along if you buy my train ticket,' Sadasivan said. 'But I only travel second class.' With a little shudder, he added, 'My constitution is quite delicate. It won't permit me to travel in those crowded third-class compartments, not if you want me to take you around Mumbai to meet special people.'

Murthy and four other students pooled their funds to buy Sadasivan a second-class train ticket. After that, they only had enough money to buy third-class tickets for themselves in an unreserved coach. The train was so crowded that there were no seats and a lot of pushing and shoving. Finally, the four of them locked themselves inside a toilet, and there they remained the entire way, while the rest of the passengers grew angrier and angrier. When the train reached Mumbai, the students took off very fast before their irate co-travellers could catch them and perhaps beat them up!

However, once they were in the big city, Sadasivan only took them to his house, and then to the office of his father, who was an audit officer. After that, he took them to lunch, but that was it. When his classmates wanted to visit the actresses he had boasted about, he hemmed and hawed and postponed the excursion, giving one excuse after another. It slowly dawned on Murthy and his friends that there were no actresses for them to meet; Sadasivan had fooled them once again!

Murthy took this trickery good-naturedly; after all, they had been to the big city and had an exciting adventure. He told Sudha, 'Upon returning, my friends and I decided that the girls in Mysore were far better than the snooty young women we had seen on the streets of Mumbai!'

———

At IIT, Murthy was part of a select class of twelve students. When he graduated in 1969, he immediately received several job offers. The Indian economy was floundering overall, but graduates from this prestigious institution, with a specialization in computer science, were a rare commodity. For some reason, though, Murthy dragged his feet. He landed offers from several large companies including TELCO, TISCO (Tata Iron and Steel Company), HMT (Hindustan Machine Tools) and Air India, but he did not accept any of them.

His professor, Dr Rajaraman, was concerned. He called Murthy to his office and spoke to him frankly. 'What's wrong? These are great job offers, with excellent salaries. You had better choose one of them. The acceptance deadlines are coming up soon.'

Murthy was equally firm. 'None of them are offering me work that's intellectually stimulating, something from which I can learn and grow. That's my priority.'

Dr Rajaraman was impressed by Murthy's goals. He thought for a while. Then he said, 'Dr Krishnayya, a friend of mine who is a professor at IIMA, is visiting the campus soon. I'd like you to meet him. He may have something that interests you.'

Murthy agreed.

Krishnayya, a highly articulate, charismatic and affable

intellectual, told Murthy about a time-sharing computer system – where multiple users could use the same computing resources at the same time – that he was planning to install at IIMA. His system would have sixteen teletypewriters, a CPU and a graphics terminal. IIMA would be the third business school in the world after Harvard and Stanford to install such a system.

'Come and work with me as the chief systems programmer,' Krishnayya offered. The job would involve building add-ons to the operating systems and developing software, especially to teach students operations research, finance, production, statistics and other subjects.

It was definitely more interesting and innovative than anything Murthy had been offered so far. But by now he had learnt to be careful. 'What's the catch?' he asked.

'The salary is Rs 800 per month,' Krishnayya admitted.

This was half of what Murthy had been offered elsewhere. He was not sure what to do. He asked for some time to think about it. He did not care about the money, but he worried that by not taking up a corporate job now, he might be shutting some important doors.

'You are only twenty-three years old,' Dr Rajaraman told him. 'You can afford to take some risks. If I were your age, I would focus on learning rather than on salary.'

Murthy felt the rightness of this advice in his gut. But he was also sensitive to the financial needs of his family. He knew that the marriages of his three sisters would need to be arranged and paid for soon, and that the family was counting on him. He sent a telegram to his father asking him for his opinion.

Rama Rao responded like a true teacher. He telegrammed back: 'Listen to your professor.'

In 1969, Murthy went ahead and joined Krishnayya in

Ahmedabad. It was a decision that would end up having a profound influence on his personal as well as professional life.

⁓

Another reason Murthy was attracted to the IIMA job was because of his leftist philosophy, which led him to care much more about the public good than money. To Sudha, who was somewhat sceptical of socialism, having seen its negative effects up close on the shop floor at work, he explained that he was influenced by Nehru, whom he had seen once as a child. Nehru's policies, in turn, were influenced by Harold Laski, the Marxist economist at the London School of Economics.

The USSR was a strong nation in those days and was considered India's well-wisher. The US had refused to help India in building a steel plant, but the USSR had accepted that responsibility. Most Indian leaders, above all Nehru, spoke of socialism as the future for India, the country's most prominent intellectuals were almost all from the left, while many of Bollywood's hit films like *Shree 420*, *Awaara*, *Naya Daur* and *Do Bigha Zamin* had socialist themes. The ideas of social equality, of the government owning much of the public infrastructure of the nation and providing a vast array of public goods to the poor, were deeply in fashion then – and these concepts, alongside a cultural leaning towards the USSR, showed itself in every facet of life, from politics to cinema, from business to academics. As an idealistic young man, growing up in this period, and also influenced by his father's lectures about Nehru, these ideas made a great deal of sense to Murthy.

Murthy also shared with Sudha his experiences with the rural poor, which influenced his philosophy as well. While he was at IITK, he would travel from Mysore to Kanpur and back two times a year. This required him to take a train from Mysore to Bangalore, wait a few hours, take a second train from Bangalore to Chennai, wait again, take a third train to Jhansi, wait some more, and take a fourth train from Jhansi to Kanpur. The journey took about thirty-six hours. It was quite an adventure since he did not know any Hindi at the time. But what impressed him was the affection and care that the poor farmers on the Jhansi–Kanpur passenger train showed to students like him even at 3 a.m. They recognized the young men as students going to Kanpur for college, and they were very kind and helpful.

'They would make space for us to lie down and sleep, sitting on the edge of the bench for hours so as to not disturb us,' he told Sudha. 'Simple and generous, they just wanted us, the students, to get a good education and become successful. Thinking of them, even now I get a lump in my throat. The IIMA job was all about making sacrifices and building a strong India. That's why I accepted it.'

Murthy would end up being the only one from his batch who chose not to join a major company. It was the first of many risks he would take in his career, choosing the road less travelled.

3

By this time, Sudha had triumphantly negotiated her way through the challenges of being the only woman at BVB College. She then joined IISc in Bangalore, known at that time as the Tata Institute. She had many friends, including other women who studied at the institute (though she was the only woman doing a postgraduate engineering degree) and, being a gregarious person, enjoyed life in the ladies' hostel to the full. She was getting ready to graduate and continue her studies abroad. Her heart was set on a PhD in computer science, and she had already received several admissions offers from the US, including some with scholarships.

Then one day in April of 1974, on her way to the lecture hall, she came across a job advertisement for engineers on the notice board. It had been posted by the Tata Engineering and Locomotive Company (TELCO). She glanced through the usual verbiage: they were looking for bright young engineers with excellent academic credentials, and they promised a satisfying career and a competitive salary. She was about to move on when a line at the bottom caught her attention: *Lady candidates need not apply.*

Sudha felt her hackles rising. Here it was again, the gender discrimination she had thought she had left behind at BVB College in Hubli. While she had no desire to take up a job, she decided to apply. She knew she had a good chance based on academic excellence – she had consistently done better than most of the men in her class. After sending in the application, she decided it was important to inform the topmost person in TELCO about this injustice and how she felt about it. So she sent off an incendiary postcard to J.R.D. Tata, head of the Tata group, describing her disappointment at the prejudicial behaviour she had just come across. She told him it was unfair and unexpected for a company that projected itself as progressive.

'Imagine my surprise,' she later told Murthy, 'when, in ten days' time, I received a telegram with an interview appointment. It invited me to come to Pune for the interview at TELCO's expense. J.R.D. Tata – who was then India's most famous industrialist – had actually read a letter written by a nobody from an ordinary, middle-class family and responded to her!'

Sudha was taken aback. She did not want the job; she did not even want the interview. But her friends at the women's hostel urged her to go. They thought it would be a fun adventure. It would not cost her anything – and she could buy them the famous Pune saris. They gave her Rs 30 each for shopping and sent her on her way.

When Sudha arrived for the interview at TELCO's Pimpri office, she saw six men lined up on the other side of the table. They whispered among themselves when they saw her. She could feel the prejudice and preconceptions rippling through the room. (Later she would realize they had also been curious about this young woman with the guts to complain directly to Jeh – JRD's nickname – in a way that had prompted him to take action.) This angered her; then, interestingly, it calmed her down. She was sure she would not get the job. With nothing to lose, she could be herself. 'I hope this is going to be a technical interview,' she told them brashly. It was, and Sudha answered every question perfectly. Finally, one of the interviewers told her, 'You performed well, but we don't hire women in TELCO because we don't know how the men on the shop floor will accept them. Also, we don't have separate trainee hostels or guest houses for them.'

'If you don't start hiring women,' Sudha retorted, 'how are those things ever going to change? You pride yourselves on being a pioneer in your field. If you think this way, how will any woman ever enter this so-called man's domain?'

'But what if you get married after you are hired,' one of them protested, 'and then leave the company and shift to wherever your husband works? Wouldn't that be a waste of all the money we used to train you?'

'Tell me, don't the men you hire also change jobs and move if they get a better offer elsewhere?' Sudha asked. 'You don't seem to have any rules against that.'

The interviewers were silenced. They asked her to wait outside while they conferred. In a short while, they called her back in and offered her the position.

On the way back, Sudha stopped at Hubli to tell her father, who was her best friend, all about her adventure. She expected him to applaud her victory on behalf of Indian women. But Sudha's father, Dr Kulkarni, didn't react as she had expected. He knew that she planned to study abroad. In fact, a thick envelope from the US had arrived at their home just a day ago. He handed it to her in silence. It was from a professor at the Massachusetts Institute of Technology (MIT), offering her work as a research assistant and promising she could soon move on to do a PhD under his guidance.

Sudha was hugely excited about this news, but Dr Kulkarni frowned as he examined the letter. 'Why do you want to go abroad to study?' he asked.

Sudha was taken aback by his question and his lack of enthusiasm because he had always been her champion where higher education was concerned. 'I want to study,' she said. 'You know that! I want to learn as much as I can, and this is one of the best engineering universities in the world. You yourself encouraged me to apply.'

Her father spoke in stern tones. 'Then why did you send that postcard to J.R.D. Tata? If you didn't want the job at TELCO, why did you waste everyone's time?'

Sudha told him she had been goaded into applying by the unfairness of the job advertisement. She wanted to show the company their assumptions about women were wrong. She had done it to prove girls could be as well qualified as boys.

'So you went through all this drama just to let J.R.D. Tata and TELCO know that boys and girls are equal, without any plan to follow through?' Dr Kulkarni asked. 'Personally, I think you have a duty now to accept the job and show them you meant what you said. Else what you are doing is just sloganeering.'

Sudha was stunned. She had not seen her actions in this light at all.

'I leave the final decision to you,' her father said as he walked out of the room.

For three days, Sudha thought hard about what she should do. With all her heart she longed to learn more, to make use of the wonderful opportunity for higher education that life had just placed in her hands. She longed to see another country and experience new adventures. But the words of her father, her role model, echoed in her ears. Finally, with some sadness in her heart, she decided on TELCO. She had started something important there, something that might make a real difference for women; she had been given a unique opportunity; she was going to follow through. It was a painful decision but, she felt, the morally correct one.

'Right after that,' she told Murthy, her voice choked with emotion, 'I tore up the letter from the MIT professor. I didn't want to be tempted to keep looking at it. I didn't want to live with regret. But it was the toughest choice I'd ever had to make.'

When twenty-four-year-old Sudha started her job at TELCO as a shop floor engineer, she faced all the challenges her interviewers had warned her about. The shop floor was a daunting space, warehouse-like, with machines lined up all along its length on both sides. It was noisy and dirty, and many precautions had to be followed to keep the workers safe. As the first woman in this environment, Sudha stood out in her salwar kameez, though it was covered by a blue engineer's lab coat. (For safety reasons she did not wear a sari.) The working-class culture of the shop floor was unapologetically unwelcoming to women. The workers gawked at her from a distance. The only women they were used to seeing in the factory were the women who cleaned up the area, women whom they could order around. They were wary and reluctant to interact with Sudha. They did not want to listen to her instructions.

The fact that she had short hair made them even more prejudiced because they thought of her as a fashionable, Westernized woman. If Sudha asked them questions about the functioning of machines or about the problems they were having with them, they would not reply. When she travelled on an assignment to Jamshedpur, there was opposition to her even entering the TELCO plant. The workers protested that no woman had entered the premises except for the prime minister, Indira Gandhi, and even she had only come once, for the inauguration. On special puja days, such as Vishwakarma Puja, or Ayudha Puja during Navaratri, Sudha was not allowed to participate.

Sudha was deeply disheartened by such attitudes, but at the same time she understood where the men were coming from. This ability to understand the psyche of those who were creating difficulties for her had helped her in engineering college, too. A quiet but determined feminist, she put up with all these troubles without complaining to the management and presented a positive and professional attitude throughout, even when she felt depressed about it in private. Just as she had in college, she focused instead on doing the best job possible. She worked hard and found that she enjoyed solving the technical challenges. After some time, the men on the shop floor, too, began to see that all she wanted was to do her job well. Slowly, they began to cooperate. They appreciated the fact that Sudha did not put on any airs. She often had lunch in the same canteen as the workers and, once she got to know them, asked sincerely about the welfare of their families.

Murthy was impressed by Sudha's story and her optimism. 'I

admire how you can move on, look ahead at the opportunities the future might hold, and make the best of the current challenges. I tend to spend a lot of time examining my past in an effort to learn from mistakes.'

Sudha smiled silently. Perhaps she was thinking that had she not sacrificed a deep personal desire and made the fateful decision to come to TELCO, she would never have met a certain 'global bus conductor' and fallen in love.

When he began his first job at IIMA, Murthy had arrived in Ahmedabad with a bit of an attitude. He believed that only students who could not handle engineering courses pursued a master's degree in management. This may have been so at some other places where management was taught, but it certainly was not the case in IIMA where the highest calibre of students could be found. Soon, he changed his mind and began hanging out in the faculty lounge, listening to the professors. Their discussions regarding organizational behaviour, politics and economic policy were fresh and illuminating, and Murthy was impressed. His horizons began to broaden, and he thoroughly enjoyed learning about the many facets of management studies. But in his new-found ardour he spent too much time there, neglecting his own duties. When Professor Krishnayya would ask him what he had done so far, Murthy would say he was still settling in.

By the third week, Krishnayya was exasperated. He cornered Murthy in the faculty lounge, in the midst of a group of professors, and said, 'Listen, young man, I keep asking you what you have done the previous week and you have nothing to tell me. So let me change the question. Please tell me what you have *not* done.'

The professors around them burst into laughter. Murthy, shamed and furious, felt like sinking through the floor. But to his credit, he got over his feelings in a couple of days and admitted to himself that he deserved Krishnayya's chastisement. He went to his office, apologized and asked him what he would like him to do. Krishnayya was planning the installation of the Hewlett-Packard 2000A time-sharing computer system, the same one he had told Murthy about when he was recruiting him. He suggested that Murthy conduct a regulation study of the voltage at the IIMA campus to assess whether the power supply was stable enough. If not, they would require a UPS to protect the system from power surges. But the UPS would have to be imported, and that was an expensive and time-consuming affair.

Murthy had not done anything like this before, but he was determined to prove himself. The problem challenged him in a whole new way, different from the academic studies he had breezed through. There was no ready reference at hand for this in the pre-internet days, but after careful thought, he came up with the idea to wire up a series of lamp loads to simulate the electrical load of the system and assess the stability. He would have to monitor the voltage over twenty-four hours. He borrowed the lamp load from the local engineering college, set up the system, tested it and eventually concluded that the voltage at IIMA was stable, never varying more than 5 per cent. Therefore, IIMA would not have to invest in a UPS system. Krishnayya was impressed by the testing and praised Murthy effusively for saving them time and money. After this, the other employees and even the professors began to take Murthy more seriously and often consulted him when they had a problem.

Murthy told Sudha, 'I saw first-hand that performance leads to recognition, recognition to respect, and respect to power.'

As the chief systems programmer at IIMA, Murthy was soon designing and building a BASIC language interpreter for a computer being developed by the Electronics Corporation of India Limited (ECIL). The work usually started at 8 a.m. and went on until 2 a.m. Besides the design work, his team was assisting 240 people, primarily students, who were using the teletypewriters to complete their assignments. A few people quit, unable to handle the load, but Murthy led his team so well that most of them enjoyed the intensity, the discipline and the sense that they were making a difference. They felt that the innovative technical work and the focus on indigenous software development were deeply important; it was an honour to participate in it.

Along with Professors Rama Rao and Ranga Rao, Murthy developed a BASIC interpreter – which is what enables users to run a BASIC program – for computers being built by ECIL. Krishnayya and Murthy also developed an interactive management game. Murthy was given enormous freedom in his job. He could present new project ideas, and Krishnayya, Professor Mohan Kaul and Murthy would excitedly try them out. It was an entrepreneurial environment in an academy with an enthusiastic adviser at the helm, the kind of thing students dream of.

Murthy never forgot the mentoring Krishnayya provided to him and he would apply many of these learnings in Infosys.

Krishnayya, who had studied at MIT and could have had an easy and affluent life abroad, had chosen instead to return to India to make a difference. An excellent mentor and true professional, he changed Murthy's self-conception about his abilities. This new self-confidence and belief in his own potential would stay with

Murthy for the rest of his life and lead him, in his turn, to mentor talented youngsters.

~

Despite all the work, Murthy managed to find time to read widely: books on operations research, economics, organizational behaviour, business policy, computer science, politics, and wealth and income inequality, including the writings of the great German sociologist Max Weber. 'Weber's central theory, that the priority of truly successful people is achieving a work ethic rather than achieving wealth, resonated with me,' he told Sudha. 'I also learnt so much about interpersonal relations, team building, organizational development and principles of business around this time. I have a feeling this is going to help me later in life.'

But Murthy was still plagued by a question. All through his childhood, Murthy's father had constantly lectured his children about the need to 'serve the country'. To have 'a bigger purpose' than just making money. But what exactly did service and purpose mean for a computer engineer?

Sudha was interested in probing in a different direction. 'Was there anything at IIMA that bothered you?' she asked.

'Yes,' Murthy admitted. 'Even though it claimed to be a collegial and liberal institution, it was very hierarchical. The faculty was at the top. The research staff was below them. There was a sense that they were there only to assist the faculty, who were the real intellectuals. The administrative and secretarial staff were at the bottom of the pyramid. There was almost no social interaction between the faculty and the rest of the staff. We at the computer centre were considered an exception, and I did make friends with several smart, young, forward-thinking faculty members.' He counted them off on his fingers. 'Mohan Kaul, Sikdar, Shamihoke, Amarlal Kalro, Shashi Mishra and Krishnaswamy. Plus some very bright students such as K.V. Kamath.' He looked at Sudha, his eyes intense with feeling. 'But it was a flawed system overall.'

'What do you mean?' Sudha asked. She had never seen a non-hierarchical organization. From her father's hospital, to her own university, to the religious mathas she had visited with her grandmother, each institution had layers and levels, with the people on top being valued more. But when she pointed this out to Murthy, he said stubbornly, 'Nobody – not even the lowliest janitor – should feel like a second-class citizen in an organization.' He made it a point to know the names of the janitors who cleaned his building and always asked after their welfare.

One day during lunch at the faculty lounge in IIMA, one of Murthy's acquaintances accused him of being a 'fake leftist'. He said that Murthy had taken the IIMA job only because he didn't get any better offers. At first Murthy tried to calm him down. Then he tried to ignore him. But the man would not stop. He challenged Murthy to get a covenanted position in a multinational and show him the appointment letter. In general Murthy was a calm individual who remained unaffected by such immature behaviour. But on this day, something ignited inside him. 'Perhaps a small part of my brain wanted me to prove to myself that I would indeed be able to obtain such a job,' he confessed to Sudha.

As luck would have it, Hindustan Lever (HL) had advertised at that time for the job of the head of the data processing cell. It fit the criteria perfectly: a covenanted grade with a good salary, accommodation and a sumptuous vehicle allowance. Murthy applied for it, went through a battery of selection tests, and was selected for the job. He was given the appointment letter by Tarun Sheth, the head of human resources, and asked to join the company soon. While on his way out, Murthy wanted to use the restroom; he asked Tarun Sheth's secretary to help him locate it. The man led Murthy down a corridor. Seeing a toilet symbol on a door, Murthy was about to go in. But the secretary interrupted him, said that was not for covenanted officers, and took him to the designated restroom.

Murthy told Sudha, 'When I was in the toilet, I started thinking whether I wanted to work in a place where there were different toilets for different classes of employees. My socialist mind was deeply disturbed by such inequality. I went back to Mr Tarun Sheth's room and regretfully told him that I would not be able to join HL after all. Mr Sheth was very surprised and asked me why, since just a few minutes back I had accepted the job quite enthusiastically. When I told him why, Mr Sheth was shocked by my thought process. He explained to me the rationale for their practice: a certain class of employees did not keep the toilets clean enough for the officers, particularly the foreigners, to use. I had a courteous but deep discussion with him on my philosophy that no organization can become strong unless there is a feeling of oneness among the employees, and that feeling of oneness cannot flourish if they are forced to use separate toilets. He tried to persuade me, but I was adamant. Finally, he said he was disappointed but understood my position.'

Murthy added, his voice resolute, 'Sudha, one day, I'll build a company where I'll ensure common toilets that are for every employee, from the chairman to the janitors. I have full faith that with proper training and instructions, we will keep our toilets clean.'

Sudha was, once again, amazed by this man. How differently he thought from every other person she knew. The uniqueness of his goal spoke to her heart. He was so different from most of the men she knew, who were focused on their office jobs, interested only in getting ahead financially, in security and comfort for themselves and their families. She looked into his shining eyes and thought, *if anyone can pull off such a utopian dream, it'll be Murthy.*

Murthy brought a copy of the offer letter back to IIMA and showed it to his cantankerous colleague, who was forced to recant his earlier accusation. The incident had an additional happy outcome: Murthy learnt that, soon after his conversation with Sheth, Hindustan Lever abolished the separate toilet policy.

4

Long before he met Sudha, Murthy, too, had set his heart on getting a PhD from a university abroad. He applied and received a scholarship to study in Israel, at the prestigious Technion-Israel Institute of Technology. He was excited and delighted because he felt that Technion would be the best place for pursuing advanced research in the field that interested him the most: concurrency. Additionally, he had long been fascinated by Israel's socialistic philosophy and hoped to experience life in a kibbutz.

But the universe had a different plan for him. Just a month before he was to leave for Israel, he was startled to receive a telex offering him a position on the eighteen-member team that was building an operating system to manage air cargo for Charles de Gaulle (CDG) Airport in Paris. This unexpected offer came about because Krishnayya had recently presented a technical paper at a conference in Italy. It had been judged the best in the conference. When one of the attendees complimented Krishnayya, he said, with his usual honesty, that the credit belonged to his co-author Murthy, who had done most of the work. The man was a senior manager at SESA, a French software company. He wrote to Murthy, offering him the CDG job in Paris.

Murthy was torn. The pay was attractive, and it would enable him to send a good amount of money home to his father, who was worried about arranging the marriages of his daughters. Additionally, Murthy was an adventurous twenty-five-year-old, and Paris with its rich cosmopolitan culture sounded very exciting. Because he kept up with world news, he knew that this was an especially exciting time in France. Post-war France was enjoying its 'Trente Glorieuses' period, the thirty years of rapid growth since 1945. Its infrastructure was burgeoning; culturally, too, it was at the top. Fashionable French singers like Françoise Hardy and Claude Francois were making music that Europeans and Americans couldn't get enough of. The French actress Brigitte Bardot had become an international icon. Murthy's friends urged him to forget the PhD in Israel and go to France.

'If I'd been older and less impressionable,' he told Sudha, 'I would have gone ahead with the PhD. Yes, I had a great time in Europe, but – like you – I'll always regret not getting a doctorate. I want one of my children to fulfil that dream of mine.'

Before going abroad, Murthy went to Mysore to bid his family goodbye. At the station, leaving, he could see the look of pride in his mother's moist eyes. Even his usually serious father was pleased that his son was going abroad with a prestigious job and showed his happiness. In Mumbai, his excited colleagues met him at the station and accompanied him to the airport. Since this was his first airplane trip, one of his senior colleagues, Professor Mohan Kaul, gave him some important pointers about air travel, including how to use the toilet.

The flight to Paris was via Heathrow. At London airport,

Murthy had his first experience with automatic doors. Seeing no handles, he stood at a distance and observed the glass doors opening and closing, and people entering and exiting the building. It took him a while to realize the doors had a sensor. 'So much for my engineering degree!' he confessed ruefully to Sudha.

Murthy was a novice when it came to living in a new country. When his French boss asked Murthy how much he wanted as a salary advance, he was too shy and proper to check with colleagues about money matters and asked for only 500 francs. Translated into rupees, it seemed like a large sum, but he soon discovered how little it was! After his hotel accommodation and daily commuting costs, he had very little left for his meals. Towards the end of the month, he survived on a single bar of chocolate a day bought from a vending machine. At night he only had tap water to drink. He was so hungry during this period that his brain was foggy all the time. The same squeamishness with discussing money matters and negotiating with his boss prevented him from asking for a raise later!

Still, Murthy found his feet soon enough. Despite his busy and challenging work schedule, he was determined to make the most of his stay in France and gather as many experiences as possible. He chose his neighbourhood carefully, renting a room for only 18 francs a day in the diplomatic quarters in the 7th Arrondissement, very near the lively Montparnasse area. It was just a few minutes by metro from the Latin Quarter and the famous Sorbonne University. He also signed up for French classes at L'Alliance Francaise because he was determined to speak with the locals and make the most of social life in the city.

But to make time for study, he had to be twice as efficient at his job and cut down on his sleeping hours. He would wake up at 5 a.m., leave for Montparnasse by metro, take a train to Versailles

Chantiers, take a bus to L'Iria, and be in the office from 9 a.m. to 6 p.m. Then he would travel back to the city and reach L'Alliance Francaise by 7.30 p.m. for his 8 o'clock French class. Once the classes were over, he would stop at an inexpensive restaurant for dinner on his way home. 'I went to the same restaurant each night,' he told Sudha, 'and each night I ordered an omelette because I didn't know enough French to order anything else.'

Sudha, a staunch vegetarian, shuddered, thinking of having to subsist on eggs for a whole month. 'Wasn't that tiresome?'

Murthy shrugged. 'There were other things that were more important to me. In any case, I cooked Indian food on the weekend and ate at home. That saved me money and allowed me to enjoy some familiar dishes.'

'I didn't know you could cook!' Sudha said, impressed. But Murthy admitted he only knew how to make rice and a basic sambar.

As his vocabulary improved, Murthy began experimenting with the menu at the restaurant he frequented. One day, as he was attempting to place an order in his stuttering French, the waiter laughingly complained, 'Life was much simpler when you didn't know any French. I always understood exactly what you wanted to eat. Now I'm confused!'

Soon, Murthy learnt enough French to hold meaningful conversations with Parisians. But he spent time with other foreigners as well. Because of his interest in Israel, he made friends with many Israelis and Palestinians and also with American students. These students were very different from the stereotypes portrayed by Indian politicians. He told Sudha, 'I'd heard so many politicians ranting against "Westerners", the "foreign hand" and the "CIA", who were all out to exploit and loot our country. But when I got close to them, I was surprised to realize that they were compassionate and generous. They often volunteered with non-profit organizations and were sceptical of interventionist US policies.'

Murthy found the work ethic at the Paris office very inspiring and, sadly, far better than what he had seen in India. The software engineering team building the air cargo system was extremely professional, constantly improving on their product to make it more efficient. There was a push for excellence everywhere, and it influenced the idealistic young man.

But what he learnt outside the office shaped Murthy in more fundamental ways. The environment of openness in debates, the role of student revolution and the freedom of expression that formed part of the cultural fabric of the French society impressed him. He saw for himself that a capitalistic country like France was cleaner, more prosperous, healthier and much more advanced than India, where leaders insisted that poverty was a virtue, and socialism and leftism were the panacea.

'For the first time – though I was still committed to socialist values – I began to doubt the Nehruvian leftism I'd grown up on,' he told Sudha.

Murthy's favourite day was Saturday, when he would visit inexpensive cafes in the Latin Quarter. He was charmed by this part of the city, every cobblestoned corner lively with people performing music or street plays. The cafes were bursting with customers having animated arguments over coffee and croissants. Murthy was amazed at how much the Parisian youth knew about politics and economics. The student revolution of 1968 had almost toppled the government, and a sense of triumph lingered in the air. Focused and intense as always, Murthy asked his new friends many questions and wrote down their answers in a notebook. He particularly liked frequenting Les Deux Magots, a cafe famous for hosting the city's intellectuals. Here, an excited Murthy came across legendary intellectuals such as Jean-Paul Sartre and Simone de Beauvoir, in spirited discussion at their favourite tables.

Murthy also met Georges Marchais, who was leader of the Communist Party in France. Marchais was a farmer's son who had been employed as a metalworker before he turned to politics. A rebellious champion for the working class, he was a popular figure on French television, given to mocking the 'guard dogs' of the intelligentsia and his fellow politicians with their fondness for three-piece suits and pocket kerchiefs. He was known for his approachability and love of banter, and Murthy, curious about communism, held long conversations with him as well as other socialist intellectuals.

'But though I liked them all as people,' he confessed to Sudha, 'I began to have serious doubts about their political stance. The facts all around me pointed in a different direction.'

Murthy's research revealed that France's gross domestic product had doubled between 1959 and 1968, thanks largely to rapid industrialization. French businesses were building a worldwide reputation in fashion, clothing and perfume. Jobs were being created at a remarkable pace. The storefronts on Parisian streets showcased beautifully packaged products with pride. Murthy saw with his own eyes that there was a better path to prosperity and people's happiness than what India was pursuing. Ideas began to take shape in his head.

Whenever he went on vacation, Murthy made sure to travel. He went to Germany, Holland, Italy and the UK. In all these countries, he observed the prosperity and freedom available to people who were running their own businesses. These ranged from modest to gargantuan, from Rome's gelato vendors to Germany's enterprising car companies, where auto plants damaged in the war and rebuilt afterwards were exporting iconic models like the Volkswagen Beetle. These countries had all become booming economies by the 1970s. For instance, in Italy, which had been an impoverished rural nation just twenty-five years ago, 66 per cent of the residents owned a car.

During this time, Murthy formulated several original ideas about how to solve India's poverty problem. He kept these thoughts to himself until he met Sudha. He told her, 'The only way poverty can be solved in India is by creating a large number of decently paid jobs giving many a good salary. And the only people who can do this are entrepreneurs, who can convert the power of their ideas into jobs. It's not the task of the government to create jobs. The role of public governance is to use tax money to run programmes of public good like education, healthcare, nutrition, defence and diplomacy efficiently. The government needs to understand this and cooperate with entrepreneurs so that they can create a large number of jobs and pay those taxes.'

It would take decades for the Indian government to see the value of such ideas.

───

As his vision became clearer, Murthy's urge to return to India grew stronger. When his project in France ended, Murthy's boss wanted him to stay on. He was willing to give him a raise because Murthy was such a responsible employee. But Murthy told him, 'I need to go back to my homeland to conduct an important experiment in entrepreneurship.' His boss heard the passion in his voice and, though sorry to lose a fine employee like Murthy, wished him the best.

However, there was one last thing Murthy needed to do before he returned to India. He wanted to experience first-hand the ground-level reality in Eastern Europe, especially the countries behind the Iron Curtain. He had saved $10,000 from his salary. But he kept only $500 for his travel expenses, sent half to his mother and donated the rest to an organization called Freres de Tiers Mondes (Brothers of the Third World).

Murthy's plan was to hitchhike across Europe. Not only would it be inexpensive, but he felt it would allow him to experience reality on the ground level. Hitchhiking was the most popular way to travel in Europe after the Second World War, and young people aged fifteen to twenty-five made 100 million border crossings in Europe annually. Rail passes and youth hostels provided a way for them to travel through the continent on shoestring budgets, and Murthy used the same strategies. He made his way east through Italy, Switzerland, Germany and Greece to Poland, Czechoslovakia, Russia, Hungary, Turkey and Yugoslavia. After that, he planned to travel through Iraq, Israel, Iran and Afghanistan. All in all, he would visit twenty-five countries over eleven months before he returned to India.

Sudha, who had not travelled much, was fascinated by the tales of Murthy's adventures. Perhaps they gave her the impetus for her own escapades some years later, when she would backpack her way alone across America.

Murthy travelled light, taking unplanned routes, relying on the kindness of strangers, eating sparingly and often sleeping in public spaces. Most of the people he met on his way were friendly and curious about this slim, brown-skinned man, his eyes shining with intelligence behind thick glasses. He got lifts from passing drivers who would often feed him a hot meal and drop him off at one of the train stations. He travelled without dwelling too much on his destination and going wherever the driver was headed, as long as it was generally in the right direction. In most cities, the train stations were where most hitchhikers congregated for temporary shelter. Murthy was fascinated by their lifestyle and personalities. A barter system prevailed among them; people traded things they had for things they needed. These young travellers were carefree, energetic and optimistic, paying little heed to where they slept that night and how little money they were carrying. Most of them were students taking a break from college to experience the world. Although a loner by nature, Murthy got on well with them.

Europe in the 1970s was largely a safe place, and the police were friendly and non-interfering, keeping an eye on hitchhikers from a distance. Murthy would put his backpack in a locker at the railway station so that his passport and money were secure. He would sleep on station benches in his sleeping bag and have a streetside coffee and croissant in the morning before wandering through the museums and other tourist sites. With glowing enthusiasm, he described to Sudha the majesty of the Golden Hall, the home of the Vienna Philharmonic Orchestra, and the incomparable artistry of the Sistine Chapel in the Vatican.

Occasionally Murthy slept in a cheap hotel or hostel – a pensione in Rome, a dormitory in Istanbul. In communist countries, he stayed at youth hostels since the police there frowned upon people sleeping on railway platforms.

'It is an interesting experience to form friendships that last a couple of hours, or an evening,' Murthy told Sudha. 'Under such circumstances, people reveal their true selves. The moral garb that we wear in our regular lives vanishes.'

———

In Greece, Murthy met a student couple from Berkeley, California: Bob and Lisa (names changed to protect identities). Lisa was around eighteen and Bob a couple of years older. The three of them hitchhiked together and were dropped off at the YMCA/YWCA in Athens. At the hostel, they found a notice for a party with free food and drinks, organized by local university students, and decided to attend. At the party, Murthy had fun people-watching, but around midnight, Lisa rushed up to him in a panic, saying she couldn't find Bob. Murthy helped her look for him for a while, but to no avail. Finally, when it got really late, he accompanied her to the entrance of the YWCA and returned to his room to sleep.

Next morning at breakfast he saw Lisa looking agitated. She had still not found Bob, and the manager of the men's hostel told her the staff had not seen him the previous night. Murthy tried to make light of it, joking that Bob may have gone off with a cuter girl, but Lisa insisted that he was not like that. She was close to tears. 'I'm sure something terrible has happened to him,' she said.

Murthy tried to calm her. 'He must have had too much to drink. He's sleeping it off somewhere.'

But by evening, Bob was still missing, and Murthy had to admit something was wrong. He went with the distraught Lisa to the police station. She had a photo of Bob, and the police told her they would get in touch as soon as they had any news. The next day, the police came to the YMCA and informed Murthy that they had tracked Bob down. He was dead. His body was found with a needle mark in his arm.

An Uncommon Love

Murthy was in shock. The police explained to him that it looked like a case of a blood sale gone wrong. Selling blood to make a quick buck was a common strategy among hitchhikers; they did it when they were short of cash. Bob was AB negative, a rare blood group. He must have needed money, and probably found some buyers at the party. It looked like they had extracted too much blood from him, causing his death. It could have been accidental – or it could have been deliberately done, the police said. It was hard to say. The body was now at a morgue.

It became Murthy's reluctant responsibility to inform Lisa of this tragedy. A devastated Lisa had no idea what to do next. Murthy put aside his travel plans; he could not leave Lisa alone in this state. He managed to get Lisa's home phone number from her. International calls were very expensive, but he phoned Lisa's parents to inform them of what had happened and where she was. It took them and Bob's parents about four days to reach the hostel. Until that time, Murthy waited with Lisa. This tragic event lingered with Murthy for days.

The last part of his Europe trip took Murthy into the communist countries of Eastern Europe, where hitchhiking was far more complicated. Since the common man lived in relative poverty in these parts, drivers usually demanded money in exchange for a ride. There were also checkpoints on the road, and people were not allowed through if they were not carrying the right papers or enough hard currency. Eventually, Murthy reached Nis, a small border town between Yugoslavia (now Serbia) and Bulgaria. A kind friend of a friend had given him a lift to the railway station. Murthy's plan was to take a train from Nis to Sofia, the capital of Bulgaria. Since the acronym of his project in Paris was SOFIA, he thought it would be fun to send a postcard to his Paris colleagues from this city!

Murthy was dropped off at the Nis railway station around 9 p.m. on a Saturday. Ready for a good meal, he went into the only restaurant there and ordered some food. But he had no Yugoslavian money and only had Italian lira. The manager refused to accept any foreign currency and asked him to leave. A hungry Murthy had no option but to doze fitfully on a bench in the station that night, keeping an eye out for the police. In the morning, he walked to a nearby bank to get his money changed or his traveller's cheques cashed. But everything was closed. He lay down again on the bench and stayed there all day to conserve his energy. He was ravenous by this time. When the Sofia Express pulled in at 8.30 p.m., he boarded a compartment which held a young woman and a man.

As always, Murthy tried to converse with his fellow travellers to learn about life in their country. They did not seem to know English or Russian, but when he tried French, the woman responded. They began a conversation. After Murthy told her about his hitchhiking trip, she opened up about her life and its challenges. A Bulgarian citizen, she had gone on a government scholarship to Kiev University to obtain her PhD in economics. While studying at Kiev she fell in love with a young man who was on a similar scholarship from East Germany.

They sought permission from their respective governments and got married. When she completed her PhD and returned to Sofia, she requested the Bulgarian government for permission to migrate to East Germany to live with her husband. But they said that since she had gone on a government scholarship, she could only do that after serving her country for five years.

Unfortunately, the East German government took the same stand with the young man. The result was the girl had to use the communist corridor via Bulgaria, Yugoslavia, Hungary, Czechoslovakia and East Germany once every six months to travel from Sofia to East Berlin to meet her husband. She grew quite emotional while telling Murthy her story; he was understandably sympathetic. They did not pay any attention when the young man who had been sitting nearby left the compartment. Later, Murthy surmised that he must have complained to the authorities that his fellow passengers were indulging in treasonous, anti-government talk.

The train had not started yet. To Murthy's surprise, four police officers suddenly came into the compartment and dragged the girl away. Murthy never saw her again and was haunted for a long time by the fear of what may have happened to her. The police ransacked Murthy's sleeping bag and backpack, seized his passport, dragged him along the platform into a bleak 8-foot by 8-foot room, and locked him in there. The room was very cold, with a stone floor and a hole in a corner for a toilet. It was the middle of winter and Murthy was afraid he would freeze to death.

He was held in that lightless room without food or water for over three days.

'I lost all hope. I was sure I would be made to die of cold and starvation in this heaven of communism called Nis,' he told the horrified Sudha.

He had despaired of ever being released or of seeing his home again when the door finally opened. Four burly Bulgarian policemen dragged him again along the rough floor of the platform and threw him into the guard's compartment of a departing freight train. They told him that his passport would be given back to him in Istanbul, and that they were letting him go only because he was from 'a friendly country called India'.

The freight train was a slow one, with multiple stops. Murthy was told by the guard that it would take about twenty-one hours to reach Istanbul. By now he had not eaten for 108 hours and was famished. But no one cared.

The journey gave Murthy plenty of time to ponder the ills of a communist regime and the injustice that it could so easily and brutally inflict on innocent people. He pushed aside his anger at how unfairly he was treated and carefully compared capitalism, socialism and communism, introspecting on his experiences over these last months. He arrived in Istanbul famished and still furious – and deeply ambivalent about the philosophy he had adhered to all these years.

Looking back, Murthy felt that his European journey – even its dark aspects – had been extremely valuable. He told Sudha, 'I was a confused leftist. My Bulgarian adventure got rid of my desire to be a socialist, but the remaining vestiges of my leftist ideology pushed me to evolve my own brand of capitalism, which I call compassionate capitalism. I also resolved to learn what it takes to become an entrepreneur and how corporations work. I am a better man today because of my experiences in Europe.'

Murthy eventually reached India via Afghanistan, which at that time was a peaceful, friendly country. The Soviet Union and the US had not yet begun their proxy war. Kabul reminded Murthy of Ahmedabad of the late 1960s – inexpensive and not too crowded. The restaurants were affordable, specializing in shareable meals that came with large slices of freshly baked Barbari bread that could be torn off and passed around the table. Murthy stayed in a dormitory which he shared with a Pakistani music troupe, street performers who earned money by singing a mix of European and Hindi songs in marketplaces. They had travelled around 2500 kilometres over three days in buses, and their happy-go-lucky lifestyle amazed and amused Murthy. But it was no longer something he wanted for himself.

Murthy returned to India in 1974, his head filled with dreams of helping to shape a nation. But within a few months, the country was plunged into the Emergency years, dark days where suspicion often led to quick imprisonment for many political leaders and journalists, not unlike Murthy's unjust and terrifying incarceration in Nis.

To make matters more complicated, Rama Rao passed away at this time, leaving Murthy with many family responsibilities. Emotionally, this was a difficult moment for Murthy as his father had been a huge presence in his life. Somewhere inside, Murthy had harboured the desire to demonstrate to Rama Rao that he was successful – but in his own unique way. He had also wanted to prove to him that his vision of compassionate capitalism, and not Nehru's socialism, that would be the solution to the problems of India. Now he would not get the chance to do it. Instead, he shouldered his responsibilities and vowed to support his younger siblings and especially his mother both financially and emotionally. To this end, he began looking for a job.

As a 'foreign-returned' computer expert, Murthy should have been in high demand in the job market. However, it did not turn out to be as easy as one would have expected, because Murthy was only interested in positions that satisfied him ethically.

Fortunately, Murthy's professor, Krishnayya, had left IIMA, moved over to Pune, and started a think tank called

Systems Research Institute (SRI), modelled on the Stanford Research Institute. He invited Murthy to join him. Murthy was happy to agree as he felt this would allow him to have some deep discussions with Krishnayya about entrepreneurship and capitalism in India. Krishnayya offered Murthy a salary of Rs 1800 per month. However, Murthy felt it was not proper for him to draw a full salary when SRI was in a fledgling state. In spite of his financial commitment to his family, he voluntarily decided to take a pay cut and opted for a salary of Rs 900 per month, though this meant that he had to live extra frugally.

At this point, in 1974, SRI had just five employees in all, including Murthy and Krishnayya. The institute applied operations research, systems theory, computer science and mathematical modelling to address problems in large-scale public systems. An early project was for Steel Authority of India Limited (SAIL). The project was to study and improve distribution of steel from the steel plants to buyers in India. In another project, SRI compared the drilling performance of Oil India Limited (OIL) and the Oil and Natural Gas Corporation (ONGC) in Assam in order to study the best practices at these units and share them to improve productivity. Krishnayya, optimistic as ever, believed that they were doing crucial work for government organizations that were keen on better outcomes.

In Pune, Murthy roomed with a colleague, Shashi, and the two were joined by his friend Prasanna, who had joined the Tata Administrative Services (TAS) and was posted for training in TELCO's Pune factory. By this time, Murthy's books had arrived from Paris – the very books that Prasanna would read on the bus on his way to work, igniting Sudha's interest.

5

By 1975, Murthy found himself increasingly happy with his personal life. He was in love with Sudha and, although he hadn't said anything formally to her, he could sense that she regarded him with great warmth. Work, however, was a different matter.

The reports that Murthy laboured so hard to produce sat gathering dust on the shelves in government offices. No actions were taken, and no changes made. There was no impact on the public sector. The lack of interest, after all the work he had done, weighed Murthy down. He had been willing to put up with a low salary, believing he was helping his country. Now he was frustrated by the meagre results. Some days, he felt like he was wasting his life. He felt a strong urge to start his own company. After all, he had the background and the intelligence for it. He had done plenty of work at IIMA and Paris in both planning and building complex software. He was certain he could do the same for corporate India.

When he shared his feelings with Krishnayya, his mentor was sympathetic. 'Whether the government uses the SRI work or not is not in my hands,' he said. 'I knew that already. But I can understand your frustration. You are much younger than me. You want rapid results.'

With Krishnayya's blessings, Murthy handed in his resignation on 19 August 1976. He had chosen the date carefully: it was Sudha's twenty-sixth birthday. The next day, 20 August, would be his own birthday. He was just short of thirty years old. If he was to create his own path, he felt, this was the moment.

He told Sudha about this significant decision that evening over a milkshake. He spoke casually, but inwardly he was anxious. He did not know how this woman, who was becoming ever more important to him every day, would react to the news of him becoming intentionally jobless.

Sudha was not totally surprised. She had known of Murthy's dissatisfaction, his frustration at pouring his talents into a black hole. Still, she was concerned by the fact that he now had no income whatsoever. She knew he did not have much money saved up, and that, since his father's death, his family had been leaning heavily on him to help with expenses.

'You seem to have made this significant decision very quickly,' she said. 'How did the dream of entrepreneurship become so important for you?'

Murthy thought for a bit. 'It's been at the back of my mind ever since I went to France. When I was growing up, I didn't really have any other models for success. I adored my father but he was always busy trying to provide for the family. So our relationship remained respectful and distant. The other two people in the family that I loved and respected the most were my mother and my older half-sister Kumuda – who was like a second mother to me – but they had not had much formal education. They loved and encouraged me, but they couldn't give me career suggestions. In a strange way, this turned out to be a good thing. Because I grew up in an atmosphere of unintended freedom, and because I had so little to lose, I felt free to dream. My dreams led me to France, where I experienced entrepreneurship in action. I became a convert!'

'Aren't you afraid of what might happen if your plans don't succeed? You have three unmarried sisters, and your mother and even your grandmother are depending on you.' Sudha shook her head. 'If I were in your place, I couldn't have done it.'

Murthy shrugged, pushing away the image of his mother's worried face. 'If I'm unhappy at a job, what is the point of staying on? I refuse to waste my time and energy writing reports for clients who have no desire to improve. That's not the kind of life I wish to lead.'

Sudha was a positive thinker, and pragmatic as well. Now that Murthy had committed to his path, she put aside her concerns – about his career and about what might happen to their relationship – and sincerely wished him the best of luck. She told him not to worry. She was sure, with his intelligence and work ethic, he would make a success of things. Then she leaned across the table and clasped his hand. 'Also, I'm here to help you in any way I can.'

A relieved smile appeared on Murthy's face. 'Let's go to Chung Fa for dinner,' he said. 'We'll celebrate both our birthdays – and the birth of my new career as an entrepreneur.'

That night, as Murthy lay in bed, thinking through all that had happened in the last twenty-four hours, he kept remembering Sudha's smiling face and the warm press of her fingers on his hand. It gave him new confidence. With her by his side, he felt he could take on even the toughest challenges.

Sudha's own way of handling professional dissatisfaction was different. Despite everything she had done to perform excellently and create rapport on the TELCO shop floor, many of the men were still uncomfortable about interacting with her. Even after several months of her being at the company, workers continued to bypass her regularly to speak to the male managers. They indicated they did not want her touching the machines because she was sure to bring them bad luck. And they told the top management they wanted her to stay away on days of special religious celebrations.

Sudha was hurt by such attitudes, especially after all the efforts she had made to get to know the workers. She had already learnt, from her experience in engineering college, not to give up just because other people wanted her to do so. Nor was she the kind of person who would quit impulsively. She knew she was learning a great deal and opening doors for other women. Stubbornly, she decided she was not going to let prejudicial or superstitious attitudes scare her away.

Her efforts did not go to waste. The management recognized her professionalism and her intelligence, appreciated her difficulties, and did whatever they could to make her job easier. This was good enough to keep Sudha going.

Over the next few days, Murthy thought hard about the kind of company he wanted to start. He told Sudha that he envisioned it as an extension of what he had built for the IIMA students and professors. He would use his knowledge of information systems to design applications for businesses. Government organizations did not seem interested in improving productivity, but surely the private sector would be. 'I feel confident about this. I've seen the impact of computerization first-hand in Europe,' he said to Sudha, who listened intently. 'Not only governments but banks and businesses have adopted these systems. The minicomputer has made computing power accessible at affordable prices. Companies like Digital Equipment Corporation, IBM and Data General are transforming entire industries with their products. Sooner or later, it's bound to happen in India – and when it does, my company is going to be in the forefront.'

Murthy decided to call his company Softronics, a word combining software and electronics. His friend Madhava Rao, who had worked with him at SRI, designed the official stationery for the company. He also promised to type Murthy's business letters in the evenings, after his regular job. Looking at the fresh ink on the newly printed Softronics letterhead, Murthy felt his heart expand with hope. He began scouting for business. He knew enough design and programming on the computers available in India at that time and was very comfortable with all the programming languages. His plan was this: once he succeeded in convincing a customer that he could develop a software system for them, he would hire computer time from data centres at companies such as ECIL in Hyderabad. He would then be able to run applications and store and process data. He could also develop his software, validate it, install it and then send in the invoice. But the reality turned out to be very different.

His lack of a formal office space turned out to be a major hurdle. When potential clients enquired where the Softronics office was, the fact that it was located in Murthy's flat rang alarm bells. Unlike in the US, where many tech giants started off in garages, in India even a fledgling company was expected to have a proper office. Murthy ran into the same problem when he tried to hire engineers. Before accepting the job offer, they wanted to see their workspace, and when they saw a table set up in Murthy's bedroom, they were sceptical. There would come a time when neither customers nor employees cared whether a company had a formal office or a co-working space or a converted apartment – as long as they had intellectual assets and demonstrable skills. But this was the 1970s and Murthy was hacking out a new path.

Even when he managed to find some clients willing to take a chance on him despite the small size of his operations, executing the projects turned out to be more difficult than he had expected. The few computers in Pune – old, outdated and glacial in speed – were useless to Murthy. And even in other cities, accessing a computer was difficult, thanks to the Indian government's severe import licensing restrictions and the small number of rudimentary, India-made, low-capacity IBM, ECIL and ICL (International Computers Limited) machines. The government wrongly believed that computers were 'labour-saving devices' that threatened to increase unemployment in India. Hence, there was massive red tape and long waiting times to purchase one. ECIL manufactured only a couple of low-powered and low-capacity models: a 12-bit computer called the TDC 312 and a 16-bit version called the TDC 316. Murthy would have been delighted even with this slow model which would have taken him twice as long as a regular computer, but they were very rare. Because of the government restrictions, only four of these had been sold to the private sector between the late 1970s and early 1980s.

To develop his systems, Murthy had to travel to other cities to use data centres there. For instance, to do the required work for his first client, Dr Beck and Company (DBC), Murthy would travel once a month to ECIL in Hyderabad and spend a week there to do his work. At other times, Murthy would have to travel to an ICL data centre in Mumbai. The computer there was free only late at night, and the centre would allocate Murthy time in fifteen-minute slots when no one else required the machine – for instance, between 2.15 and 2.30 a.m. Murthy worked alone in the data centre, compiling his code. If he made an error in his code, he had to wait two frustrating days to get another time slot to rectify it.

These were tough odds: travelling from Pune to Mumbai to use a computer for fifteen minutes in the dead of night at an exorbitant price. It cost Murthy Rs 550 for each hour of computing time; additionally, he was exhausted from all the back-and-forth travel. The computer available to him, the ICL 1901, was very slow, taking fifteen minutes to compile a COBOL program of a thousand lines. His revenues were eaten up by high business costs that made it increasingly unlikely that he would turn a profit.

The biggest challenge, Murthy realized with a sinking heart, was that access to computers – especially a faster computer – was unlikely to improve any time soon. The Indian government's motto, at that time, was 'self-reliant, indigenous development'. If an entrepreneur did not want to use the Indian ECIL computers, the authorities made procuring anything else from abroad very difficult. The US firm Digital Equipment Corporation (DEC) had emerged as the top minicomputer manufacturer in the world, providing customers with smaller, cheaper general-purpose computers that would have been perfect for Murthy's projects. But the government made their import into India almost impossible. Because of the lack of computers, Indian businesses did not yet recognize the value of information systems and therefore were reluctant to pay good prices for the kind of service Murthy could provide.

Faced with a slew of problems beyond his control, a frustrated Murthy was finally forced to admit that his first foray into entrepreneurship was not going well. This created in him a crisis of conscience. He felt he had no right to involve Sudha in such an uncertain future. After agonizing over this for weeks, he made a decision. When they met after work one evening, he startled her by blurting out, 'I think we should break up.'

Sudha was both shocked and hurt. 'But why?' she asked him.

'My venture is failing. You are a beautiful woman with a shining future. I can't drag you down with me,' he said. 'I'll be happy without money, I don't care for it. After all, I grew up on the edge of poverty. But I don't want to spoil your life.'

Sudha's heart sank. She had been planning to tell her parents about him and to introduce him to them soon. But she hid her feelings and narrowed her eyes at him. 'What makes you think I care about money any more than you do?'

Murthy, however, would not listen to her arguments. He cut off all contact with her. In the following days, he started hanging out more than ever before with friends with socialist leanings, but this only confused him further. Within his heart, the ideals of Marx battled with the examples presented by Gandhi and by his best-loved epic hero, Karna the Generous. Out of this turmoil would finally emerge a clear philosophy of compassionate capitalism, but the interim was painful and bewildering.

Sudha could have made Murthy feel guilty for abandoning her after spending all this time with her or pursued him aggressively, but she had too much self-respect to respond in an over emotional way. But neither was she willing to just give up. Though she was upset, she knit him a white sweater – perhaps because she knew his propensity towards giving away his clothes to the poor. It took her a long time because she was not deft with handicrafts. But finally she completed it and sent it to him with their common friend Vinay. This silent gift of love did its job. Murthy, who had been missing her terribly, reached out to apologize, the two of them got back together, and in the dark days that followed, Sudha became the single source of brightness for Murthy.

Sudha helped Murthy through this tough time in a number of ways. When she realized he was running out of savings, she quietly loaned him some money every month. When he protested, she told him he could return it when things got better. She even bought him a shirt so that he would be better dressed at meetings. She knew their evenings together brought him a great deal of solace because she was a good listener and he could unload whatever was on his mind. But she also realized he no longer had money to eat out regularly. So she started paying for their dinners – and Murthy, though usually proud about being self-sufficient, accepted. She sometimes asked probing questions about what he was doing to grow his company, but overall, she was supportive and encouraging. Murthy, who could never speak to his own family about his work problems, grew more attached to her each day.

When Sudha visited her family in Hubli – something she liked doing every few weeks – Murthy would accompany her to the train station. 'I'll see you off,' he would say, but when the train arrived, he would get on it with her because he wanted to spend as much time with her as possible.

The first time this happened, Sudha, who was a law-abiding

individual, was scandalized. 'Murthy,' she said, 'you don't have a ticket!'

'It's okay,' he reassured her. 'I'll get down at the next station.'

But he did not get down at the next station – or the next, and they continued on, chatting all the way. When the ticket collector came to check their tickets, he fined Murthy. Sudha was the one who ended up paying because Murthy did not have enough money! This happened several times. Finally, Sudha stopped protesting and just bought a ticket for him. She understood this was a way for Murthy to spend some extra time with her. Soon, Murthy began to accompany her all the way to Hubli, an eleven-hour trip each way. Her home was walking distance from the station. He would wave goodbye and wait patiently at the station for four hours for the next train back to Pune.

Most of Sudha's friends did not approve of this relationship. None of them came from entrepreneurial families. They could not understand how Murthy could live with so much uncertainty, not knowing where his next paycheque would come from. More importantly, they could not understand why Sudha, who was from a respected and well-to-do family, held a good job, and was attractive and intelligent, would want to be with him.

'You can have anybody,' they protested to her. 'Why do you want Murthy, who is little more than a vagabond?'

In response, Sudha would just smile.

One day, Sudha's friend Surckha went to Pune station to catch a train and was horrified to find Murthy sleeping on the platform. The train he was supposed to take to visit his mother had been delayed. So, the international hitchhiker had rolled out his sleeping bag, which was zipped up all the way to his face, and gone off to sleep. Indians were unused to such behaviour from educated, middle-class individuals. Surekha joked about the incident to Sudha, but perhaps she was also warning her friend. 'If you plan to marry him, watch out! You and your children may be sleeping on a platform, too!'

Sudha was too confident to be troubled by her friends' comments. She saw great potential and courage in Murthy. She watched with sympathy as he struggled for customers and tried to stretch his savings from one month to the next, and she never lost her faith in him. She was willing to give him all the time – and the support – that he needed.

In February 1977, six months after Murthy had resigned from SRI, he was forced to face a bitter fact: his business was failing. While greatly disappointed and perhaps a little ashamed, he was not a man to avoid the truth. He knew he needed to shut down Softronics without further delay in order to minimize his losses. As always, he spoke frankly to Sudha about his decision – and his frustration at being forced to make this decision. 'Softronics isn't going to be able to scale up,' he admitted. 'Everything is against it. I don't have sufficient access to computers, and buying a computer is out of reach for a small company like mine. Banks don't understand the importance of software development and have refused to give me a loan without a physical collateral. There just isn't a venture capital culture – a culture of risk-taking – here in India.'

Sudha felt for him, but she was, ultimately, a practical and positive person who always looked ahead. 'The real market for you is the international one,' she advised him. 'You need to join a software exporting company, and understand the market and the industry. When the time is more conducive, you can try again.'

Boosted by Sudha's encouragement, in June 1977 Murthy closed down Softronics after fulfilling his obligations to all his clients. He told Krishnayya what had happened and explained that he wanted to work for a while in a software export company in Mumbai to gain experience. Krishnayya promised to recommend his name if any opportunity arose.

6

Now Murthy focused on his next step: finding a job. The search took time; several months passed, but he did not find anything suitable. Being unemployed was difficult for him, both financially and psychologically. He could not send much money to his family. By now Sudha was taking care of many of Murthy's expenses, including getting him clothes that were suitable for interviews and renting a bicycle, apart from paying for dinner when they went out. The loans quickly piled up. Murthy told Sudha to keep track of everything, and she wrote it all down in a notebook – but neither of them seemed overly concerned about this.

Murthy was confident he would be able to pay Sudha back eventually. After all, he had a computer science degree, and he had seen the size of the computer industry in Europe. He felt it was only a matter of time before his fortunes changed. Sudha, too, had full faith in him, though she liked to joke about how large his debt to her was growing.

A different issue troubled Murthy more deeply. He was in love with Sudha and felt certain she was the perfect life partner for him. But he agonized over the fact that, given his present situation, it would not be fair to entangle her further in his uncertain destiny. Finally, though, he felt he could not wait any longer.

On this particular night, Sudha and Murthy had gone to have dinner at the cantonment. On their way back, they decided to take an autorickshaw as Murthy needed to meet with an ex-client after dropping Sudha off at Mahila Niwas. It was a clear night, and Sudha's face shone in the light from the moon. An intense emotion arose in Murthy's heart. It made him clasp Sudha's hand. As she glanced at him in surprise, he took a deep breath and rushed into speech. 'I'm no hero – just a short man with a squint and thick eyeglasses and no job. You, on the other hand, are beautiful and smart. But I love you, and that gives me the courage to ask this. Will you marry me?'

Sudha was taken aback. Not many people, after all, propose in a rickshaw! But then, Murthy was not like most other people – and neither was she. This man, with his deep intelligence and limitless dreams and intense desire to bring a lasting change to his country, was the only person she wanted as her husband. For his sake, she was willing to face as many challenges as necessary.

Murthy was watching her with some trepidation. It looked like he was holding his breath.

'Yes,' she said. 'Yes, I will.'

A huge grin spread over Murthy's face. 'I've never been happier in my life,' he told her.

Sudha, too, felt her heart expand with joy. But she was a practical person. 'Don't get too excited too fast!' she quipped. 'We can't get married until our parents bless the union.'

'There will be no issues from my side,' Murthy said confidently. 'My mother is easy-going, and she will be very happy about our match.'

'I'm pretty sure that my mother, too, will be fine with it. But my father' – Sudha shook her head, grimacing – 'that might be a different story!'

As he dropped her off at Mahila Niwas, though, Murthy didn't worry too much about her warning. His heart was singing as he went to meet his client, and his steps were light. Sudha had said yes – that was the most important thing. How hard could it be, he thought to himself, with his solid educational and past employment record, his intelligence, work ethic and his high ideals, to get Sudha's father to agree that he would be a suitable partner for his daughter!

During a recent trip to Hubli, Sudha had indicated to her parents that she was leaning towards a young Kannadiga man in Pune as her life partner. Soon after that, Sudha's parents decided to pay a visit to Pune. They said they wanted to spend a few days with their daughter, but in reality, it was to scrutinize the young man their daughter had talked about so warmly.

'Invite him over so I can take a good look at him,' Sudha's father told her.

Murthy knew how close Sudha was to her parents. Her father, whom she lovingly called Kaka, was her number one hero. She had already told Murthy she would not marry anyone without his consent, so he felt the pressure to make a good impression on him. At the same time, because of his independent nature, a strange rebelliousness rose in his heart. He decided he would wear a red shirt – the symbol of communism – to the meeting, perhaps because he was still holding on to the vestiges of the leftist philosophy that had inspired him for so long. In addition, instead of taking an autorickshaw, he decided to ride his bicycle.

This was a bad decision. Caught in Pune traffic, he arrived sweaty and late. Sudha knew this was unlike his usual meticulous and punctual nature, but Dr Kulkarni did not. He was displeased and interpreted the lateness as purposeful. To him, Murthy's attitude showed a lack of respect.

At first, as they conversed, the situation improved a little. Dr Kulkarni was impressed by the breadth of Murthy's knowledge. He was able to discuss Dr Kulkarni's job with him in some detail because of the books he had read on medicine and surgery. Dr Kulkarni had to admit that the young man sitting in front of him was intelligent and well educated. But those qualities, by themselves, did not seem enough to assure him that Murthy would be a husband worthy of his exceptional daughter who had broken so many glass ceilings.

He frowned as he probed further. 'What are your goals in life?' he barked.

Murthy did not like being cross-examined in this way. Though he was totally focused on finding a steady job in technology so that he could learn what he needed to become an entrepreneur, something made him say, 'I'm not sure yet.' When Dr Kulkarni raised his eyebrows, Murthy added rashly, 'Maybe I will contest elections and start my own political party.'

'I see,' Dr Kulkarni said coldly. 'That is a worthy ambition, indeed. However, how will you take care of a family? Are you going to take up a job on the side?'

Murthy was searching for work day and night, but that stubborn streak made him say, 'No. Instead, I would like to start an orphanage.'

The meeting was not a success. Dr Kulkarni walked out of the room, indicating clearly that he had nothing more he wished to say.

After Murthy left, Dr Kulkarni told Sudha. 'He wants to start an orphanage and run as a candidate in an election. Where, in this equation, is his plan for supporting a family?'

'Kaka,' Sudha pointed out, 'I, too, can support a family.' But her father did not want to hear any more of such talk.

Later, Murthy apologized to Sudha. 'I don't know what came over me. I guess I just didn't like being interrogated as though I were a boy and not a grown man.'

But the harm was done.

Sudha, as Murthy had guessed, was already certain she did not want to marry anyone else. However, because she cared so much for her father, she needed to win him over. This was not going to happen easily. Dr Kulkarni, as stubborn in his own way as Murthy, considered his daughter to be a gem of a woman who deserved the very best – but now she had her heart set on an unemployed, stubborn leftist! If that was not bad enough, her father also knew she had lent Murthy a substantial amount of money. This upset him further as he wondered if, blinded by emotion, she was being taken advantage of.

'You are a Kulkarni,' he told Sudha in ensuing conversations. 'You come from a lineage of accountants. Accountants know that transactions are supposed to be clear-cut. Do you know if he will ever pay you back?'

'I know he will,' Sudha said, though the loan was not important to her. She told her father that the qualities that troubled him – Murthy's impracticality and impulsiveness – were the same ones that attracted her. 'Just the other day,' she added, 'when he saw my hostel watchman without a sweater, he took off his own – the only sweater he owned – and gave it to him.'

Murthy's generosity had touched her. She thought it would touch her father, too. After all, Dr Kulkarni often took care of his poor patients without charging a fee. But her father turned away. From his stern face, she could see he was not ready to listen to her arguments.

Things were now at an impasse. A disheartened Murthy regretted his earlier brashness and wondered what he could do to make up for it, but Sudha, who had a more optimistic nature, told him to be patient. She was confident that things would work out. She had already spoken at length to her mother, telling her she was certain that Murthy would be a good husband and, more importantly, that he was the only man who could make her happy. Her mother had not agreed, but at least she had listened carefully. And her brother Shrinivas, Murthy's staunch supporter from day one, was on her side.

Shri had been the first member of Sudha's family to meet Murthy – and he had got to know Murthy well. As a student in IIT Delhi, Shri would travel from Hubli via Pune to Delhi. He would break his journey in Pune to spend a few days with his sister. Because she was staying in Mahila Niwas, and later renting a room as a paying guest with a family, Shri would stay in Murthy's flat, where the two men would have intellectual discussions late into the night. Murthy was deeply interested in the classes Shri was taking at IIT, and later, in his career plans. Shri was impressed by Murthy's intelligence, focus, breadth of knowledge and discipline. From the first, the two of them clicked, and Shri told Sudha that she could not find a better life partner.

Shri and Murthy would become lifetime friends and keep in close touch even when oceans and continents separated them. Murthy thought of Shri as his own brother. When Shri went to the University of California at Berkeley to do his PhD, because of the stringent foreign currency rules in India, he did not have enough dollars even to buy winter clothes. Murthy, usually reluctant to ask for favours, contacted a friend in California and asked him to loan his brother-in-law enough money to tide him over until his first assistantship cheque arrived. After Shri got a job, whenever he visited India, he would always ask Murthy what he could bring for him. Murthy was not interested in the usual luxury items that people want from a foreign country. The only thing he wanted was floppy disks for his computer because they were hard to obtain in India! Later, when Sudha wanted to buy a plot in Bangalore to build a house, Shri would share in the investment and pay for part of the cost. Through the years, Murthy continued to value Shri's opinion, and whenever he came to India, Murthy would take him to the Infosys offices and ask him for his opinion on various ideas and projects.

One evening when Murthy was feeling dejected about Dr Kulkarni's refusal to give his consent, Sudha consoled him by saying, 'Don't worry. You just stay focused on looking for jobs. I have faith that things will turn out well. After all, when God closes a window, He opens a door.'

Despite his socialist leanings, Murthy was a firm believer in God. He decried the caste system, refused to wear a holy thread and detested any external show of piety – but he was a staunch devotee of Raghavendra Swamy, his family deity. However, he was very private about his spiritual life. Only after he grew close to Sudha did he tell her about his deep faith in Raghavendra Swamy and take her with him on a trip to the Raghavendra Swamy temple in Mantralayam. It was the first of several pilgrimages they would undertake to that village together.

The journey had allowed Sudha to see another side of Murthy, head bowed in prayer in front of Swamy's statue in total humility, with all his defences down. Sudha, whose father and brother were both atheists, was startled and impressed. As a child, she had accompanied her grandmother on several religious trips to temples and enjoyed the experience of circumambulating their family temple 108 times. But she had always felt she could not share that side of her nature, her religious faith, with anyone else in her family. After this trip she felt that Murthy and she held a very important common value. From that time onwards, she began to talk to him about trusting God, especially in challenging times.

Sudha's comment about trusting the divine went deep into Murthy's heart and gave him great solace. He continued his job search with renewed vigour. Perhaps serendipitously, very soon after this, he got a call from Professor Krishnayya. Ashok Patni, a graduate of IIT Bombay who had, along with his brothers Narendra and Gajendra, founded Patni Computer Systems (PCS), was looking for an experienced software professional to be the general manager (GM) for software development for exports. Would Murthy be interested?

Murthy's heartbeat speeded up. He knew about PCS. It was one of the first companies, alongside Tata Consultancy Services (TCS), to provide IT services to the domestic market. Now PCS was about to start software exports from India to the US, and Ashok was looking for a person to head that function. It fitted his expertise perfectly and was exactly the kind of learning experience he was looking for.

'I'm extremely interested,' he told Krishnayya, who was happy to connect him to the company heads. They wanted to meet him right away. With Sudha's best-of-luck wishes echoing in his ears, an excited Murthy made his way to Mumbai.

From the moment Ashok Patni shook hands with him and took him into the company boardroom for the interview, Murthy had a good feeling. Already he appreciated the fact that the Patnis had paid for him to travel in second class and had put him up in a three-star hotel. Murthy did not care for comfort or prestige, but he could see this behaviour indicated that the Patnis took good care of their employees, even potential ones. This matched his own professional philosophy. Now, he sat up tall in his chair and answered all of Ashok's questions – on computer architecture, software development, project management, people management and leadership – with ease. From the first, he had taken a liking to Ashok, who was polite, friendly, intelligent and genuinely enthusiastic about computer programming. But while he really wanted the job, Murthy felt he had to be totally open with the Patnis.

'I must warn you that my ultimate aim is to start my own company,' he informed his startled interviewers. 'While my first venture, Softronics, failed, in about six months, I'm going to try the entrepreneurial experiment again. You need to know this before you decide whether to hire me – or not.'

In spite of Murthy's warning, the brothers offered him the position right away.

'We'd like you to be the general manager of the software team,' Ashok said. 'Your salary will be Rs 4800 a month.' (About Rs 130,000 today.)

This was a generous offer – five times what he was making in Pune! – and quite a bit more than Murthy had expected. The first thought that came to him was, surely Sudha's father would now consider him a suitable partner for his daughter!

The position would formally begin in February, but meanwhile, the Patnis hired Murthy as a consultant. He visited Mumbai once a week, soaking in all the knowledge he was exposed to, excited about all the new things he was learning. He immersed himself in the manuals of the Data General (DG) computer that Ashok was importing and accompanied him to meetings with potential export and domestic customers. An added benefit was that since he only had to be in Mumbai part-time, he had plenty of time to spend with Sudha. And now *he* could pay for their evenings out!

But then there were new developments. Ashok informed Murthy that, soon after his official start date, PCS wanted to send him abroad for six months to get training on DG's minicomputer machines and to discuss export projects with various prospective businesses in the US. He would have to leave for Boston in the first week of March 1978.

'We must get married before that,' Murthy told Sudha with a new urgency, and she agreed.

An Uncommon Love

However, Sudha still had to get her parents' permission. While her father had been apprehensive about Murthy's financial future, her extended family, especially her grand aunt, had been reluctant because of a very unusual reason. Murthy's family was from the south of the Tungabhadra river. This was a big deal for Sudha's relatives, who lived on the river's northern side, because they felt that the cultures on each side were completely different from the other.

'Marrying across the river' was considered to be scandalous behaviour by traditional Kannada families. The winding Tungabhadra, which reaches a width of 25 kilometres at some parts of its journey, had served as a boundary between Karnataka's north and south for a long time. It marked a distinct separation in culture, language and cuisine. Sudha's people, for example, ate millets, and considered the rice-based diet of those from the southern side a reason for their weakness. People from north Karnataka had tea in the morning, the southerners had coffee; one side called married women 'amma', the other used the word to describe widows. And so it went. In many ways, it was easier for Sudha's community to marry Maharashtrians than to cross the river and wed someone from south Karnataka. Sudha would realize this after her marriage, when she would face significant communication challenges with Murthy's family.

While visiting home in November for Diwali, Sudha decided the time had come – now that Murthy had a good job – to tell her mother exactly how she felt about him. She added, 'I will not marry without your permission, but I refuse to marry anyone else.' Shrinivas, who was also home, supported Sudha. 'Don't worry about Sudha,' he told their mother. 'She's marrying a living computer. I can't think of anyone more suitable for her.'

Sudha's mother, Vimala, was persuaded and brought up Murthy's proposal that night during dinner, but Sudha's father continued with his meal as though he had not heard her. So Sudha had to write and inform Murthy, who was waiting impatiently, that she had not yet received an answer. She said she would try again during her visit home in December. Murthy, though disappointed, was optimistic. *No answer is better than an outright no,* he wrote back. *Plus, I have complete belief in your powers of persuasion.*

He was not wrong. Sudha's mother advocated for Murthy over the next few weeks, backed up by Shrinivas, and by the end of the year, Dr Kulkarni had given his reluctant consent.

Next, a delighted Murthy visited his widowed mother, who was now living in Bangalore, to get her permission. He had thought it would be a breeze, but to his surprise, he, too, was faced with a hurdle. His mother had met Sudha when she had visited him in Pune. While Murthy had introduced Sudha to her only as a 'good friend', she had probably guessed her son's feelings. So she was not too surprised when Murthy told her his plan. Being a very traditional woman, she was not thrilled at the thought of a 'Westernized' daughter-in-law who wore pants and T-shirts and had short hair. She said yes, but she insisted on one thing.

'Who you marry is your choice,' she said, 'but you must get married in Bangalore.' When Murthy asked why (since traditionally marriages took place in the bride's home town) she, too, pointed out that Sudha's family, who lived on the other side of the river, were practically foreigners.

'Kulkarni is not a surname that is well known this side of the

Tungabhadra,' she said. 'Our relatives will not be comfortable travelling all the way to the other side to attend the wedding.'

Murthy did not want to refuse this request from the woman who had supported him so often through his tough growing-up years. But he, too, had some requirements for the marriage ceremony. Neither he nor Sudha wanted the pomp and show and unnecessary expenses that occurred during the usual Indian wedding.

'I want the wedding to take place in your home in Jayanagar,' he said, 'not in some costly banquet hall.'

The house was a rental, and not in the best shape. Plus, it was very small. Murthy's mother protested, pointing out all the inconveniences, but he was adamant. 'That's why we'll invite only twenty guests from our side, and Sudha will do the same.'

'How will I feed everyone in this tiny space?' his mother cried.

Murthy had already thought this through. 'After the wedding, we'll go to the temple of Raghavendra Swamy – it's not far from here, and in any case, I want his blessings. We'll follow up with a simple lunch for all the guests there.'

Now Sudha had to go and tell her parents that the wedding would have to be in Bangalore!

Sudha's parents were not too happy about this flouting of tradition.

'A marriage must take place in a bride's home. Everyone knows that,' Mrs Kulkarni said. Already they were facing a lot of pressure from the extended family. The same aunts who had predicted that Sudha would be forced to remain a spinster if she studied engineering now muttered that, as the oldest of her generation, she was setting a bad example for her cousins by marrying someone from all the way across the river! 'It's as though you are marrying a foreigner,' they complained. And when some years later, Shri would marry a Japanese woman, they would shrug and comment, 'What else can you expect? He's following in his sister's footsteps.'

Finally, Sudha's parents agreed to the Bangalore wedding, but they had a stipulation of their own: the reception would have to be held in Hubli.

Sudha and Murthy, who did not believe in pomp and show – or traditions that did not have meanings or values attached to them – were exasperated by all these complications.

'We want a simple wedding,' they protested. 'Why are you making things so unnecessarily complicated?'

But their families were adamant about this issue. 'It'll be simple,' they responded. 'A simple marriage – just spread across two events, one on each side of the Tungabhadra.'

Sudha and Murthy finally gave in, but they reiterated their desire that both events be kept very simple.

The extended family members did not like this 'cheap behaviour'. Sudha's aunts were particularly indignant. 'How can you have such a modest celebration for the first marriage among the seventy-five Kulkarni cousins in the family?' they complained. Naturally, all the cousins would want to attend!

Sudha and Murthy, however, refused to compromise further. Murthy, who had five sisters, and whose marriages had required the family to mortgage everything they owned, was particularly against wasteful pomp. He remembered, with deep sadness, that his mother had had to sell all her jewellery to meet the demands of the marriage ceremonies. Sudha – though her family was financially well-off and quite able to afford a fancy wedding – agreed with him that a display of wealth was vulgar and wasteful.

'I would rather have you donate money to a worthy cause than waste it on unnecessary lavishness,' she told her father. He agreed, though not very happily. As a result, when the reception was held at the Hubli Woodlands Hotel, the guest list would consist mostly of the extended family, and Sudha's mother would cook some of the dishes herself.

———

Ultimately, Murthy and Sudha insisted on paying for their own wedding ceremony. After some calculations, they figured out that if they were careful and planned well, they would only need to spend a total of Rs 800 on the event. This amount they decided to share equally; the sharing would symbolize their life together, which they envisioned as an equal partnership. Instead of designing a wedding card, they sent a FYI letter to their few friends, announcing the wedding date. This no-nonsense invitation was printed by his friend B.M. Rao, who had taken care of Murthy's Softronics letterheads. Sudha's and Murthy's friends joked that they were probably the only couple in India of that era who sent an 'information card' for their marriage! Many members of the extended family were offended that there were no proper invitations, along with gifts and formal visits to their homes requesting them to attend, but Murthy and Sudha did not care to follow fussy niceties that they did not consider important.

Knowing that Murthy didn't have a suit for the reception in Hubli, and that he would need this when he went to Boston, Sudha gifted him one. The two of them spoke ahead of time to the priest and asked him to finish the ceremony in half an hour. Since Sudha knew Sanskrit, she looked over the slokas the priest had planned to recite and removed the ones she did not agree with, such as verses on female passivity and male dominance.

And she refused to have demeaning rituals like the one where the bride's father has to wash the feet of the bridegroom.

Finally, ever the feminist, Sudha pointed out that since Hindu men did not have to announce their marital status with matrimonial signs like sindoor or particular kinds of jewellery, she would not either. 'No mangalsutra for me,' she declared.

Murthy had no issues with this – he was an egalitarian individual – but his mother was upset. A woman with deep traditional beliefs, she worried that skipping the mangalsutra ceremony during the wedding might bring the couple bad luck. As a compromise, Sudha agreed to allow the ceremony to take place. But once she was back in Pune, she put her mangalsutra away. In fact, she went back to dressing in her preferred outfit, jeans and a T-shirt, and continued to wear her hair short. It was only years later, after she started on her project with sex workers as part of her work with Infosys Foundation, that she would wear a mangalsutra again, along with a sari and flowers in her hair, so that the women she was helping would feel comfortable with her.

Before her marriage, Sudha made another decision: she would spell her last name differently from Murthy's. She told him 'Murty' was the correct way to spell the name as that was closer to the original Sanskrit pronunciation. She had always loved Sanskrit, to which she had been introduced by her grandfather, and she wanted its authenticity to shine through her new name. Murthy, who was easy about such issues, did not mind. When, after some years, the children were born, he was agreeable to having their last name match Sudha's. Sudha appreciated his laid-back attitude in this matter. Most of the men she had come across would not have agreed to any of this.

On 10 February 1978, on a chilly morning when mist

An Uncommon Love

shrouded Bangalore's trees, a quiet wedding ceremony took place at Murthy's mother's house. It began at 10.15 a.m. and ended – as scheduled – in thirty minutes. The entire event, including lunch, was completed by noon. Murthy, thirty-two, had married Sudha, twenty-eight, from across the river.

There was one final wedding gift that Sudha gave Murthy: she tore up the notebook she had used to keep track of the money he had borrowed from her, which by then had run up to Rs 4200.

7

'Shall we go on a honeymoon?' Sudha asked Murthy once they were back in Pune after the wedding and settled into Murthy's old apartment.

Murthy, always up for a travelling adventure, was enthusiastic. 'Why not! Our married friends keep telling us how much fun it is, and romantic, too. And this is the best time, before we get busy with work again.'

They researched possible destinations. Their friends had gone to exotic locations such as Kullu Manali, Jaipur or Goa, but being frugal spenders, the two of them settled on the nearby hill station of Matheran.

'Let's go for a week,' Sudha said and, after some research, she made reservations in a clean but modest hotel, choosing a room without a view to keep costs down. Once there, the two had an enjoyable time, going sightseeing to waterfalls and scenic lookout points on the hillside filled with birdsong. At night, they ate out at simple restaurants and watched movies, and went on long moonlit walks, holding hands. They had brought their favourite entertainment – books – with them, and they spent some of their free time snuggled in bed, reading. After they turned off the light, they chatted companionably in the dark about their future life. There was much to talk about and imagine. Murthy was excited about going abroad to the US again. And Sudha, who had never been outside India, was excited to accompany him. She had already started putting aside money for this purpose.

However, after two days, they both concluded – practical as ever – that they had seen all they needed to see in Matheran. 'Everything else which we are enjoying, we can keep enjoying in Pune – for free,' Sudha said. Murthy agreed. So, on the third day, the newlyweds packed their bags and went back to their little city apartment. They had learnt an important lesson that would help them through the coming years: all they really needed in order to have a good time was each other.

―⁀―

Only three weeks now remained before Murthy's departure for Boston, so PCS very thoughtfully allowed him to work from Pune and commute one day each week to Mumbai. This enabled him to spend the maximum amount of time possible with his new bride. This was a good thing because all of a sudden Sudha's trip to the US seemed uncertain. The PCS visa consultant felt that, PCS being a fledgling company, Sudha and Murthy applying for B1/B2 visas together would cause suspicion.

'I advise you against it,' he told Murthy. 'The US government might surmise that you and your wife were both secretly intending to stay on in the US. In that case, even you would be denied a visa.'

This was a great disappointment to both Murthy and Sudha. Sudha, especially, left behind all alone so soon after their marriage, was saddened. But there was no recourse, so she made plans to stay busy. She took on extra projects at work to keep herself occupied and asked family members on both sides to come and visit her once Murthy left, so that she would have company and positive distractions.

The interim period in Pune was an interesting experience for Murthy, a lifestyle different from anything he had known until then. Sudha would go to TELCO on the company bus at 7 a.m., while Murthy would work from home, learning everything he could about the DG computer – hardware as well as software – that PCS was planning to import. He would then create reports to share with Ashok. He would also prepare his lunch and most of the dinner ahead of time so that Sudha would not have to cook after she came back from work in the evening. In any case, he was a more enthusiastic cook than Sudha, who only prepared food when she was forced to. Murthy did not know a lot of recipes. His staple dishes were sambar, a simple vegetable curry made with whatever was in season, and rice, but he cooked them with the enthusiasm of novelty. Rice was not something Sudha was used to eating every day. In her family, chapattis were eaten more regularly. 'We only eat rice when we're sick and need something bland to settle the stomach,' she said to Murthy. But she was a good sport and appreciated Murthy's efforts.

Murthy was enthusiastic about his role as house husband. Perhaps this was because he knew it would end very soon, so that it was almost like a game to him. Each morning he would go, along with the women who lived in that block of flats, to the vegetable vendor who came by with his cart at 9 a.m. The women haggled to reduce the price of the vegetables, but Murthy (still a leftist at heart) felt it was unfair to the poor vendor. He always paid whatever the man asked for. Because his Marathi was not the best, sometimes he misunderstood the vegetable seller and paid him more than the man had asked for!

The women of the neighbourhood eyed Murthy with great suspicion. He could hear them whispering to each other, 'Look at this good-for-nothing fellow. His wife is working her fingers to the bone all day in a factory – and he's lazing around at home. He can't even speak Marathi. On top of that, see how he's throwing away his wife's hard-earned money carelessly by paying extra!'

Sometimes, the more outspoken ones would give him unsolicited advice. 'Get a job, young man,' they would admonish him. 'Aren't you ashamed of wasting away your life like this, shamelessly eating the food your wife is earning with such difficulty?'

Murthy would listen meekly, nodding his head at the right moments. When Sudha came home, they would share the dinner he had cooked, and he would have great fun enacting these scenes for her, making her dissolve into laughter.

In March 1978, Murthy left for Boston for training on Data General Corporation's computers and software systems along with two other colleagues. Arriving at the Logan International Airport was quite a shock for Murthy. The biting cold brought back traumatic memories of his Bulgarian Imprisonment. To make things worse, it was snowing heavily. Fortunately, Naren Patni, who was coordinating sales from the PCS offices in Boston, was a considerate man who had planned ahead. He met them at the airport with overcoats for all three men. But, even after bundling up, the new arrivals were freezing.

When Naren took the men to the apartment they would share, near the DG headquarters in Westboro, Murthy was impressed. Used to his tiny apartment in Pune, he thought this apartment was quite luxurious, with wall-to-wall carpeting and three separate bedrooms, each with a bathroom of its own. (Later he would learn this was nothing special – most apartments in the US had all these features, and more. Still, his early gratitude would remain.) He was touched, too, by Naren's thoughtfulness: he had stocked milk, coffee, tea, vegetables and Indian groceries in the apartment before their arrival. That night, curled up in his warm bed while a winter storm raged outside, Murthy wrote to Sudha (who was missing him terribly and waiting anxiously for his news), 'Don't worry about me. I've reached safely and couldn't have asked for a more welcoming host. I feel confident that, if any difficulties arise, Naren will handle them.' In a later letter he would write, 'I will always remember the Patnis with gratitude and fondness for their caring attitude towards their employees. I hope to emulate them when I have a company of my own.'

Without Murthy, Pune had lost its charm for Sudha. Wandering its streets alone, or walking past the places where they had spent so many happy evenings, only made her feel bereft. Murthy's apartment, where they had spent so many happy days after marriage, seemed cold and cavernous. She contacted the appropriate people at TELCO to ask for a transfer to Mumbai, which was approved. Murthy returned in August. The separation of six months just a few days after marriage had felt like ages. He was to go to the US again in April the following year. This time he was very keen that Sudha should join him in Boston. Fortunately, based on Murthy's past travel record, Sudha got her visa to the US without any problem. Now Sudha had to meet with the personnel office and explain that she needed a little time off to join her husband abroad. TELCO was surprisingly understanding about this, and soon Sudha found herself on her first flight, on her way to meet her husband. She was so excited that she could barely eat or sleep throughout the journey. When she finally glimpsed Murthy at the airport in Boston, waiting outside the customs area to receive her, she ran all the way across the baggage claim area and threw her arms around his neck.

Murthy's house was very well located, in the Porter Square area of Cambridge. He shared it with a younger colleague and two American girls studying at Harvard. It was a great place to explore Boston from. But soon Sudha realized that her trip was not really going to be the shared vacation she had envisioned. While he was delighted to have her with him, Murthy was extremely busy. All day he was busy discussing the details of the software project. In the evening, he went over the material with his colleague. They compared notes and shared their understanding and observations. Often, they discussed complex issues late into the night until they were exhausted, and then fell into bed and slept like the dead, leaving Sudha pretty much to her own devices.

At first Sudha was disappointed because Murthy did not even have the time to take a simple sightseeing trip around Boston with her. Another new bride might have sulked about this, but when Sudha saw how hard he was working, she could not be angry. 'Don't worry,' she told Murthy, who was feeling guilty about abandoning her in this manner. 'I can go around Boston by myself.' By reading guidebooks and asking questions, she quickly learnt to use the public transportation system in Boston and made a list of the places she was interested in visiting.

The first trip she took was on the subway's red line to MIT. Sudha stood before the imposing limestone structure of the entrance with its iconic dome and tall white Roman columns and felt a strong wave of emotion. Here it was, the world-famous institute of her dreams, the university she had chosen not to attend even though it had welcomed her with open arms. Incidents from her past flashed before her eyes. She remembered seeing the job flyer from TELCO with those incendiary words: *No women need apply*. She remembered her outraged postcard to Mr Tata himself, which had landed her a job interview at TELCO. She remembered the interview where she had aced all the questions and successfully parried the interviewers' objections to hiring women. She remembered the triumphant moment she was offered the job – though the job itself had not been important to her. She remembered her father's stern words to her, which had led her to choose TELCO over MIT, slamming shut the door on what she had long believed to be her true vocation.

Sudha was not one to regret past decisions and lost opportunities. And how could she regret a decision that had led her to Pune, and to Murthy, the love of her life? But she was only human. Now, though five years had passed, she was shaken by her old desires. She felt again how badly she had wanted to attend MIT and receive a PhD. She sat down on the steps to the entrance to the institute with its iconic dome and did something that was rare for her: she wept.

Sudha spent the rest of the day walking through the libraries, turning the pages of books she would never read. She stood at the doorways of labs and watched hungrily as students consulted with each other and with their professors. The breadth of resources available to the students at MIT astounded her. She could not stop thinking of the opportunities she had lost. Books and libraries and education had always been her passion, and even though she realized she had accomplished many important things by remaining in India, regret kept sweeping over her like a tidal wave.

When Sudha returned to the apartment that evening, she was very quiet and went to bed early, without eating dinner. But she couldn't sleep. She tossed and turned and couldn't stop thinking of all she had given up. When Murthy, sensitive to her moods, asked her what the matter was, she was unable to keep her feelings bottled up any more. Tears came again to her eyes as she told him how regretful she had felt while visiting MIT, how much she had loved the place. Murthy gently turned her towards him. Cupping her face in his hands, he said, 'It isn't too late. If you want to study at MIT, I will continue working at Patni and support you. You can still do your PhD.'

Sudha knew Murthy never said something unless he truly meant it. This was a serious offer he was making. He was willing to give up his dream of entrepreneurship for her sake. That's how much she meant to him. Looking into his resolute face in the shadowy bedroom, she felt her heartache receding. What she had gained with this man was far more than any degree that even the most prestigious institute could confer on her. This was what love really was, not the dramatic dialogues filled with poetic exaggerations, or the exchange of sultry glances, or the dances around the trees in the movies she loved to watch.

She pulled Murthy close. 'You are my PhD,' she whispered into his ears.

One of the things that troubled Sudha as she watched Murthy working so hard in Boston was that he had stopped reading for enjoyment. The man who had valued his well-thumbed books above all his earthly possessions did not even have ten minutes in his day when he could relax with a treasured writer or explore a new one. The only books he had time to read were the technical documents required for his job. Remembering how the works of Mikes had brought them together, Sudha felt sad.

'Don't you miss reading?' she asked him.

Murthy shrugged. He was not one to regret what could not be helped. 'Books for me have always been a way of learning about the world. Interacting with people from other countries allows me to learn the same thing, just in a different way.'

Many years would pass before Murthy would once more have the leisure to turn to books just because they gave him pleasure.

This American trip was Sudha's first excursion outside India – she had taken a three-month leave for it – and who knew if she would ever come back, or ever have the luxury of this much time. Murthy was still too busy, but she decided she was quite capable of travelling by herself around the US.

Inspired by Murthy's stories about hitchhiking through Europe, Sudha decided to backpack across the US for three months. She bought a Visit USA plane ticket for $400. With it, she could travel all over the country. She planned her itinerary carefully, going over a map with Murthy, circling cities that were at once interesting and budget friendly. 'I can stay with friends and family in Chicago, New York, New Orleans, Niagara Falls, Washington, DC, Dallas, Los Angeles and San Francisco,' she told him. Murthy, an adventurous traveller himself, thought this was a great idea. He asked only that she check in with him every day from wherever she happened to be. She promised to do so.

With her short hair and her customary T-shirt and jeans, Sudha blended in well with the Americans around her. Often, people thought she was Hispanic. In her large backpack, she carried her money, her IDs, a camera – and, often, a tiffin box with curd rice! In New York, she stayed with Murthy's cousin in Queens and particularly enjoyed visiting the museums, especially the Metropolitan Museum of Art and the Met Cloisters. Being a history buff, she also explored many historical sites.

One evening Sudha was caught in a terrible traffic jam that gridlocked most of the roads leading out of Manhattan. Finally, though Murthy's cousin had warned her not to do this, she was forced to take the subway. Her train compartment was empty except for two men who kept staring at her.

Sudha grew increasingly uncomfortable. It was 8.30 p.m. Darkness had descended. She became very conscious of the $200 she had in her backpack. She was afraid the men were thinking of robbing her. She moved to the next compartment but that, too, was empty. What was worse was that the men followed her there. By now she was sure something was very wrong. Her heart thudded in her chest and her hands began to sweat. Even though she did not know this part of town, she decided to get down at the next stop. Perhaps she could find an all-night diner, she thought, where she could wait until morning. But when she exited the train, clutching her backpack tightly to her chest, the men got off as well. She tried to run, but before she could get far, one of them caught up with her and grabbed her arm.

'You need to come with us,' he said, flashing his badge at her. They were undercover cops! Sudha didn't know whether to be relieved or even more anxious. What did they want with her? she wondered. Had she broken some unknown American law?

The men marched her to the Railway Police office and

questioned her as to where she was from and what she was doing in New York. They opened her bag and searched it thoroughly, but the only unusual thing they found in there was a half-empty container of curd rice! After checking her IDs to make sure they were not fake, they told Sudha that she matched the description of an Italian drug dealer they had been looking for. Her nervousness on the train, her tight grip on her backpack, and her attempt to 'escape' had made them certain she was carrying drugs. They let her go after strictly cautioning her not to travel alone so late at night. Violent crime, drug dealing and street prostitution were serious problems in the city, with many criminals carrying guns.

When she finally found a bus and reached the house, Sudha called Murthy to tell him about her misadventure. He was very concerned and made her promise not to stay out that late again while she was in the city. It was only later, after researching New York further and learning that its subway was considered the most dangerous transit system in the world, that Sudha realized the full extent of the risk she had taken and how lucky she had been.

Sudha soon recovered from this frightening encounter and continued with her itinerary, and when she reached Arizona, she decided to make her way to the bottom of the Grand Canyon. It would be a lifetime experience, she thought as she stood on the edge of the immense, red-rimmed valley with the silver thread of the Colorado river glimmering below. A good planner, she had plotted her trek carefully, estimating the distance to be 9 kilometres. She started her descent, confident she would reach the valley by midday.

After a while, however, she realized she had made a serious miscalculation. The distance was more like 14 kilometres and the path a rocky incline full of loose stones that forced her to slow down. It was dark by the time she reached the bottom of the valley. She knew that if she tried to go back up, she might encounter a wild animal, or slip and fall, breaking a bone.

Sudha was nervous but she knew she could not afford to panic. Taking God's name, she walked along the river's edge. In a little while, to her great relief, she saw a few people. There were two young men who had been rowing down the river and had set up a tent for the night. There was also an older couple, campers who spoke no English. They offered her a blanket to sleep in and the only vegetarian food they had, a pack of biscuits. Sudha was thankful for their kindness. She devoured the biscuits in minutes and was still terribly hungry. As the night progressed, everyone disappeared inside their tents. Sudha wrapped herself as best as she could in the blanket. But the night had turned very cold, the ground was hard and bumpy, and sleep was impossible. After a while, she sensed something, and when she looked that way, there was a massive cat – perhaps a cougar – crouched not far from her. It was the most frightening thing she had ever seen. She covered her head with the blanket but was too tense to even think of sleeping. Each time she peered out from under the blanket, there the creature was, watching her with its glowing, tawny eyes. Perhaps it was considering if it was hungry enough to go to the trouble of attacking her. It seemed to Sudha that this hellish night would never end!

As soon as the sun rose, Sudha returned the blanket, thanked the campers, and climbed back up as quickly as she could. By the time she reached her hotel, Murthy, who had been keeping careful track of her itinerary, had called the hotel several times, trying to figure out where she was. He had left increasingly anxious messages asking her to call him as soon as she returned. When she did call him, he gave her a stern lecture on taking too many risks. Love had changed the man who had once blithely hitchhiked, without a single thought for the future, into Iron Curtain territory!

Sudha listened meekly and promised to be careful. Then she reverted to her usual cheerful self and described her night's adventure to him in colourful detail. Now that she was safe, she could laugh about the entire experience, and her descriptions of herself peeping out at the big cat from under her borrowed blanket made Murthy laugh, too.

Sudha's nature was to look at the bright side of things, and she usually managed to make Murthy see things her way. At times when Murthy was worrying about a significant risk he was about to take, she would say to him, 'What's the worst that can happen!' Because of her calming influence, Murthy would phone her to discuss important upcoming decisions even if she was in another city – or on another continent. Her positivity reassured him, and her down-to-earth attitude gave him the confidence to follow his dreams even when they seemed out of reach.

Once Murthy's work was completed, he and Sudha decided to visit Paris together before returning to India. Murthy wanted to show his bride the city that had shaped his outlook on the world. It was a magical experience for Sudha. She loved the old churches, the grand palaces, the roadside cafes where she could sit and people-watch, or the many bridges from where she could look down at the Seine winding its way through the city. She was particularly excited by the museums, especially the Louvre, filled with famous paintings and statues that she had only read about, and seen pictures of, in books.

'I can't believe that I was able to stand in front of amazing works of art such as the *Mona Lisa* and the *Winged Victory*, and look at them for as long as I wanted!' she exclaimed in awe to Murthy.

Murthy did not share her enthusiasm for art, but he encouraged it. He waited for her in a cafe, drinking coffee and happily reading a book, while she spent an entire day at the Louvre.

By the end of their sojourn abroad, Murthy and Sudha recognized something important about each other that would contribute to the success of their relationship: they were very different from each other, and that was fine. Murthy appreciated Sudha's cheerfulness, her willingness to face the world with her arms wide open and her ability to bounce back quickly even if things did not turn out the way she imagined. It sometimes took her to dangerous places like the bottom of a canyon or into a crime-ridden subway! Still, her enthusiasm prompted Murthy to engage with the world more than he otherwise would have. Sudha, on the other hand, appreciated Murthy's strict discipline, his sharp intelligence, his deep store of knowledge and his eagerness to always learn more. She was moved by his thoughtfulness, adherence to values and fairness when dealing with people. She particularly admired the fact that he was unaffected by status and posturing.

On the flight back to India, Sudha told Murthy, 'In many ways, you remind me of my grandfather, who was a very principled man. That's one reason why I love you.'

Murthy said, 'You, however, don't remind me of anyone. You are unique and unlike any woman I've ever met.' With a grin, he added, 'And that's why I love you!'

8

Mumbai was a whole different world and a whole different lifestyle for Sudha and Murthy. Because of their new jobs and their new responsibilities, they both became busier than ever before. While it was an exciting place, Mumbai was larger and more confusing than any city they had lived in until now – and it was a commuter's nightmare. For Murthy, especially, the workday was very long.

The PCS data centre was located at the computer centre of the Associated Cement Company (ACC). PCS was allotted two time slots for their use of the DG computer system there: 6–8 a.m. and 8–11 p.m. Murthy and his team also had to provide software support to ACC and other PCS domestic data centre customers during normal office hours. Because of this, Murthy would leave for work at 5 a.m. and reach the office in time for the morning slot for software development work. He stayed at work all day and then worked through the late-night slot, which was devoted to solving problems for international clients. He would reach home exhausted and get only about four hours of sleep before his workday started again.

To add to their difficulty, the apartment they had rented – the only one they could afford – was all the way across the city in Santacruz East, next to the railway line. It was tiny and cramped and up on the fourth floor. There was no lift. But at least it had its own bathroom, something their first flat didn't have. However, the Mumbai trains ran past their windows till 1.30 a.m. and started up again at 4 a.m. The noise of the trains kept waking Murthy up, and as a result he was always tired. He found himself getting short-tempered, which was unlike him. He was also losing weight. Sudha grew worried as she watched this punishing schedule beginning to take its toll on her husband's health. She wondered aloud whether he should start looking for a different job with better hours, one which would allow them to move into a better flat, hopefully something closer to work.

As providence would have it, right around this time their old friend Prasanna got in touch with them. He had done very well for himself since moving from Pune to Mumbai and was now the HR head at Wipro.

'I think I might have something at Wipro that will be just right for you,' he told Murthy. 'Why don't you and Sudha come and have dinner with me, and I'll give you all the details.'

Sudha was excited at the thought of a better opportunity. She was also impressed by Prasanna's flat on Nepean Sea Road. It was in a lovely part of the city, with wide roads and high-rises and parks from which you could see the ocean. Being a movie buff, she was particularly taken by the fact that it was close to the luxurious Malabar Hill area, where many Bollywood stars lived.

Over a sumptuous dinner, Prasanna told them that Azim Premji, the chairman of Wipro, was planning to start a technology division and was looking for someone to head it.

Prasanna suggested that Murthy apply for the job. 'You'll be perfect for it,' he assured Murthy. He promised to get him an interview with Premji.

Sudha was excited by the idea. She said, 'If you get the job, maybe we could move into a noise-free apartment.'

Soon Prasanna scheduled an interview with Premji for Murthy. Murthy did not have any formal wear; nor did he think such attire was necessary for a technical interview. He showed up in a clean shirt and a pair of brown pants. Premji, who was immaculately dressed in an expensive suit with a foreign cut, was very polite, but he was clearly a little taken aback. He took Murthy to the Willingdon Club for a luncheon interview. Murthy had never been inside such a fancy venue in India and was a little awed by his surroundings – including the many pieces of cutlery arranged beside his plate. He could see that his world was very different from that of Premji, who was clearly from a very privileged background. He answered all of Premji's questions accurately and smartly, but perhaps Premji sensed his unease with his surroundings. Perhaps it made him feel that Murthy would not fit in with the other sophisticated heads of departments. He did not offer Murthy the job.

Years later, Murthy would learn that Premji regretfully referred to this decision as one of his gravest errors of judgement.

Luckily the management at PCS recognized how Murthy's living conditions were impacting his health. They also realized that if they did not do something about this unsustainable situation, he was likely to take up a job elsewhere. Therefore, they allotted him a company apartment in Bandra West. To Sudha's delight, it was a far quieter place, with its own bathroom, and not far from the sea. It seemed the ultimate luxury! Their new home was certainly an improvement, but Murthy barely saw the place since he came home primarily to sleep. Apart from taking care of his own work, he spent a good amount of time training his team. He had already recruited a talented group of engineers, but he continued to add more people to his team. Within a couple of years into his job at PCS, he would have over a hundred people working with him, including many graduates recruited from IIT Bombay – most of them not computer engineers – whom he would train in the basics of computer science and software engineering.

Sudha was also busy with her work, but overall, she had a saner schedule. It was important for her to spend quality time with Murthy whenever possible, but she did not want to stress him. *If the mountain would not come to Muhammad*, she said to herself with a shrug, *then Muhammad must go to the mountain*. So she would come home from work and quickly cook something – usually a simple meal of rice, sambar and vegetables from her slim repertoire of recipes. She would jump on the train to Churchgate, with the food packed in a tiffin carrier, and arrive at Murthy's office around 9 p.m. After a while, all the cleaners and the night crew knew this bustling, friendly young woman, and the security people would wave her through with a smile. She would spread out their dinner on Murthy's table, and the two of them would have a leisurely meal.

Sudha took Murthy's mind off work troubles by telling him about interesting events at her office, or funny things she had seen on her commute. She was sensitive to his moods, and on days when she felt he was extra tired, they ate in companionable silence. For special occasions, she would cajole him to pause work for a bit and join her at a small restaurant nearby in Bandra, the

Pamposh, which reminded them of their romantic Pune days. On Sundays, if Murthy was not too tired, they would go for a movie because Sudha was still just as crazy as before about seeing films as soon as they were released. Money was tight for the young couple – Murthy was saving for the upcoming wedding of one of his sisters. But the cinema was one of the few treats they allowed themselves. One of their happier memories of this busy time was enjoying movies such as *Rajnigandha* and *Chitchor*. Sudha discovered a new film star she liked very much: Amol Palekar. His 1979 romantic comedy *Baton Baton Mein* would become one of her favourites.

At times when Murthy's work responsibilities grew too heavy, he would be unable to spend even this small amount of time with Sudha. She did not like it, but she understood. Meanwhile, her own work at TELCO was engrossing and enjoyable. In Pune, she had constantly been made to feel conscious of her unusual position as the first woman on the shop floor. The Mumbai head office was, in comparison, a cheerful corporate environment where her colleagues, both male and female, were accepting and friendly.

One evening, while they were eating dinner at Murthy's work, he apologized to her for abandoning her to her own devices. 'Don't worry,' she replied in her usual cheery way. 'Thanks to my father, I'm quite used to workaholics. There were many nights when my father would see patients until three in the morning. My mother never berated him for it. She lived a full and interesting life herself and enjoyed her solitude – and watching her, I learnt to do the same.'

Sudha found new ways to make positive use of her time. She visited relatives and friends in the city and was quite content to go alone for the plethora of activities that were available to cultured Mumbaikars. She attended art exhibitions at the Jehangir Art Gallery, attended Marathi plays in Vile Parle, went to Karnataka Sangha in Matunga, and visited the Chhatrapati Shivaji Museum (called Prince of Wales Museum at that time) regularly. At other times, she was happy curled up in bed in the quiet of their apartment, reading books by well-loved authors, such as Jerome K. Jerome or George Mikes, which she would have picked up at the Strand, one of her favourite bookstores. Mumbai was a friendly place, easy to get around and safe for women. She quickly grew fond of the city and began to think of it as home.

~

Meanwhile, Murthy was putting a lot of energy in gathering the right kind of team around him. He was an out-of-the-box thinker when it came to recruitment, and his interview process was strikingly innovative. Instead of quizzing the interviewees on the knowledge they had gathered and could easily regurgitate, he created puzzles. In order to solve these puzzles, interviewees had to be able to recognize patterns and use logical reasoning. He termed these 'learnability' tests.

Sudha, who liked to keep up with what was going on in Murthy's work life, was curious. 'What are these tests and how do they work?' she asked. 'I've never heard anyone talk about learnability.'

Murthy said, 'To me, learnability is the ability that allows you to extract generic inferences from specific instances and use them in new, unstructured situations to solve new problems. It's far more useful than having knowledge, which can get outdated fast, especially in the rapidly changing IT industry. We'll be going from country to country, developing new applications for new domains. What my team needs is flexibility to learn new things quickly and the ability to think nimbly.'

Clearly, Murthy was on to something. Some of the people he hired using this method were Nandan Nilekani, K. Dinesh, S.D. Shibulal, Ashok Arora, Madhav Mutalik, Arvind Kher, Madhusudan Gaikaiwari and Kamlesh Gandhi. Most of them were very young – just one to two years out of college, many of them would go on to play a role in Infosys.

In addition to training his team rigorously, Murthy took the time to develop a relationship with these much younger men. He cared for them and took the time, no matter how busy he was, to give them advice if they asked for it. He often told them, 'The team must have trust for each other. Trust is the strongest glue.'

Sudha did not begrudge the fact that Murthy's care for his mentees would cut into the few precious moments she had with her husband. She understood the importance of team building. Being more of a people person than the serious Murthy, she was good at conversing, laughing and joking, and getting to know each one of them and their families. She organized fun weekend activities such as picnics, day trips and cinema outings. Sometimes they all went to eat at a restaurant, where they pulled smaller tables together to create one large table where everyone could sit. In this way, the core team grew close to the Murthys and felt a strong bond with them. When Murthy would leave PCS to start Infosys, several of them would also quit without a second thought – mostly because they wanted to continue working with Murthy. They would form his core team and stand by him through the company's stormy early days.

Other important things were happening for Murthy as he worked at PCS. He was gaining valuable insights into the likes and dislikes of global IT customers. He was learning how to negotiate terms for developing the software they required. And most of all, he was learning about the challenges of providing international firms with India-based software support. The 1960s and 1970s were not an easy time for building overseas customer bases. Foreign companies were wary of having an Indian outfit oversee their technical issues. India had a bad reputation in the world; headlines related to India, in American and European newspapers, were mostly about food shortages and requisitions for emergency aid. It hardly seemed like the ideal tech destination. They preferred the software support to come to them. So Murthy had to undertake a great deal of international travel; but travelling abroad was slow and frustrating because it required several weeks of waiting for the Reserve Bank of India's (RBI) approval, and visas from the consular offices were not easy to get.

Murthy could see that one of the major hurdles for Indian tech companies was procuring a computer. IBM had left India in 1977 due to the 1973 amendment to the Foreign Exchange Regulation Act (FERA) that capped foreign equity at 40 per cent, and this had made it much more difficult to get its coveted mainframe computers. Obtaining a licence to import computers took several visits to Delhi, and there was no guarantee of success. The difficulty of convincing Delhi bureaucrats that you needed a mainframe computer meant that Indian engineers had to come up with workarounds. They used minicomputers and superminicomputers like DEC, Prime and DG, and connected low-cost PCs and smaller workstations in data networks to approximate the power of bigger computers. These minicomputers were cheaper than a mainframe and represented an early and essential wave of affordable computing. Competition was also growing: PCS, TCS, Tata Burroughs and Hinditron, all based out of Mumbai, were fighting for a foothold in the tech export market.

'So many challenges!' Sudha said, worried, when Murthy explained these things to her. 'How will you manage, when even the big companies are having problems?'

But Murthy was not disheartened. 'Understanding challenges,' he would say 'is the first step towards finding a solution.'

Sudha was about to face her own challenges on the home front.

In 1979, roughly one year after marriage, she became pregnant. She had not really planned it; she discovered the fact when morning sickness sent her retching to the bathroom in the fourth week. She was happy and excited, of course, but also distressed because suddenly the healthy body she had taken for granted all her life refused to obey her. Her terrible morning sickness persisted all through the pregnancy. She wrote to her mother: *I'm still throwing up after every meal, every day.* She was reluctant to eat anything, so persistent was the nausea, and she lost so much weight that she began to worry about the baby's growth. Still, she was determined to work for as long as possible – partly because she loved her job and wanted to fulfil her responsibilities before taking off, and partly because she wanted to save her maternity leave for after the baby was born. So she kept going to the office even as her delivery date drew close.

Murthy, while excited about the impending arrival of the baby and worried about Sudha's health, had been given several new responsibilities that kept him very busy at this time. He had to tell her, apologetically, that he would be unable to take time off to help her. Sudha was deeply disappointed. This was, after all, their greatest adventure together, their most exciting creation. But she could see he had no option. Instead of bemoaning the situation, she decided to lean on her family. This was something she would continue doing for the next decade.

Luckily, Sudha's family was supportive and resourceful. Her older sister, Sunanda, was by now an experienced obstetrician. She was quick to respond to Sudha's call for assistance. She took time off from the hospital and travelled to Mumbai from Hubli to give her sister company and moral support. A petite and soft-spoken woman, when necessary, she could be a pillar of strength – and that's what she became for Sudha. She watched over her sister's health with an eagle eye, not hesitating to scold her if she felt Sudha wasn't eating or resting properly. When the delivery date approached, she brought Sudha back to Hubli to give birth in her parental home, as was the custom. This was wonderful for Sudha. Once home, she could relax and enjoy her mother's pampering. Her father was also at hand to watch over her health. And Sunanda, of course, was keeping a careful eye out for any complications.

For some reason, Sudha had been certain that the baby was going to be a girl. Diligent as always, she had collected over 500 names for a girl! Her final choice was 'Akshata', which refers to the auspicious rice grains used in weddings or pujas. Murthy had his doubts about this name.

'Akshata would be too difficult to pronounce anywhere outside India,' he protested.

But Sudha could be stubborn when she wanted, and Murthy finally conceded.

Baby Akshata arrived on 25 April 1980. It was an easy birth that took very little time. Dr Kulkarni drove Sudha to the hospital, and within an hour or so, Sunanda delivered the baby and placed little Akshata in Sudha's arms. Together, the sisters gazed at the addition to the family, marvelling at the perfect fingers and toes, the tiny face that seemed to Sudha to be the prettiest in the world. Since the Murthys did not possess a home phone, Dr Kulkarni phoned the PCS office to inform the new father about the arrival of his daughter. But Murthy had just left the office. Luckily, one of his colleagues, Arvind Kher, was still there and took the message.

Around 9 p.m., Arvind made the long trek to Murthy's home to tell him that he now had a baby daughter. He then asked Murthy, 'How does it feel?'

Murthy was speechless with emotion. He was shaken by a joy that was different from anything he had ever felt – and burdened with a responsibility larger than anything he had ever imagined. Finally, he said, 'I'm going to have to be a better human being from today, now that there's a little person who might hero-worship me.' He took a deep breath and added, 'It's a huge responsibility. It's kind of frightening.'

From that day on, Murthy tried his best to be a good role model for Akshata. Years later, he would write to her: *Your birth raised the benchmark of my life in every aspect. My interactions at the workplace became more thoughtful and measured; the quality of my transactions with the outside world more considerate, dignified and mature. I felt a need to deal with every human being more sensitively and courteously.*

The very next day, Murthy rushed to Hubli. Unsure of what to bring for the newborn, he bought a dozen feeding bottles. He did not realize that a nursing baby would not need any of them! Holding his daughter close for the first time, he teared up. His father-in-law smiled at this show of paternal emotion, but he could not resist quipping, 'It seems the robot has a heart, after all!'

Murthy's relationship with his father-in-law had settled down since the early days. However, though the two men respected each other's intelligence, Dr Kulkarni, who was very protective of Sudha, felt that Murthy spent too much time chasing his business dreams and burdened Sudha with all the family responsibilities.

All that day and the next, Murthy watched in fascination as the baby kicked her arms and legs. 'How smart she is!' he kept telling Sudha. 'She's so active.' Her tiny hands seemed to him to be the most perfect things in the world. But despite his ebullience at seeing his daughter, Murthy was only able to spend one weekend with Sudha and Akshata. He apologized profusely, but that was the longest amount of time he could get away from work, where the pressures had grown enormous.

Though Sudha missed Murthy and would have liked to share the exciting experiences of early parenthood with him, she stayed on at her parents' home quite happily during her six-week maternity leave. Akshata was a calm infant, easily soothed. With her parents and sister around her to help, and no job demands, Sudha had a relaxed and cheerful time, enjoying the baby.

When Sudha needed to return to TELCO, she turned to her mother, Vimala, for assistance.

'Will you come to Mumbai with me and help me look after Akshata until I find a good nanny?' she asked.

Vimala, who had grown attached to her granddaughter, readily agreed. This was a great help for Sudha as she could go to work without worrying or feeling guilty.

Akshata was an undemanding baby. She ate well, slept well, and gave little trouble to her caregivers. Returning to work was good for Sudha because she loved her job and had missed it during her leave. She threw herself back into work and did not mind when she had to stay late because she could count on her mother to be there for Akshata. Still, coming home was the most exciting time of the day for both her and Murthy since little Akshata would entertain them with her excited babbling.

Meanwhile, Sudha was searching everywhere for a full-time nanny so that her mother could return home. Not satisfied with anyone she came across in Mumbai, she finally chose a woman who agreed to come to Mumbai from Hubli. The plan was that Sudha's mother would train this woman, and she would take over Akshata's care when Vimala returned to her own home. The woman seemed to like the Murthys and was excited to experience life in the big city.

But things didn't go as planned. Soon after Sudha's mother left, the nanny grew homesick. She wept every day and finally insisted on returning to Hubli. Sudha searched around desperately but could not find anyone she felt she could trust with such a small baby. She had no close family in Mumbai whom she could ask for help. There wasn't even a phone in their house that a nanny could use to call her in case of an emergency. On top of it, she missed her baby dreadfully when she was away at work. She held several long and tortured discussions with Murthy about the problem.

At one point, she asked him, 'Do you think I should quit my job?'

Murthy had no objections. 'If you would like to stay at home with Akshata,' he said, 'I'll make sure I handle the expenses.'

But Sudha knew that would be the wrong choice. They had taken a substantial loan and put money down for a flat in Pune, and she knew, despite Murthy's assurances, that it would be very difficult to make ends meet. Another factor, though less important, was that she loved her work and was not ready to quit.

The couple finally reached a tough, heart-wrenching decision. Sudha phoned her parents and once again asked for help.

'Could you keep Akshata with you for a while, until I can find reliable childcare?' she asked them. She felt guilty about burdening them – especially her ageing mother – with the responsibility of caring for a baby. But her parents reassured her that they were delighted to help.

'Don't be so formal with us,' her father said gruffly. 'Are we not your family?'

Her mother added, 'Akshata is our first grandchild. It will be wonderful to have the opportunity to keep her with us for a while and watch her grow.'

Sunanda, too, got on the phone and promised to help. 'I brought Akshata into the world. She's like my own baby. We'll all take good care of her. You have nothing to worry about.'

Sunanda's reassurance resonated in Sudha's ears. She knew that Akshata would be safe in the loving embrace of her aunt and grandparents. Still, her heart was heavy as she took Akshata and caught a flight to Belgaum, which was the nearest airport to Hubli, two hours away from her home town. Akshata's ticket was only Rs 20, 10 per cent of the regular fare, because she was so small. Luckily, she did well on the aircraft, sleeping most of the time. Sudha held her daughter close through the flight and kept looking at her, trying to imprint her face in her memory. When she got down at Belgaum airport, Sudha's parents were already waiting, along with Sunanda.

Sudha reluctantly handed the baby to them and turned away, trying to hold back tears. Though she knew Akshata would be taken care of perfectly, she couldn't help feeling that she was abandoning her baby. She was still breastfeeding Akshata, and both her body and mind rebelled at being separated from her child. She wept all the way back to Mumbai, her breasts swollen and aching. Later that day she told Murthy, 'It's the hardest decision I've ever made in my life.'

Sudha and Murthy took turns catching the overnight bus to Hubli every Friday to visit their daughter. They would reach Hubli early Saturday and spend the weekend playing with Akshata, making sure she did not forget them. They would leave the town on Sunday afternoon and try to get some sleep, perched on the uncomfortable seats of the bus. When they reached Mumbai at 5 a.m. on Monday, they would go straight to work, no matter how exhausted they were. Though it was a punishing schedule, they forced themselves to get used to it. They also had to get used to not being able to spend any leisure time with each other. On days when they were extra tired, or missed Akshata more than usual, they reminded each other that they had many blessings to count.

'We're both making good money,' Sudha would say.

'We're lucky to have jobs that are challenging and satisfying,' Murthy would add.

'Our colleagues are friendly and helpful, and the senior management are appreciative of our contributions to the company,' Sudha would continue.

'And most importantly, Akshata is healthy and happy in the heart of her loving extended family,' Murthy would end.

But when they lay down, the bed seemed too vast, and they

were very aware of the empty space between them where a little person used to sleep.

In a while, things returned to an equilibrium for the couple. Sudha became a senior engineer in the ancillary development department at the TELCO headquarters in Nanavati Mahalaya. This was a far cry from the shop floor where she had worked in Pune. Her colleagues were from many backgrounds – Parsi, Maharashtrian, Gujarati and Bengali – and they were well read and open-minded. She could discuss books and movies with them, and sometimes they went out together to eat or to see a movie or a play.

Murthy, too, was enjoying his job at PCS and felt that he was finally flexing his intellectual muscles to the full. His team was in charge of completing two major projects, the distributed real-time process control system for the Rourkela steel plant, and the CAMP project, an application software for the apparel industry, for Data Basics Corporation, a New York-based company headed by a tall, energetic and intelligent American businessman with a shock of dark hair, named Donn Liles.

Still, from time to time, Murthy's entrepreneurial dream would raise its head. Many nights, Sudha would wake to find him lying sleepless next to her. She knew that he was analysing, once again, his failure in Softronics, meticulously going over his mistakes. He would spend time during the train ride from Churchgate to Bandra figuring out what he would do differently if he had a second chance. While riding back, he asked himself tough questions. Had he given up too quickly the first time? Could he have pursued a different path, one that allowed him to find some financial support to sustain himself for a longer period? Should he have waited a while for the computer import policy in India to change? And most importantly, was it time to try again?

Murthy knew that, if he decided on that route again, this time the stakes would be higher. He would be leaving an excellent job where he had a dream boss, challenging work opportunities, and wonderful younger colleagues who looked up to him. A decision to start his entrepreneurial journey again would require him to move out of Mumbai, where renting an office was prohibitively expensive. This would mean risking Sudha's promising career at TELCO and gambling with Akshata's future. It would be more hazardous this time because – many of his friends had already warned him of this – he was considered too old to risk the entrepreneurial track. Each day, he felt more strongly the inexorable passing of time.

All these conflicting thoughts caused a great deal of turmoil within Murthy, but he hid it carefully from his colleagues and bosses. Only Sudha, who lay awake with him, knew his restless dreams and his disquieting belief that, by choosing the safer, more popular career option, he was selling himself short. She would put her arm around him, offering silent comfort.

9

It was an unusually balmy morning in December. Murthy and Sudha had a pleasant breakfast together before he set off for work. He took his regular route from his Bandra West apartment to his office: the bus to Bandra railway station, then the suburban train and, finally, a taxi from Churchgate station to Nariman Point. He had no idea that in a few hours his life was about to take a very different turn.

At this point, Murthy was the head of the expanded software group at PCS, his seniority second only to Ashok Patni, who never treated him as a subordinate. In addition to his responsibilities for software exports, Murthy supported the sales force at PCS who were selling DG computers in India.

Ashok Patni was in Pune for a few months, so Murthy had a meeting that day with one of the relatives of the Patni family in the office. Like most Indian companies, PCS was a family firm, with all the hierarchy that came with it. The senior management consisted of the three Patni brothers and a few relatives. The family member with whom Murthy was to have a meeting was usually a pleasant, kindly man. But for some reason that day, when Murthy entered his office, he was irritable. He waved at him to sit down and continued his work while Murthy waited. Finally, he told Murthy to prepare an import application for a DG MV/8000 computer for PCS's data centre in Mumbai.

The Rajaraman Committee had recently recommended allowing computers to be imported by fledgling Indian software export companies as long as the firm was committed to exporting 250 per cent of the customs duty, insurance and freight cost of the computer in foreign currency by software services. However, a computer import application was only the first step of a gargantuan bureaucratic process at the Department of Electronics (DoE). Murthy would have to fill out the application with great care, justifying the application and providing details of possible customers and future software export opportunities, among other things. If anything was missing or incorrect, their application would be rejected. But when Murthy started asking questions related to these areas, the Patni relative grew irritable and raised his voice.

'Just do what I asked you to,' he said. 'It's not your job to ask so many questions. You're just an employee.'

His brusque tone shocked Murthy. No one at PCS had ever spoken to him in this rude manner and he had only been treated with professional courtesy. His boss, Ashok Patni, had always treated him as a respected equal. When Murthy returned to his own office, he tried to continue with his work but could not. The unfairness of what had just happened agitated him. He had often argued with his colleagues at PCS about treating everyone – including the newest, wet-behind-the-ears engineer – with respect and affection. He had never believed in family-run businesses, feeling they didn't allow for the growth of professionals working in that firm and because, generally, family privilege allowed mistreatment of employees. *I can't be part of such a system*, he told himself. *I must walk away from this job. I've lived without much money before; I can do it again. A fat paycheque isn't essential to my happiness, but respect is.*

Resolutely, he wrote a resignation note on a sheet of paper, took it to the Patni family member, and informed him of his decision. He left the paper on the desk of a very startled man and returned to his office.

Once he was alone in his office, the enormity of what he had done struck Murthy. He had just quit the best-paying job he had ever had in his life. He had a nine-month-old daughter and an elderly mother to support. He had been the primary wage earner for his extended family – his mother and sisters – for a long time. He led over a hundred young men and women, most of whom he had hired, in the software group. Many of them had told him they were joining Patni only because they wanted to work with him. He had promised his team they would do challenging and fulfilling work at PCS. More importantly, he had not discussed this huge decision with Sudha, taking a leap which would have an enormous impact on her. He wondered, *did I act too rashly?*

Just at this time, the Patni relative walked in.

'I'm very sorry about what happened earlier,' he told Murthy apologetically. 'The Patni brothers value you very much. There should be no question of your leaving, particularly in Ashok's absence. I'm willing to do whatever is needed to have you stay on.'

Here was the perfect opportunity for Murthy to agree graciously and return to the status quo, possibly with an advantage. But he remembered all his conversations with Sudha about his entrepreneurial dreams, and how encouraging she had been. Now that destiny had unexpectedly opened that door for him, he decided he should walk through it.

Murthy politely told the Patni relative that his mind was

made up. When the man asked Murthy to keep his resignation confidential until Ashok was back in the office, Murthy told him this would not be possible since he had to discuss his decision with his wife and probably a few close friends.

As he went through the day's work with various teams, Murthy was still agitated. But he began to think that this incident, negative though it had been, might also be a blessing. By pushing him out of a comfortable situation, the universe was forcing him to start afresh and to challenge himself anew.

That evening Murthy went to Bombay House to pick up Sudha and take her to Swagat, a restaurant they both liked. There, he sat silently, picking at his meal, wondering how best to break the news of his impulsive decision to her.

Sudha, who had a sixth sense where he was concerned, said, 'I can tell something's bothering you. What is it?'

'I've quit my job,' Murthy blurted out. He described, to his startled wife, what had happened at the office and why he felt he could not continue there. 'This might be the perfect opportunity to get back to my entrepreneurial plans,' he added. 'What do you think?'

Sudha was dismayed by this bombshell. They sat in the restaurant until it closed, debating what the decision would mean for their family. Sudha's only personal experience with businessmen was with a cousin of hers who had owned a grocery shop in Hubli. She described to Murthy how he would reach the shop at around ten in the morning and spend the first hour reading the paper, sometimes refusing to serve customers until he had finished. He also tended to criticize customer purchases. He would, for instance, scold customers for buying tea powder late at night, asking, 'Is this a time to drink tea?' Not surprisingly, his business failed, and he ended up with a lot of debt.

Murthy laughed. 'I'm never going to be like that,' he declared with full confidence.

Sudha knew he spoke the truth. Still, the memory of his first failed enterprise hovered over her like a dark cloud. And things were different now: there was a little child who depended on them.

'Are you sure you want to take this path?' she asked. 'We don't have deep pockets like the Tatas or Birlas. At the end of the day, we shouldn't become bankrupt. We also need to think about Akshata's expenses.'

Murthy's voice was firm. 'If I don't take advantage of the software revolution right now, I'll never produce anything worthwhile. You're a lover of history. You know how, in the 1800s, after the industrial revolution in Britain, India became a mere supplier of raw material. We can't let something like that happen again.'

Sudha capitulated. 'I'll support you while you chase your dream,' she said. After all, she had married this man because he had such dreams and visions. She had by now been promoted to a senior engineer in the ancillary development group at TELCO. Additionally, while Murthy was occasionally a spendthrift, she had put aside savings religiously every month and managed their budget with care. 'I'll keep working so that we have a steady income. We are simple people with simple needs, and we can tighten our belts. If we give up a few things – eating out less and watching fewer movies – I'm sure we can make it on one person's salary.'

She ended with a statement that Murthy would remember always, and a promise that he would have to call upon soon. 'I want you to be like the trapeze artist in a circus and take a spectacular leap of faith. I'm willing to be your safety net.'

―――

As soon as Ashok Patni returned to Mumbai, he called Murthy to his office. He had been shocked to hear about Murthy's resignation and tried his best to convince him to stay back, offering him a higher salary and more perks. Knowing Murthy's fondness for challenging projects, he also offered him more responsibilities.

'You're walking away from the chance to do extraordinary things here,' he said. 'We work so well together. Look at all that we've achieved together in just four years.'

Murthy knew this was true. Additionally, he had always liked Ashok, who was unfailingly kind, empathetic, fair and supportive. However, his mind was made up. He said, 'You've been an excellent employer and a true friend. But I must build something of my own.'

Ashok was disappointed. However, he respected Murthy's determination. After all, he, too, was an entrepreneur. He wished Murthy the best. Then, with a worried look, he confessed that he was stressed about an important issue. PCS had signed two bank guarantees recently, together amounting to three times the net worth of the company, for projects with the Rourkela steel plant and the Bombay Electric and Suburban Transportation Company. They had done it on the assumption that Murthy would take the responsibility for these hugely challenging technical projects.

'Don't worry,' Murthy promised. 'I'll leave PCS only after we get project acceptances from both these customers and after PCS gets the bank guarantees back.'

Ashok's face cleared and he breathed a deep sigh of relief.

Though he didn't discuss this much with Sudha, Murthy was concerned about whether this was the right moment for his entrepreneurial journey. Some events that had occurred earlier had put him in an advantageous position. In 1977 the Janata Party government had come to power and forced out the international computer firms IBM and ICL. Over 1200 former IBM employees were without work, and numerous engineers had been laid off from ICL. They were the perfect workforce for firms like the one Murthy had in mind. On the other hand, in 1980 Indira Gandhi had returned as prime minister, and the licensing regime was in full force. Often, licences were granted in exchange for favours. Indira Gandhi's son Sanjay, for instance, was notorious for using the licensing system to reward friends and punish enemies. The environment was anti-market and pro-establishment.

Moreover, people like Murthy who were middle-class professionals didn't start businesses in this period – having neither access to capital nor government networks to get favours. It was the business families and their offspring who dominated this area. This made Murthy's venture riskier, and he was hesitant to involve anyone from his team at PCS in his endeavour. However, he felt he could not in good conscience leave without informing his closest colleagues about his resignation.

When he told his assistant manager, N.S. Raghavan, about his resignation, Raghavan, serious, hard-working and steadfastly loyal to Murthy, immediately said, 'If you're leaving, I'm coming with you.'

Murthy was taken aback and a little concerned. 'It may not be wise to follow someone who has no idea where he's going. I don't even have a name for my company!'

Raghavan shrugged. 'I joined PCS because of you. I'll follow you wherever you go.'

That evening, Murthy and Sudha visited Raghavan at his house in Chunabatti, hoping to change his mind. Raghavan had a wife and two children in their teens, and the Murthys did not want their lives to be turned upside down. But Raghavan's mind was made up. He had convinced his wife Jamuna as well, and they would not be swayed by Sudha's or Murthy's warnings.

Back at home that night, Murthy was racked with anxiety. 'I no longer have the freedom to fail that I had with Softronics,' he said. 'People – and their dependants – are counting on me to be a success. I can't afford to make mistakes.'

Sudha laid a hand on his arm. 'You'll probably make some mistakes. Everyone does.' Then she quipped, 'Just don't make the same ones again!'

⁌

Sudha and Murthy strategized carefully about what his next steps needed to be. Softronics' mistake had been in targeting an Indian software market. 'This time,' Sudha told him, 'you must focus on export markets such as the US, where tech is expanding rapidly, and government regulation isn't throttling companies.' She had researched and discovered that the US government was aggressively encouraging the growth of Silicon Valley firms and often becoming their biggest customer through purchases for defence and other departments. 'That should be your first target,' Sudha said.

Murthy agreed. 'I've been observing several entrepreneurs obtain licences for importing an advanced computer for software export, establish a data centre and earn a decent revenue from large corporations. I feel confident that I, too, can create a similar centre, and invest my profits in an export business. I can also lease computing time to large Indian companies and use the profit from that to scale up the export business. All I need to do is import the right kind of computer.'

Sudha thought it was a sound plan. 'Plus, it will create jobs for young Indian engineers,' she said enthusiastically.

But Murthy was to discover that importing an advanced computer was nowhere as easy as he had believed. Such an import required navigating a complex Delhi bureaucracy that did not trust small entrepreneurs. So far, only large companies like TCS, PCS and Tata Burroughs had fulfilled their contract with the government by using the profits from their data centre operations to scale up their software export business. The smaller entrepreneurs would merely make some quick money with the data centre operation and then shut down their enterprises without fulfilling the export obligations.

But Murthy was confident that his new company would be one of the exceptions. He knew he had the software expertise needed to target export markets. However, he would have to convince the bureaucracy of this.

Sudha and Murthy worked late each night, figuring out how to build the new firm. Despite her demanding job at TELCO, Sudha was with Murthy every step of the way, patiently hearing his plans, giving him valuable feedback. Because she knew the people he worked with, she gave him excellent suggestions as he tried to figure out who should be on his new team.

Murthy reached out to the brightest engineer he had – twenty-five-year-old Kris Gopalakrishnan. Kris was a whip-smart engineer at PCS who was instrumental in designing and building a complex process control software system for the Rourkela steel plant. Rather soft-spoken and shy, he was an innovative software architect and a creative thinker. The system he built was possibly the most complex at the time in the country; it greatly improved steelmaking in the Rourkela plant's furnaces. Steelmaking involves heating cast iron, mixed with slag and minerals, to about 1500 °C. The computer system that Kris designed automated this entire process while being housed in an environment that reached furnace-level temperatures.

Kris said yes immediately when Murthy asked him if he would be interested in joining his new venture.

'Don't you need to check with your wife and parents?' Murthy asked.

Kris shrugged. 'I'm used to taking risks. I come from a business family.'

Murthy's next choice was Nandan Nilekani. Educated at Bishop Cotton School in Bangalore, this twenty-six-year-old with a dashing moustache was versatile, sociable, articulate and fluent in English. Murthy and Sudha liked him because of his intelligence, humour, sociability and debating skills. Nandan reminded them of Sudha's brother, Shrinivas; they were both 'ideas men' who liked to back up their arguments with good data. When Murthy broached the subject with him, Nandan agreed right away.

Nandan had just got married to Rohini, a young journalist with *Bombay* magazine, whom he had met at an intercollegiate festival. Murthy asked him to consult her and her parents before taking any steps. He did not want Nandan to regret a hasty decision or experience conflict at home. Soon enough, an embarrassed

Nandan asked Murthy if he would be willing to have dinner with his uncle Mr Divgi, who ran his own metalworking business in Pune. Divgi wanted to discuss Murthy's venture. Murthy later learnt that Mr Soman, Rohini's father, was worried that his son-in-law was planning to give up his promising career and join 'some crazy, middle-aged fellow'! He had requested Divgi, an established entrepreneur, to assess Murthy's business idea. Murthy understood why the Sonams were so concerned – after all their new son-in-law was young and had very little experience.

It was also important for him to make sure everyone on his team was comfortable about joining his fledgling company, so, despite his busy schedule, he agreed to subject himself to some cross-questioning by the Nilekani family elders. Sudha came along with him to meet Divgi for dinner at the home of Nandan's grand-uncle. She and Nandan's grand-uncle hit it off because both had studied at IISc. Their laughter and jokes lightened the atmosphere.

Murthy spoke to Divgi at length about his plans to target the export market with custom-designed software. He patiently explained how the use of the superminicomputer in commercial applications would soon result in the explosion of IT demand in the US, and how Indian companies were well positioned to compete with their talent and price advantages. He said, 'We're at the cusp of something huge and dramatic. The software revolution will transform the world in offices, factories and at homes.'

Murthy ended by stating, 'You shouldn't worry about Nandan. He has just started his career. If this new company does not work out, he will find another job easily with his skills and degree. Look at the far greater risks I am taking. I'm giving up a highly paid general manager's job – and I have a baby daughter. Having closed a business once, I wouldn't give up working at PCS without considering it carefully. But I feel very confident.'

Murthy's speech had the desired effect. He won the argument and Nandan got the green light!

While he was confident, Murthy had little idea that day of the gargantuan growth that would take place over the next thirty years – a growth of which he would be one of the key architects. The Indian software industry would employ millions of engineers and log annual growth rates of 30 to 40 per cent in revenues between 1994 and 2005. From fewer than a thousand in 1978, the number of computers in India would jump to 80,000 by 1990. And Murthy's company would ride the crest of this wave.

Murthy invited a few other trusted colleagues to join him. Dinesh and Shibulal, both talented programmers, came on board, as well as Ashok Arora who, Murthy told Sudha, wrote programs that 'looked like beautiful poems'.

Murthy now had a talented team of six. As an incentive to join, he offered them directorships. But the consultant advising Murthy on company law pointed out that seven directors at an early stage of a small start-up might be rejected by the registrar of companies. Dinesh, Shibulal and Ashok consequently joined as senior project managers.

The group was full of enthusiasm and energy – but they did not have any clients yet, in either the export or domestic market. Nor did they have an import licence, or the money needed to import and install an advanced computer for data centre operations. For the moment, they were forced to wait impatiently for something to open up.

During this uncertain time, Sudha was a great help. Impatient to launch his new business, Murthy was working harder than ever to complete the two pending projects at PCS. He put in twenty hours a day through the weekdays and the weekends. In addition to handling her own job responsibilities, Sudha did everything needed to keep the household running, and she made sure Murthy ate healthy meals and got at least a little sleep.

Thinking ahead to the money they would need once Murthy started up his firm, Sudha decided that their long-term financial situation would improve if they were able to buy a flat of their own. Murthy agreed with her. Sudha's parents also promised to pitch in with funds. Despite everyone's help and encouragement, Sudha was nervous. She had never taken a loan before. At the back of her mind were memories of her childhood holidays with her maternal grandparents in Shiggaon. There she had seen first-hand how badly the local moneylenders treated borrowers, hounding them for payment. She had grown up believing that being in debt was a negative thing, and that only morally weak people found themselves in such situations.

But Murthy reassured her, pointing out that their situation was different. 'We are both hard-workers and professionals, and you have an excellent job. We're going to do this using an established bank or financial organization, with whom we will have a contract,' he said.

Sudha did her research and found a good housing loan company, Housing Development and Finance Corporation (HDFC), which treated her and Murthy with courtesy throughout the process. They were given a loan of Rs 1 lakh, which would be repayable in monthly instalments of Rs 1224. Murthy and she agreed that if there was one world-class company in pre-1991 India, it was HDFC. Years later, Murthy would reminisce, 'They made us feel truly wanted. I haven't had such a customer experience anywhere else in the world.'

Once she bought the flat, which was being built in an upscale part of Pune called Deccan Gymkhana, Sudha's responsibilities increased. Every weekend when she did not go to visit Akshata, she travelled to Pune to check on the building's progress. She did not mind the extra pressure. It was a labour of love. Watching the flat take shape gave her comfort and security amid many uncertainties. Now, she thought, even if the company on which they had pinned so many of their hopes failed, there would be a roof over their heads and a place for their children to call home.

This tiny flat was to become the place Sudha loved most, and the place in which she was the happiest. It was the first home they owned, and what made it extra special was that she had bought it with her hard-earned money. It was a simple two-room affair – the fanciest thing about it were the built-in wardrobes in the bedrooms – but she would remember it forever with fond nostalgia.

The responsibilities Sudha juggled during this period of her life exacted a heavy price. They forced her to miss, with many pangs of regret, several key moments of Akshata's childhood. Sunanda, who lived with their parents, wrote down all these precious moments in a notebook which Sudha would pore over hungrily when she came to visit.

When Sudha read about the time when Akshata had taken her first step, or when she spoke her first word, calling Sudha's mother 'Akka' (sister), she laughed and cried at the same time, trying to imagine the scenes. Her mother-heart was wrenched as she realized anew all the things she was missing. Akshata was a happy and contented child, and her sweet nature endeared her to her Hubli family. She was extremely close to her grandparents and aunt. Sudha was thankful for that, and for the fact that she did not have to worry about Akshata's upbringing. But, paradoxically, she was also sad because of this.

Sudha felt torn as she suffered the pain many working mothers share. It was hard to be a long-distance mother, and to hear about her daughter's milestones through letters from Hubli. Sometimes, she would read Sunanda's letters over and over, trying to imagine her little girl doing things she could barely imagine – climbing stairs, or eating lunch by herself, or speaking in short sentences. Simple things that most mothers took for granted but that seemed miraculous to Sudha because she did not get to see them when they first happened. As her daughter grew older and more active, running around the house, Sudha felt bad for a different reason. Often, her mother would be running after Akshata, trying to keep her out of trouble. Though her mother did not mind, Sudha felt guilty about making her mother look after a small child in her old age. Even the fact that it was imperative for her to hold on to a steady job at this risky entrepreneurial moment did not make it emotionally easier for Sudha.

Akshata did not miss Sudha. In fact, she did not even know who Sudha was. This made Sudha miss her daughter twice as much. For quite a while, Akshata thought Sudha was merely a friendly lady who visited their home occasionally. This upset Sudha deeply. Sometimes she was tempted to hug her daughter close and blurt out, 'I'm your mother!' But she knew that would be confusing and perhaps traumatic for Akshata. So she bit her tongue, put up with her heartache, and remained silent.

Sudha noticed Akshata going through different stages in her efforts to understand who her mother was. At first Akshata thought Sudha's mother was her own mother. She would say that her mother was different from other kids' mothers because she was grey-haired, unlike the dark-haired women who came to pick up her classmates in her playschool. Later, Akshata assumed that Sunanda was her mother. She would say that her mother was different from other mothers because she went to the hospital every day instead of staying home and doing housework. This hurt Sudha, but she also realized that her daughter's confusion was, in a way, the result of being loved so deeply by so many people. She took her family's advice and waited (though impatiently) for the special day when her daughter would figure out who Sudha was.

Sudha had to wait for a long time. It was only when she was almost four years old that Akshata eventually realized that Sudha was her mother! Sudha had thought this moment would bring about an immense and immediate change in their relationship, but to her disappointment that did not happen. Though Akshata was fond of Sudha, she remained closest to her grandmother and aunt. It would take Sudha a great deal of effort, and a prolonged stay in Hubli (after her second child's birth), to build a true relationship with her daughter.

Akshata would remain very attached to her grandmother and aunt throughout her life. Every year, when she gave Sudha a Mother's Day card, she made sure to send one each to the other two. And when they were finally reunited in Bangalore – Sunanda having moved there in 1985 and the grandparents in 1986 – a delighted Akshata would often opt to sleep in their flat, which was downstairs from her own.

One change did occur after Akshata learnt who Sudha really was. When it was time for Sudha to go back to Mumbai after having spent time with her daughter, Akshata would ask her to stay back. 'I wish you could stay for a hundred days and play with me,' she would say, hundred being the biggest number she knew. Such moments made leaving even harder for Sudha, tugging at her heart. She had to use all her self-control to hold back her tears. Akshata would get distracted by other things soon after Sudha left, but Sudha carried the pain of separation within her all the time.

10

It was 1981 now, and in Mumbai, Murthy was making plans for the new company even as he finished up his projects at PCS. This meant finding suitable clients. He had been meticulous about not courting any of PCS's existing customers; this scrupulousness presented him with additional challenges. But finally, fortune smiled on him in the form of Donn Liles, the American owner of Data Basics Corporation who had worked with PCS to develop CAMP, an application software for the apparel industry. Murthy knew him well and had a good relationship with him. After the project was completed, Donn decided to start his own software company at the Santa Cruz Electronics Export Processing Zone (SEEPZ) in Mumbai. Since Donn was no longer a client of PCS, Murthy felt that his new software venture presented Murthy and his team with a unique opportunity. As always, he checked in with Sudha – as well as Nandan, who was by now a close friend. They discussed the matter over dinner at Swagat. Both Sudha and Nandan thought it was a good idea.

Murthy, Nandan, Kris and Raghavan set up a dinner with Donn at Golden Dragon, the iconic Chinese restaurant at the Taj Hotel in Colaba, a favourite space for striking deals and holding business meetings. At the dinner, Donn loudly expressed his frustration at trying to get his company off the ground. He was bewildered by the reams of red tape he was facing. He complained that the Indian government was sloth-like in getting anything done. He was also finding it hard to hire good talent and get any work going.

After letting Donn vent for a few minutes, Murthy jumped in. 'Would you consider closing your Indian company,' he asked, 'if you got a group of experienced people here to work exclusively for you and take care of your problems in India?'

Donn was surprised but willing to listen.

'If you had a team in India working on software development,' Murthy continued, 'you could focus on what you do best, which is selling CAMP software on bigger machines to an even larger number of customers in the US.'

Donn was intrigued. He was tired of getting lost in the unfamiliar maze of a developing country's laws, bureaucracy, languages and cultures. This could be a win-win, with more sales and better work.

'If such a team existed,' Donn asked, 'where would I find it?'

Murthy began his pitch about his new company, pointing out his team members' relevant technical experience. Donn knew all of them from the PCS projects.

'We would be privileged to have you as our very first client,' Murthy said. 'We have the talent and the skills. We will apply the latest ideas and tools to produce a technology package for the apparel sector. It will be the best in the industry and you'll be able to sell it profitably.' As an additional incentive, he offered exclusivity to Donn for six years if Donn guaranteed a certain level of business every year.

Donn must have seen something special shining in Murthy's

eyes. Even before dinner ended, he began hashing out financial terms and advances. But towards the end, he made an unusual demand: 'If I'm closing down my company to work with you, I want 20 per cent equity in the new firm.'

Murthy was taken aback, but he said, 'If the Reserve Bank of India agrees, I am fine with it.'

Fortunately for him, the RBI, when approached, would refuse. But by then Donn was enthusiastic enough about the project to go ahead with it anyway. Within a few weeks of that momentous dinner, Donn contacted Murthy to inform him that he had closed down his company in SEEPZ. They were ready to go.

Being able to convince Donn to put his faith in Murthy's start-up rather than in his own gave Murthy a huge confidence boost. He was now ready for the next step.

Now that the new company had a client, it had to go through the legal process of incorporation. But there was a problem: two of his colleagues – Raghavan and Shibulal – did not have the money needed for equity. Fortunately, Murthy had a rock-solid source for funding to fall back on: Sudha! He knew she had been putting some money aside each month, though he did not know how much.

Over dinner, Murthy went straight to the point. 'I need some money to get the company started,' he told Sudha. 'Can you help?'

Sudha was taken aback. 'But I don't have the kind of money needed to establish a company!' she cried. 'And we have so many expenses to meet each month. We must support ourselves as well as your family in Bangalore. And let's not forget Akshata.'

'Heavy industries require large amounts of money,' Murthy explained. 'Software companies need much less. But without your help, I can't do it.'

That night, after Murthy went to sleep, Sudha lay thinking. Her mother had advised her to be cautious and save some money – money that even her husband did not know about – not to buy gold or silver but to use if there was a disaster. Sudha had saved Rs 10,250 in three years. For a while it frightened her to think that if she gave it away there would be nothing left in case of an emergency. Then she said to herself, resolutely, *This has always been Murthy's dream, and now it is so close. I must help him. What's the worst that can happen? The business will fail. In that case, he can always take up a job. And I will be working, too.*

The next day was Thursday, dedicated to Sri Raghavendra Swamy. Sudha considered it to be especially auspicious. She stood in front of Swamy's photo, prayed sincerely, then handed Rs 10,000 to Murthy (worth roughly about Rs 200,000 in today's currency) keeping only Rs 250 for herself. She told her husband, 'Regret is worse than failure. So let's go for a wild ride! It doesn't matter whether it's joyous or bumpy. We'll be on it together.'

Murthy was speechless with emotion – he had not expected Sudha to give him all her savings – but Sudha could see the love and gratitude in his eyes. When he finally managed to stammer his thanks, she said, 'No need to thank me. After all, it's my company, too.' Years later, she would joke that, though she had never been good at economics, she had turned out to be one of the best angel investors in India. She had invested Rs 10,000 in Infosys, and it had grown to billions!

Murthy did not want Raghavan and Shibulal not listed as shareholders on the day of registration since that could have created problems for them. Nor did he want them to feel singled out. So, he decided that Sudha would give money as a loan to all seven of them. The money Sudha thus gave to Murthy was used to create the equity pool of the company. In time, as and when they could, they all repaid Sudha. Every one acknowledged that without her help, it would have been impossible to bring a sense of unity to the team. They remain grateful to Sudha even to this day.

Sudha and Murthy's marriage had its ups and downs. Murthy was so focused on work responsibilities that he was rarely home to support Sudha, who had her own hectic work schedule. As a result, they were unable to raise their daughter together. They had to budget their money carefully, as they were trying to buy a home. Now came a development that was exciting but also stressful: the starting of a new company, which required all of Sudha's savings.

Many relationships have foundered because of such tensions. What was it that allowed the Murthys to succeed? Partly this was due to Sudha's optimistic nature, her faith in God, and her ability to focus on the present moment even as she planned for the future.

But one thing helped them above all others.

Often, when Murthy talked to her about new ideas, Sudha would spot potential problems and raise a red flag. 'As your friend, I feel I must inform you that this is my view,' she would caution. Sometimes he listened, and sometimes he did not. Sudha respected his decision, even if it was risky or impractical. And once he made it, she supported him ungrudgingly. Murthy did the same for her. That was the best part of what they called their 'partnership'. They never tried to stop each other from doing what they wanted to do.

The area where Murthy made perhaps the most unusual decision about his new company was in dividing up the equity. Though the idea and initiative for the venture was entirely his, and he was senior to all the others and had taken the biggest risk in giving up a job in which he had been highly placed, handled huge accounts and made a great deal of money, he kept just 30 per cent of the equity for himself. He gave N.S. Raghavan 19 per cent, and Kris and Nandan 15 per cent each. Dinesh, Shibulal and Ashok received 7 per cent each. Such an act was unheard of, and many of Murthy and Sudha's close friends felt he was being unnecessarily generous to his junior colleagues – and perhaps even foolish – in giving them such a huge share of the equity. They pointed out that giving people with hardly two years of experience, such as Kris and Nandan, as much as 15 per cent equity was unfair to Murthy's own family. Even one of the accountants with whom they were registering the company with, pointed this out. The norm in those days was that the founder would mostly keep the entire equity or at least 67 per cent of it so that he had the controlling interest. Wasn't Murthy giving up a coveted senior position at PCS, which was at least five to six levels above that of his colleagues? It would be difficult for him to get another suitable job if his new venture did not work out, whereas it would be relatively easy for his colleagues to find alternative employment. And what about the fact that while Murthy took a huge salary cut of 90 per cent, he ensured that his junior colleagues got at least a 20 per cent salary increase?

They also felt it was unfair that his colleagues would all be going to the US to work with Donn, while receiving a higher salary plus a stipend to perform duties that were quite similar to what had been required of them at PCS. Meanwhile, Murthy was the one staying back in India to do the difficult entrepreneurial stuff – getting the licence to import a computer, getting a computer centre client, and arranging a bank loan.

But Murthy did not care about such things. What was important to him was to create a company that was an embodiment of his deepest ideals and philosophies, things that, over the years, he had learnt the hard way. The adversities he had experienced, growing up in a poor family where he was unable to fulfil his dream of going to IIT in spite of his receiving a scholarship, along with his mother's kindness, had made him into a compassionate man, someone eager to share his good fortune with younger colleagues. His father's many talks on equality and fairness, and his own experience of the disrespectful way he'd been treated by a Patni relative, made him determined to break down nepotism and treat his colleagues with respect and generosity. So deeply held were his beliefs on caste and class that he had given up a great job opportunity at Hindustan Lever because of their class-based washroom policy. Now he was determined to not allow a similar hierarchy to creep into the workplace he was envisioning. And finally, he was still, at heart, an enlightened socialist.

'I want to create a professional company that is truly employee-owned,' he declared. 'I want my team to have a sense of this ownership. Having a loyal and committed team that wants to work with me means more to me than keeping most of the wealth for myself. You are all acting as though I'm doing something exceptional. But I'm only putting into practice my belief in the democratization of wealth, the culture of enlightened meritocracy and compassionate capitalism.'

The friends turned to Sudha. 'Surely you don't agree with this craziness!'

Sudha shrugged. From the beginning, she had decided she would not interfere with Murthy's decisions about his company.

It was his baby, and she was willing to let him nurture it the way he wanted. In case the company, or one of the employees, or their families, required any assistance, Sudha was ready – and happy – to help. In case Murthy wanted advice, she would speak up. But otherwise, she was a silent supporter, especially where money was concerned. Wealth had never fascinated her, so she had no problems with Murthy distributing it as he saw fit.

'I grew up with a simple lifestyle and strong values and am more comfortable, anyway, with such a life. I agree with Murthy that the most important use of money is to help others live better,' she told their friends.

The friends threw up their hands. 'You're each as crazy as the other!' they exclaimed.

Now came an exciting moment: what to name the new company? Since this was an Indian company developing information systems primarily for the US market, Murthy knew that the ideal name would be one that clients outside India could easily connect with. Something that sounded forward-looking and was instantly recognizable as an IT company. He asked Nandan, who was the most fluent in English, to think of a name, but after a week of intense brainstorming by the team, they still had nothing satisfactory.

One afternoon, Murthy sat at his desk, feeling frustrated. Stacks of papers had piled up on his table, and he decided he would put them away. Perhaps a clear desk would lead to a clear mind, he thought. In the pile, he came across a magazine titled *Infosystems*. The first half of the title, 'Infosys', leaped out at him. He knew right away that it was the perfect name for the company. It was simple and communicated what the company planned to do: developing and maintaining information systems for customers.

Next, the company needed an accountant. A chartered accountant had been recommended to Murthy, so he went to meet him at his apartment, taking Sudha along because he wanted her opinion. The accountant lived in a high-rise building in an affluent neighbourhood near Shivaji Park. 'I was told the cricketer Dilip Vengsarkar lives on the third floor,' Murthy whispered to Sudha in the elevator.

They went up to the fifth floor to meet the accountant, who suggested that he enter into an equity arrangement with the company. 'I'll be your sleeping partner,' he said. Something about him made Sudha suspicious. She asked Murthy in Kannada, 'What does he mean by sleeping partner?' The accountant explained that he would stay uninvolved in the day-to-day business operations, primarily providing advice in exchange for equity in the company.

Sudha was unconvinced by his speech and unimpressed by his lavish flat with its expensive decor and false ceiling.

'That man is too fancy for us,' she told Murthy on the way back. 'He lives in a Dadar high-rise building on the fifth floor with Vengsarkar staying below him. Plus, do we really want a person who isn't excited about getting involved in growing the company?'

'I trust your instincts,' Murthy said. He decided to not go ahead with the proposal, which turned out to be a good thing, as giving away more equity in Infosys would have cost him a great deal in the long run.

Infosys was formally registered on 7 July 1981, with an equity base of Rs 10,000. Raghavan, Kris, Nandan and Murthy were directors, and Dinesh, Ashok and Shibulal were senior project managers. Murthy was embarking on this new venture at thirty-five while the others, with the exception of Raghavan, were in their mid-twenties. They celebrated the exciting occasion with dinner at the Gaylord restaurant in Mumbai. When the restaurant's famed dessert, custard, arrived, Murthy made an important announcement.

'As soon as my responsibilities at PCS are fulfilled, I'm going to move to Pune to establish the Infosys office there.'

Everyone cheered. Pune was a much cheaper city with excellent living conditions; that would be great for a fledgling company and its employees. There was no turning back now!

But on the way home after the festive dinner, Murthy was unusually silent. He felt the burden of being a leader and an inspiration to his younger colleagues, several of whom had just started family life. They had left secure job situations because they trusted him implicitly. How could he take this responsibility lightly? He knew that, despite his team's enthusiasm and hard work and his expertise, things might not turn out well. In entrepreneurship, sometimes luck plays a bigger part than talent, competence, strategy, hard work and commitment. Adding to his uncertainty was the fact that the early 1980s was a volatile time in India. Oil prices were rising, impacting India's import bills, and the Indian government had signed up to borrow close to $5 billion from the International Monetary Fund – the IMF's largest ever loan. Prime Minister Indira Gandhi was bitterly criticized by the national media, while the outgoing finance minister, R. Venkataraman, told his successor, Pranab Mukherjee, 'I pass on my sleepless nights to you.' Murthy could foresee that his start-up would face a triple challenge: a weak economy, political hostility to business and import restrictions on a range of computing products that Infosys needed. *Without Sudha's wholehearted support,* he thought, *I couldn't take such a risky leap.*

Sudha could sense the turmoil in her husband's mind. She, too, was concerned because she knew she would have to leave her secure position at TELCO, which she had been counting on all this time. Who knew what the future held for their little family – as well as the larger Infosys clan. But whatever it was, they would face it together.

She slipped her hand into Murthy's and gave it a squeeze, and together they walked up the stairs to their flat.

By the time Murthy was done with the two projects he had committed to seeing through to Ashok Patni, it was 17 March 1982. The other Infosys members had quit PCS much earlier – most of them in September 1981. From the day Murthy turned in his resignation to the day he left PCS, it was fifteen months. Murthy jokingly called it 'the longest notice period in the history of corporate India'.

There would be one final episode before the Murthys left for Pune. The Murthys' Mumbai flat, acquired for them by PCS, was a coveted apartment in a prime location. Several people at PCS (though never Ashok Patni) had been apprehensive that Murthy would refuse to part with it. Maharashtra tenancy laws in the 1980s made it very difficult to evict a tenant if he or she had stayed seven years in an apartment, and people often refused to vacate their homes even after leaving the company that had originally given it to them. Many at PCS had expected that their head of software engineering would act similarly. When Murthy found out about this, he was amused, though it was an amusement tinged with sadness that his co-workers would believe such a thing about him when he was giving up so much money, prestige and security to follow his dream.

Murthy and Sudha sat side by side as their train made its way from Mumbai to Pune. Usually, they liked to chat when embarking on a journey, making the most of their time together. And certainly, today there was a lot to discuss: their new flat, setting up the office, hiring employees and so much more. But they were quiet as they mulled over all that they were leaving behind and the unknown future into which the train was carrying them.

Murthy thought about Ashok Patni, who had insisted they could do great things together at PCS. Murthy knew that was true; he liked and respected Ashok a great deal and thought he was the best boss he had had. He was already missing the friends he had made at PCS, especially S.R. Manik, head of the hardware group, and his assistant, Harish Tandon. Manik, whom Murthy affectionately called Manik Saab, was the most generous person he knew. Manik had taken Murthy and Sudha under his wing when they had first moved to Mumbai, helping the young couple in many ways as they got used to the metropolis and inviting them often to his home. Harish, with his deep intellect and knowledge of facts and data in their field, was a man after Murthy's own heart, someone Murthy would go to whenever he needed advice or information.

But there was a deeper reason. Murthy was worried because this was his second stab at entrepreneurship. He was thirty-six already, and he wasn't sure if he would be able to survive another failure. This time around, there was greater pressure on him because of his six junior colleagues. He worried about all of them, but he was particularly concerned about Raghavan, who had been the most insistent about joining Murthy. Raghavan was the kind of person who would never have considered a start-up venture on his own. He was older, had teenage kids, and would find it difficult to transition if this venture failed. And finally, Murthy worried that he was jeopardizing the futures of his wife and daughter. He felt particularly guilty because his decision had forced Sudha to resign her job at TELCO, which he knew she had loved.

Murthy kept these doubts to himself because he did not feel it was right to pass on his misgivings to any of these people. Already, he was experiencing the loneliness of being a leader.

~

Sudha, who was seated next to the window, stared out at the sylvan scenery streaming past her – fields of grain, deep green groves of trees, little villages with their thatched huts – but she did not notice any of it. She was too busy thinking about the job she was leaving behind at TELCO. She knew that Murthy's decision to start the new company in Pune made sense. Their flat could double as an office, while employees would find apartments more affordable there than in Mumbai. But there was a pang in her heart as the train carried her further from Mumbai with each minute.

Sudha had thoroughly enjoyed her tenure at TELCO Mumbai, which had an amicable office culture, and she had made good friends who came from various cultural backgrounds. For the first time, she got to know the Parsi and Gujarati communities closely and enjoyed learning about their customs and eating their food. Being a people person, she loved the work she did in vendor development and connected well with her co-workers and customers. People were very caring, especially during her pregnancy when she was sick every day. She recalled a touching instance when she was heavily pregnant and the meeting she was supposed to attend was on the third floor. The elevator was not working, and it took Sudha quite some time to make it up the stairs. When she apologized, out of breath, for being late, her boss, Mr Mulgaonkar, stopped her and apologized in his turn, saying that had he known of her situation, he would have been happy to move the meeting down to a room on the ground floor.

One of the reasons Sudha had enjoyed working next to Bombay House was because that was where J.R.D. Tata had an office. She had got to know him over the years, and he impressed her with his caring attitude and kindness for his employees, who affectionately called him 'appro JRD' or 'our JRD'. She often spoke admiringly of him to Murthy, so much so that Murthy once quipped that he was getting an inferiority complex, like Professor Parimal (in one of Sudha's favourite films, *Chupke Chupke*) whose wife Sulekha sang constant praises about her jijaji.

One evening after work, Sudha stood on the steps outside her office, waiting for Murthy to pick her up. At that time, JRD was leaving the office and happened to see her.

'Kulkarni,' he said – that was what he always called her – 'why are you here so late?'

When she explained she was waiting for her husband, he said, 'It's getting dark, and there's hardly anyone around. I'll stand here with you until he comes.' It was a surreal moment for Sudha. JRD was hugely wealthy, respected and successful, and known and admired throughout India. Still, he did not hesitate a moment to spend his time to ensure the safety of an ordinary employee. Though Sudha felt bad that she was inconveniencing him, she was deeply moved by this great man's considerateness for all the people in his company.

When Murthy, who had been caught in the infamous Mumbai traffic, finally arrived in a taxi, she thanked JRD and hurried down the steps.

JRD called after her, 'Young lady, tell your husband to never make his wife wait again!'

On the day she resigned, Sudha bumped into JRD on the stairs of Bombay House. He stopped and asked, 'So what are you doing Ms Kulkarni?'

'Sir, I am leaving TELCO,' replied Sudha.

'Where are you going?'

'Pune, sir. My husband is starting a company called Infosys, so I have to shift.'

'Oh! What will you do when you are successful?'

Sudha smiled and said, 'Sir, I don't know whether we will be successful or not.'

JRD looked at the young woman intently and said, 'Never start with diffidence. Always start with confidence. When you are successful, you must give back to society. Society gives us so much, we must return it. I wish you all the best.'

His words left an indelible mark on Sudha's heart. She remembered them often over the next years. 'On that day,' she would later tell Murthy, 'JRD gave me the best, most valuable advice.'

Sudha had experienced crossroads moments in her life before this. Choosing to study engineering instead of medicine, which her family would have preferred, was one such moment. Deciding between starting work at TELCO and going to MIT, which had long been her dream, was another. Marrying the man she loved, though her father had called him 'an unemployed communist', was a third. She had faced them all confidently, with an indomitable will. But this time was different. This time she was making a choice based on someone else's dream, and that caused her to feel a new kind of anxiety. She was used to being the planner, but this time it was Murthy at the helm, making decisions she couldn't fully foresee.

As the train sped across the ghats of Maharashtra, she wondered what the coming years were going to be like now that she had left TELCO. Though she would never say this to Murthy, she imagined that at best Infosys would be a modest success, enough for them to pay off the loan on their two-bedroom apartment and own a scooter. Additionally, she couldn't help worrying about her own career. She was already thirty-two, an age where she needed to build on her strengths and cement her position in a company. Was this a huge backward step for her? And most importantly, how might this move impact her daughter's life?

Many spouses of start-up founders must make such sacrifices, leaving behind careers, friendships and even entire lives. They are often the unsung heroes of these modern-day odysseys.

Part 2

'I'll Be Your Safety Net'

11

Murthy and Sudha stepped into their modest apartment in the Deccan Gymkhana area of Pune without any fanfare. They looked around it carefully. As they stood there, taking the scene in, both thought of the lovely song by Jagjit Singh, *'Yeh mera ghar, Yeh tera ghar'*. It was a simple two-bedroom flat, empty, with bare bulbs hanging from the ceiling. But the fact that it belonged to them, that it was the first place they owned, and that she had overseen the building of it, meant a great deal to Sudha. Unpacking their suitcases did not take long. Even after they put away their clothes, the wardrobes were largely empty. That did not bother them; they were used to spare living. The doorbell rang. The deliverymen had brought the tables and chairs they had ordered. The Murthys set them up in the spare bedroom, which was to become the first operational office of Infosys. It was a far cry from the large, busy and fancy workspace Murthy had been used to at PCS.

Another man might have felt he had moved down in the world, but Murthy was ebullient. 'I'm one step closer towards achieving my dream,' he declared to Sudha.

Murthy became busy right away, putting together the

infrastructure he needed to get the business started, hiring an assistant, and getting his telephone line set up. (He still had his old phone, which he had left with a friend when he went to Mumbai. This was a great help, since new phone lines were very difficult to come by.) Meanwhile, Sudha took up a job as an analyst in the computer department of an engineering company to ensure that the family had a steady income.

This was a very different company from TELCO, and much less to Sudha's taste. The management was less progressive than the Tatas. It was more of a traditional family business where it was considered acceptable for the family to use corporate resources for their own benefit – exactly the kind of structure and environment that Murthy detested and wanted to offer an alternative to. TELCO had been a large-hearted, cosmopolitan company where Sudha felt appreciated and respected. At her new job, most of the employees were from the interior of Maharashtra, and non-Maharashtrians were looked upon as outsiders. The expectation here was that employees should fear the boss, and the environment was not open-minded, with no opportunity for sharing ideas or solutions. Some employees spied on their co-workers and reported their behaviours and conversations to the bosses. All the bosses were male. After a week at work, Sudha told Murthy, 'I feel like there's always a man keeping an eye on you.'

Sudha's immediate supervisor was a particularly suspicious individual who watched her constantly. If she was even a couple of minutes late at returning from her half-hour lunch break, he would note it down and point it out to her – even though he knew she always made sure to finish her work before going home. Once, just before the weekend, she took a rose from a bouquet of flowers in the office that was beginning to wilt. Somehow, he found out and chastised her about it. He loved to boast about his accomplishments and often stated that he had won a gold medal from BVB Engineering College in a particular year. Sudha knew he was lying because she was the one who had won the gold medal that year. She asked politely to see his medal, but of course he could not produce it. This incident made him even more annoyed with Sudha, and he made her life as difficult as possible.

Sudha was not happy in this negative atmosphere, but she put up with it. She was a pragmatist, so she focused on the present moment and did the best she could with it. One of her favourite sayings was 'How much masala I have, that much sambar I make.'

Sometimes, though, she could not help but think longingly of 'aapro JRD' in Mumbai and how he had stood with her on the steps of Bombay House so that she would not have to wait by herself in the dark.

―⁂―

Once she had settled into her new flat, Sudha told Murthy, 'It's time to reunite the family by bringing our daughter to Pune.'

Murthy, too, felt this was important as he missed his daughter a great deal. Akshata was almost two, and he did not want to lose out on any more of her childhood.

'But I'll have to plan the transition carefully,' Sudha said. 'Akshata is so attached to her grandparents and aunt. I don't want her to go through a shock.'

With the aid of Sunanda and her parents, Sudha carefully explained the upcoming move to Akshata, presenting it as a fun adventure. While Akshata seemed excited and curious, Sudha wanted to make sure the change would not be traumatic in any way. Once again, she leaned on her mother and sister.

Sudha's mother accompanied Akshata to Pune and stayed with them for two weeks. Each day, despite the pressures of her new job, Sudha would visit the apartment during her lunch break and spend some time with her daughter, telling her stories. Building a strong relationship with Akshata and keeping her happy was the greatest priority for her. When Sudha's mother left, Sunanda came to Pune and stayed for a couple more weeks. Luckily for the Murthys, Akshata continued to be a cheerful child, easy to please; she was not given to tantrums and was content to spend time by herself with her dolls and her books. By the time Sunanda left, Sudha enrolled Akshata in a playschool and found a nanny to take care of her while she worked.

Murthy was of course extremely busy during this time, setting up the India office of Infosys and sorting out the application for the import of the computer. His six colleagues were busy, too. They were already in the US, working on the first Infosys project at Tropical Garments, a client of Donn's company Data Basics Corporation (DBC), in Tampa, Florida. The work would keep them in the US for a while, but unfortunately, they were unable to take their wives along. Murthy had explained that Infosys was more likely to be granted their visas if their spouses did not apply. 'That was how it was when I went to the US for training,' he explained to them. 'I, too, had to leave Sudha behind even though we were just married.'

The team members had been excited to travel to the US and start their first Infosys project, but the reality was not as pleasant as they had imagined. Somewhat crestfallen, they informed Murthy that Tampa was swampy and humid, and their cheap apartments nowhere near the luxurious accommodations they had expected to find abroad. Worst of all, Donn Liles turned out to be a temperamental client.

Perhaps because of Murthy's refusal to compromise on what he felt were the rights of his team members, Donn was especially unpleasant to Murthy at times. He would often delay payments when he could, and Murthy would then be the target of his ire because he would hold his ground, refusing to budge on timely payment for services. Or Donn would not provide timely authorization for Murthy and his Infosys colleagues to book hotels when they had to visit him in Manhattan. Once when Murthy visited the US for client work, Donn made him sleep on a large box in the storeroom, surrounded by cartons, though his home had four bedrooms. Additionally, Murthy had to manage Donn's many last-minute demands for resources.

Murthy put up with Donn's behaviour for the sake of his fledgling company, but the box incident truly shocked him. He had been brought up to treat guests with special respect. 'My mother used to say that a guest was like God, and the way you treated your guests revealed what kind of person you really were,' he told Sudha. 'When my father invited someone over without advance notice, she often served the guest her own food and went to sleep without dinner. And here was Donn enjoying a good night's sleep in his luxurious bed after making me spend the night on a big box in a windowless storeroom!'

Sudha was furious when she heard about how her husband, who was working tirelessly for Donn's benefit, had been treated. While she was often willing to shrug away bad behaviour when it was directed at her, she was very protective of her family members. She told Murthy she would neither forget nor forgive this rudeness.

An additional challenge for Murthy was to send his team in the US their monthly allowance in a timely manner. At that time, thanks to Indian bureaucracy, the process was highly convoluted. Infosys had to first bring the foreign exchange earned from the team's services each month into India. Only then could Murthy use up to 50 per cent of that amount to send his team members their maintenance allowance for the next month.

Thus, at the end of each month, it was a stressful race against time to manage these payments for the US-based team. Murthy and one of his colleagues – usually Nandan or Dinesh – would pressurize Donn to send the money he owed them to the Saraswat Co-operative Bank. Murthy would collect the Inward Remittance Certificate from the bank after the money reached them, submit it to the RBI in Mumbai, a journey that took four to five hours each way. He would then wait in its corridors for hours over several days to get half of the money released so that he could send it back abroad for the Infosys employees.

Sudha, who helped out with Infosys administrative work in the slender window of spare time available to her, accompanied Murthy whenever she could so that he would not have to wait alone. She knew how unpleasant and frustrating these monthly visits were and how much of Murthy's energies were being wasted on them. But she could do nothing about it. Occasionally, she brought Akshata to the RBI so they could spend a little extra time with their daughter. The officials would smile at the little girl; then they would go straight back to being rude and unhelpful to her father!

'I wouldn't wish this monthly torture even on my worst enemies,' Murthy would often tell Sudha.

This ongoing hassle of chasing Donn to get the payment and then persuading the RBI bureaucracy to release the maintenance allowance was a constant headache for Murthy throughout the pre-liberalization period. A less resolute person may have become disheartened in the face of this constant irritation and given up, but that was not Murthy. But he had to draw on all his patience and resolution to keep going. When he felt particularly discouraged, he would repeat to himself one of his favourite quotations from Jawaharlal Nehru: 'Life is like a game of cards. The hand that is dealt for you is determinism. The way you play it is free will.'

Murthy continued to play the hand he was dealt, but the tension that he constantly laboured under took its toll on him. This was the time when he – only in his mid-thirties – started developing health issues such as indigestion, hypertension and diabetes, which would plague him all his life.

Another major obstacle Murthy faced in the early days of Infosys was obtaining the licence to import a DG MV/8000, the superminicomputer (colloquially referred to as a supermini). This computer, essential for software export work and for running a domestic data centre, was essential to Murthy's strategy of quickly building a steady stream of revenue which Infosys could then invest into scaling up software exports. Murthy decided on this strategy after studying several US companies (such as Microsoft) that had developed a steady revenue from a product, and used part of that money to invest in new product R&D. For example, the profits earned from early products like DOS were reinvested by Microsoft to build highly successful software like Windows and Office. The logic was to invest money earned from a steady, reliable source of business into riskier new innovations.

But getting the licence to import a supermini was extremely difficult at the time. The Rajaraman Committee report, which recommended to the government that companies should be allowed to import computers as long as they followed up by exporting software, had made things somewhat easier for India's young software industry, but entrepreneurs still faced a long-drawn-out battle to import a computer, especially the supermini.

Sudha, who accompanied Murthy many times to government offices and banks, noticed the negative attitude of the officials. Whenever Murthy requested a bank for a software business loan, or asked government officials for the computer licence, it angered her to see that he was treated with contempt. Bureaucrats judged entrepreneurs – especially in the field of software development – to be crooks out to cheat the government of taxes, thwart regulations and sell products illegally. Faced with such prejudice, Infosys had an uphill battle.

Murthy wasn't the only Indian entrepreneur to be treated in this way by the government. Most Indian businesses resolved their issues by paying bribes. Murthy had resolved to never pay one. That this was part of the Infosys corporate vision was itself an innovation. But these were the moments where he had to pay for his values.

'They're already certain – even before they speak to me – that I'm a thief,' Murthy told Sudha after a particularly frustrating and fruitless visit. 'They've already convinced themselves that Indian companies can't compete in the US market.'

Still, he refused to give up. He had earlier, while still in Mumbai, got hold of an application form to import a DG MV/8000 and filled it out in his usual meticulous style. He had then taken the application to Delhi by train. Travelling in an overcrowded, unreserved compartment, he reached Delhi two days later, staying in a rundown hotel next to the Old Delhi railway station until he could hand over the form in person to the appropriate official.

The director in charge of computer imports for software exports at the DoE – a Mr Singh – was familiar with PCS. He was surprised – and not particularly pleased – to see that a PCS employee had now started his own company. He accepted Murthy's application with clear reluctance. Murthy sensed the negative vibes, but he had no option but to work with him.

Several months passed by in total silence while Murthy waited. He did not know – and had no way of enquiring – whether his application was making its way up the ranks, or whether it was lost forever at the bottom of a gargantuan pile of similar forms. Finally, when he had almost given up, he received an interview call from the DoE computer licensing committee, which would be deciding whether Infosys could receive a licence. As usual, he made the uncomfortable, crowded train journey from Pune to Delhi, this time on Valentine's Day. He hurried to his inexpensive hotel room, took a quick shower to clean off two days' worth of grime and rushed to the interview. As he waited at the reception for his turn, he noticed that none of the other candidates were from the software industry. He knew they only wanted to set up a data centre for the quick money it would provide. They planned to lease computer time 24/7 to Indian corporations that needed computing power. Once these five to eight year data centre contracts were completed, they would shut shop. Some of them even bribed the lower-level government employees to burn these agreements. They were the reason the government was so distrustful of entrepreneurs.

During the long interview, the group of officials (which included Mr Singh) bombarded Murthy with personal questions. Why would someone like him who had a steady job with excellent pay give it up? Why would he start his own firm and go through all the growing pains? Why would he take so much risk when there were no guarantees and not even a history of entrepreneurs who had made it in this field?

When Murthy shared his dream of creating 'India's first company of the professional, for the professional and by the professional', they found it naïve and amusing. Several of them laughed, derisively slapping the table. Singh openly told Murthy that it was impossible to succeed in India without connections and money.

Only one of the interviewers listened carefully to Murthy's words and encouraged him. 'I think you have a good chance,' he told Murthy. This was Dr Seshagiri, a computer scientist who was an early champion of liberalization and passionate about technology. He would, in a few years, head the National Informatics Centre, which provided technology-driven solutions to problems faced by the central and state governments, and would play an important role in framing the country's IT policy. When the interview ended, he took a moment to shake Murthy's hand and wish him luck. Murthy held on to his kind and encouraging words through the next months as he waited for a decision.

In the US, the fledgling company was experiencing a whole new set of problems. Donn Liles declared that he found Raghavan, whom Murthy had placed in the primary leadership role abroad, inadequate. Though angered at Donn's interference in the workings of his company, Murthy could not take the tough stand he would have liked to adopt here. Infosys was, for the moment, entirely dependent on a single client. If Donn erupted and brought their whole engagement to an end, it would be a mortal blow for Infosys. So, Murthy suggested that Nandan take his place. Donn agreed.

Murthy conceded, but it was a setback in terms of his vision for the company. He had designated Raghavan as number two, given him the second highest equity of 19 per cent, and had expected him to contribute more than other colleagues. Nandan would go on to do a fine job; but Raghavan, perhaps because of Donn's interference, lost his confidence. He would never lead any software projects abroad and would fall woefully short of the potential Murthy had envisioned for him.

In April 1982, the mailman brought an envelope to Sudha and Murthy's flat. Instead of a sender's name, there was a DoE stamp in the corner. Murthy called to Sudha to come and join him and, while she whispered a prayer, he opened it with trembling fingers. It was the coveted computer import permit! It had taken nine months from the date of application for the approval of the computer import to come through. Still, both Sudha and Murthy realized they were very lucky. Applicants usually had to wait far longer and were often denied. Given the inhospitable climate in India towards entrepreneurs at this time, it was a breakthrough.

Sudha and Murthy were exhilarated, and so was the Infosys team in Tampa.

'This deserves a special celebration!' Sudha announced. She and Murthy decided they would commemorate the occasion. They did not have to think long about what to do or where to go. With Akshata seated between them, chattering away with excitement, they took an autorickshaw to Chung Fa, the Chinese restaurant that had been their favourite during their courtship years. It was the perfect place. To the many happy memories that the Murthys had of this place was added another one – that of Infosys's first major victory.

12

Now that he had cleared one hurdle – receiving the import approval for a supermini computer – Murthy was immediately faced with another two. He had to find a major Indian client for the data centre operations of Infosys, and he needed to get a bank loan of Rs 50 lakh to import the DG MV/8000 supermini and set up a data centre.

The experience with bank managers in Pune and Mumbai did not give Murthy much hope. The managers that the couple met with – sometimes with Akshata sleeping in Sudha's arms – didn't understand what software was and were deeply sceptical of a business where nothing tangible, like a chair or a television set, was produced. As far as their understanding went, software was 'vapourware'. They couldn't fathom how such a product could be built in India or be exported.

Once, a manager even took off his spectacles and shook them at Murthy, saying that the glasses were a more saleable product than Infosys's software. Sometimes Murthy was so disheartened that Sudha did the loan presentation instead of him, carefully explaining their vision for the future of the company – but to no avail. Eventually a chance meeting with Mr K.R.S. Murthy, the Chairman of Karnataka State Industrial and Infrastructure Development Corporation (KSIIDC) provided Infosys with the funding, that too without having the endless rounds of meetings and the many cups of coffee! KSIIDC had an extraordinary set of officers, and it partnered with Karnataka State Financial Corporations (KSFC) to facilitate the loan in record time. Murthy had finally found some government organizations to be proud of.

With the Infosys US project work being handled by the Tampa team, Murthy suddenly had a pocket of leisure – something he was unused to, especially after the hectic pace of his final days at PCS. Though he spent a good amount of time and effort each day searching for a possible data centre client, his evenings were free. Guessing that this opportunity would not always be available, he spent as much time as was possible with his family. Their uncomplicated company was just what he needed.

When Sudha returned from work, they would make a simple dinner, blending South Indian cuisine with Maharashtrian: rice and roti, sambar and a vegetable. Neither of them cared to spend the little leisure they had struggling with dishes that demanded complicated prep. They would sit and eat together with Akshata, who kept them amused with tales of her playschool adventures. She was already quite musically talented and performed songs and dances for her adoring audience.

Despite these happy moments at home, Murthy was restless and concerned. He knew he needed to find a major data centre client before he bought his computer. Every day he reached out to his network to see if there was a prospective client he could approach. He spoke to former classmates, friends at the Computer Society of India, and several business contacts. But for a long time, he found nothing.

Around this time, Murthy began to have a recurring dream which continues to this day. In the dream, he was alone, lost in space, drifting through emptiness. He interpreted it as a symbol of the loneliness of the Indian entrepreneur, of a man with a vision and work ethic shared by very few. But perhaps it was the dream of a man who was feeling lost and alone and a little fearful, not knowing where he would end up. Though he shared most things in his life with Sudha, this dream was too disturbing. He kept it to himself.

After a couple of worrisome months, things seemed to turn around for Murthy, and he got a lead. TI Cycles of India in Chennai was on the lookout for a data centre arrangement. Murthy travelled to Chennai, checking into a budget hotel and requesting a meeting with the information systems head at the company. The manager, Subba Rao, agreed to meet with him, and Murthy made a two-hour presentation to him and his team on the technical superiority of Infosys's DG MV/8000 computer.

Subba Rao and Murthy then met the finance director at TI Cycles. Rao batted for Murthy. He took the director through the details of the computer and its use for their applications. By the end of the meeting, the director was enthusiastic and asked Rao to work out the details of the contract. Murthy was ecstatic as they shook hands. Rao promised to meet Murthy the next morning in his hotel to start discussions. Murthy floated on a cloud all the way back to the hotel and called Sudha and his colleagues with the news. Everyone was super excited.

The next morning, however, there was no sign of Rao. He called Murthy later with apologies, stating he would meet him the following day to discuss the contract. But Murthy sensed a guardedness in his manner. When Rao called next, it was to inform him that the management had changed their minds. Murthy tried to get a second meeting with the finance director, or an explanation as to why he had been turned down, but he failed. With a heavy heart, he informed Sudha of this unexpected reversal.

Sudha, too, was disappointed and worried, but she pushed aside her own feelings as she often tended to do and assured Murthy that something else would turn up. In an effort to cheer him up, she reminded him of one of her favourite stories from the Ramayana. 'Look at Lord Hanuman. He had to carry an entire mountain of herbs across to Lakshmana, who was dying. He was small in size, so his solution was to grow giant-sized so that he could transport the mountain easily. That's what you should do. Grow bigger than the problem. Then the solution will come.'

In spite of Sudha's words, Murthy left Chennai with a heavy heart. But on the way back, he began to think through his failure and delineated some lessons he could learn from it. The first was that a start-up needed to be in touch with the senior management of a potential client rather than its mid-level or junior managers. The second was that Murthy's presentation needed to strongly differentiate Infosys from its competitors both in technical competence and in business value – otherwise a large company would not take a small start-up seriously. The third was that the vendor had to demonstrate unusual strengths in areas where the customer was weak.

I'll use these techniques next time, he vowed.

⁓

The Infosys team in the US continued to expand and needed more assistance. Three young engineers from IIT Madras joined Murthy in Pune in July 1982. But Infosys still had no office space, and Murthy worried that the three would be disappointed with this and decamp even before their US visas arrived. So he came up with an intensive training programme to teach them a business language, the operating system, and the file management system on the DG MV/8000. The three recruits were kept very busy, leaving them no time to wonder why they had joined a company that operated out of a spare bedroom!

When Sudha returned from work in the evening, she would help the new employees with their technical assignments and often invite them to dinner, where they would all enjoy Akshata's antics. But Sudha was not satisfied with this minor supportive role. Being a fine engineer, she knew she could contribute far more solidly to Infosys than helping with only the odds and ends that Murthy assigned to her.

One evening, when it was just the two of them at the dinner table, she told Murthy, 'I want to be involved with Infosys in a more significant way. I'm not satisfied with just running errands and being your girl Friday. I know I can't quit my job until the company is more stable, but I can start coding. You know I'm more experienced than any of our new hires.'

Murthy stopped eating, and though his plate was still half-full, he pushed it away. There was a pained look on his face. Sudha was surprised. She had made mooli-sambar, one of his favourite dishes. For a moment, she wondered if she had forgotten to add salt.

Then Murthy said, 'I'm sorry. You can't work at Infosys.'

Sudha could not believe her ears. She had to ask Murthy to repeat himself – and he did. Even though he looked apologetic, his voice was resolute. 'The two of us cannot be in the same company.'

Looking at his face, Sudha could see that her husband felt terrible about turning her down. But she could also see that he was dead serious.

'How is this fair?' she asked, more upset than she had ever been with him. And hurt. Even when he had tried to break up with her, she had not felt this deep hurt, turning inside her like an iron skewer. She knew she shouldn't say any more while she was so angry, but she couldn't stop the words that poured out of her. 'Who was it that supported you all along, when no one believed in your crazy vision? Who accompanied you on those hundreds of frustrating visits to the RBI? Who advised you to target the international market? Who encouraged you when you felt desperate? Who held you when you couldn't sleep at night? Who gave you the money for the equity for the company? Even today, the company is operating out of the apartment I bought with my savings.'

A part of Sudha hated herself for saying these things. What she was really trying to say was that Murthy had broken her heart and shattered her dreams.

Murthy looked more unhappy than ever, but he said, in a steady voice, 'You did all of it – and more. I admit it fully. Without you, Infosys would not have been born. But it still would not be right for you to get formally involved with the company. You know what happened to me at PCS, with Ashok's relative. You've heard the same horror stories about family-owned businesses as I have, and you're experiencing some of them right now at your job. I don't want Infosys to be looked at in the same way. I didn't go through all these traumatic ups and downs just to have Infosys perceived as dynastic or nepotistic, like so many of the large companies in India.'

Sudha understood what he was saying. She believed in the same things and dreamed the same dreams as her idealistic husband. But all this while she had also believed that Infosys belonged to them both. Equally. And now Murthy was saying it did not. Feelings she was unable to express raged in her chest.

'You're extremely well qualified,' Murthy continued. 'Nobody at Infosys has ever been invited to be a research assistant at MIT. And no one has your kind of determination. However, if you join us, Infosys will become a husband-and-wife firm rather than a professional company. I just cannot let that happen.'

Sudha stared at her beloved husband, numb. Ever since Murthy decided to leave PCS, she had envisioned working side by side with the man she loved, putting to use all her talents and knowledge, building the company she saw as the culmination of her career. All her battles – as the only female student in engineering college, at the TELCO plant, where she broke the barrier against women, and finally at her last job, where she had to put up with her supervisor's demeaning behaviour – had been leading her, she believed, to this ultimate dream. All these months, when things were difficult at work, she had consoled herself by telling herself that soon she would join Murthy and never have to put up with an employer's tyranny.

And now this?

Murthy saw the deep hurt in her eyes. His face, which had been filled with distress, grew strangely calm. 'If you really want to be at Infosys, that's fine with me. You can lead the company. I know you're fully capable of doing that successfully. But I'll have to leave – and I'm ready to do that.'

A reluctant admiration rose through the agitation in Sudha's breast. Her husband was absolutely serious – she could see that. He cared so much for his principles that he was willing to turn over his beloved company, his lifelong dream that he had worked so hard for, to her rather than compromise his values.

She was still very upset, but she remembered what her grandfather had taught her: 'Silence is the best medicine for the disease of anger.'

She went into the bedroom and shut the door, leaving her uneaten dinner on the table. She did not sleep all night, not even after Akshata came in and curled up quietly next to her.

Long after this happened, Sudha said to her children that if she had been older and more mature, she would have argued further that night – and possibly over the next few days, too – and pushed harder. She would have challenged Murthy's opinion, using logic to point out that not all family-run companies had to be like the ones they had encountered. That even if they both worked at Infosys, they could set a new record for professionalism. Perhaps she would have managed to make him see her point of view. Instead, she accepted Murthy's premise that it was a binary system they were looking at, the very basics of computer science, which she had loved so much and excelled in: either she could be in and Murthy out, or Murthy could be in and she out.

The other thing that swayed her was her family. She visualized the daily lives of Akshata and the second child she hoped to have some day soon. If she were to head the company and deal with all the hassles that sent Murthy rushing across the world several times a year with no notice at all, what would happen to them? She could take care of Infosys; she was confident of it. But could Murthy take care of the children as well as she would have?

Her Ajji's comment from decades ago resonated in her ears: 'A woman can do a man's job. But a man cannot do a woman's job.' Sudha knew her husband. She knew that, at least in this case, Ajji's evaluation was correct.

Sudha mulled over these thoughts for a night and a day. By the time she came to a decision, she was calm. She came to Murthy and said, 'I've made my choice. You can head Infosys. I wish you all the best with it.'

Murthy was very thankful. He apologized again, but Sudha

shrugged. Once she made her decision, she believed in moving on. 'I'll always be a part of Infosys whether my name is on the letterhead or not,' she told him. 'Whether anyone else is aware of that doesn't matter. I know it, and that's enough.'

But people *were* aware of her decision. Years later, Nandan would put into words what was in the hearts of the entire Infosys board when he acknowledged Sudha's contribution publicly, saying, 'Sudha's sacrifice formed the foundation on which all our careers and success were built.'

The days after the TI Cycles deal fell through were agonizingly slow as Murthy scoured his database, trying to connect with potential Indian clients. Then suddenly one day the phone in the office rang, startling him. He had been sitting at his desk, looking dejectedly at a list of the names of companies, many of which were crossed off. He let out a sigh and picked up the receiver.

On the other end was his friend H.R.S. Murthy, who used to be the head of information systems at TELCO in the mid-1970s when Sudha worked there as an engineer. HRS, who knew Murthy's plight, got to the point right away. 'MICO in Bangalore is looking for a data centre arrangement. They're considering two computers, the IBM 4341 and VAX 11/750. They'll be making their decision in a week. It's a very long shot, but I thought I'd tell you about it.'

An excited Murthy thanked HRS warmly. MICO (Motor Industries Company), associated with Bosch, was a company he knew and admired. It had the reputation of choosing its vendors purely on merit, not because of contacts – a rarity in India. It was a long shot, but he was getting desperate. He called

MICO right away and managed to get in touch with the head of MICO's information systems department, V.M. Venkatarajan. Venkatarajan was not particularly encouraging. 'We've already done a lot of research and decided on a vendor,' he said.

'I'm not asking you to change your decision,' Murthy replied. 'I'm just asking for a meeting where I'll present you with a mathematical method to evaluate the architecture of computer systems. This can only help you make a better choice.'

Venkatarajan must have been impressed by Murthy's confidence. He agreed to a meeting but warned Murthy it would have to be very soon. Their deadline for the decision was fast approaching.

Murthy dropped everything to focus on a presentation that would highlight the crucial advantages that Infosys could offer but the competitors could not. He worked for three days, barely pausing to sleep. His intention was to build mathematical models to demonstrate that the architecture of the DG MV/8000, which Infosys would offer MICO, was superior to the offerings from competing vendors. He created a detailed presentation on perspective sheets, researching carefully. He even used data from the papers of John Hennessy, the famous computer architecture professor who would go on to become the president of Stanford University. But even after all this work, he felt something was lacking. Knowing that Sudha was better than him in advanced mathematics, he showed her his analysis.

'What do you think of this?' he asked.

Despite their recent disagreement, Sudha was quick to help him. She pointed out weaknesses in the presentation and helped Murthy improve his models. In between, she supplied him with breakfast, lunch and dinner, and as many cups of coffee as he needed. Akshata, too, helped. When Murthy felt that his brain was jammed and he couldn't think any more, she made him smile by singing the newest rhymes she had picked up in preschool.

Murthy dipped into their meagre funds and took a flight, rather than a train, to Bangalore as the deadline for MICO's decision was very close. He met Venkatarajan and his colleague Rajeev Lal. Both managers were cautious during the first meeting. They reluctantly agreed to sit through his presentation but warned him not to have any expectations.

Murthy's presentation, 'A Quantitative Approach to Evaluating Computer System Architecture Using DG MV/8000 as a Case Study', was probably the most thorough sales pitch MICO had seen. Murthy outlined how the DG MV/8000 would allow their applications to run more efficiently compared to the other architectures they were considering. He walked them through his mathematical models and even wrote down technical questions they should ask competing suppliers. He told them, 'You shouldn't look just for financial or organizational strength but also for technical expertise in software development for advanced international markets. It's important to gauge how well and how quickly the vendor can develop your applications on the new machine. The values and work ethic of the founder are also important.'

He dwelt at length on the solid backgrounds of the Infosys team and spoke about how he had been part of an eighteen-member team who had built a real-time operating system for managing 400 terminals to handle air cargo in Paris. He described how his tech team had built a state-of-the-art online information system for the US apparel industry.

The meeting, scheduled to end at 1 p.m., went on for nine hours and finished at 8 p.m.!

The younger members of the team were openly enthusiastic.

They told Murthy, 'We've never met a group like yours among the data centre vendors.' Venkatarajan, more cautious, only said, 'I'll talk to my boss to see if we can reopen our vendor search. Call me on Wednesday.'

Murthy stayed in his mother's home in Bangalore for the next few days. This presented its own challenge as it was never his habit to cause concern to his mother, a simple woman who would not have understood what was going on. So he had to hide his worries and converse with her as though all was going well. Additionally, he did not want to bother Sudha, who had her own work troubles to handle. He did not sleep well at night as scenarios of failure kept crowding his mind. Later, he would tell Sudha that these few days of waiting with nothing to do was the most stressful time he had ever faced because so many people's futures depended on him.

On Wednesday morning he called Venkatarajan's office promptly at 9 a.m. Venkatarajan was cheerful – a good sign – and invited Murthy to meet a couple of MICO directors for lunch at noon. This itself was significant. Murthy had made the senior management at MICO reconsider what they had thought was a final vendor decision. Large companies did not take such U-turns casually.

Murthy reached the MICO office early, as was his wont, and was taken to the directors' floor. The tech and commercial directors that he met asked him questions for two hours. Murthy was upfront about the size of his company but pointed out that the strength of Infosys lay in their superior hardware and software offering and their unmatched ability to support MICO technically.

After the meeting, the MICO team asked Murthy to sit in another room while they conferred among themselves. Murthy settled himself with a book, expecting a long wait. But they were back in fifteen minutes, offering him their congratulations. Venkatarajan, circumspect until then, had a smile on his face. He shook Murthy's hand while telling him, 'Watch out! We are tough negotiators when it comes to commercial terms.'

Murthy could barely contain his happiness. The first person he thought of was Sudha.

'May I call my wife and tell her?' he asked.

When Venkatarajan agreed, he phoned Sudha right then from the MICO offices. 'It was your help with the presentation that took me over the finish line,' he said.

Later, Murthy and Sudha went over his pitch carefully to gauge what had helped him to succeed. The first factor was emphasizing the superior technology that Infosys brought to MICO. The second was demonstrating that Infosys brought strong complementary values in the quality and experience of their team. The third was using mathematics and formal computer science methods to build models to show the superiority of the Infosys solution.

Murthy told Sudha, 'This third factor is rare in the corporate world. Thanks to you, it helped me beat the competition.'

'Well, then,' Sudha advised, 'you must train your younger colleagues to do this in all their sales pitches. But I think what swayed them just as much was your strong work ethic.'

The MICO contract ended up being far better than the TI Cycles project in terms of both its revenue and duration. MICO agreed to pay for computer time even if they did not use it during periods of company strikes, as long as the computer was made available for use by Infosys. This would give Infosys an uninterrupted stream of revenue. The MICO office being in Bangalore was an additional advantage. It helped simplify Murthy's decision of where to locate the data centre and the Infosys office. Additionally, since rents were very manageable in Bangalore, the employees would find decent places to live there.

When founders talk about why their start-ups succeed, they mention hard work, to the point of obsession and choosing the right business for the climate as two of the key ingredients. But they also mention another factor, one that is more intangible: luck. Something going your way at a crucial moment. MICO was an example of the kind of luck entrepreneurs sometimes need.

But just as the Murthys were feeling ebullient about Infosys's success, matters became complicated on the home front. The nanny Sudha had hired disappeared without giving notice, and Sudha could not find anyone suitable to replace her. She was very busy with her own job, as well as with helping Murthy with Infosys work in the evenings. Her supervisor refused to give her any time off. Sometimes she had to take Akshata along if there were evening meetings. Finally, she capitulated and phoned her mother.

'I have to ask for your help one more time,' she said. 'Will you keep Akshata with you in Hubli?'

Vimala was willing to have her granddaughter live with her, but she was concerned about all these rapid changes in Akshata's life. 'Children need stability,' she told Sudha sternly when she came to Pune to pick up Akshata. 'I'm not sending Akshata back until I feel you are properly settled.'

Sudha was crestfallen. She had worked so hard at getting her daughter acclimatized to her life in Pune and to living with her parents. Akshata had settled in well and had even picked up Marathi. She loved her playschool, where she had made many friends. She had grown attached to her parents. Had it all been for nothing?

Sudha did not want to be separated from her daughter. But she was also feeling the effects of the pressure that comes with building a company from scratch. Murthy was working very long hours, travelling at short notice, and unavailable to his family for significant stretches. Sudha had her own job with its many demands. Additionally, in spite of the argument that Murthy and she had had about her working at Infosys, she was spending many of her evenings helping him plan Infosys's future. Her mother was right – she just did not have the time and energy to look after a small child at this moment. What was worse was that she did not know when things would stabilize. She was forced to agree with Vimala that Pune was not the best environment for Akshata.

Sudha's heart was heavy as she accompanied her mother and daughter to the train station. In the past few months, she had grown very attached to her little girl. She had saved up her money carefully and bought two little gold bangles for Akshata for Rs 1700. When Akshata performed her dances and songs, Sudha always thought the bangles looked so pretty on her daughter. But when she was forced to hand Akshata to Vimala and bid them a teary goodbye, and Akshata waved to her, the bangles glittering on her arms, Sudha thought her heart would break. Paradoxically, it made her even sadder to see Akshata going off quite cheerfully with her grandmother. It was as though the little girl sensed that her real home was the old family house in Hubli, not this Pune flat upon which Sudha had lavished so much care and attention.

13

One day, when Sudha returned from work, it was almost dark. Just before she was supposed to leave, her boss had given her a new task and insisted it was urgent, so she had had to stay on longer. Now, entering the flat, she was surprised to find that Murthy had not turned on the lights. She found him sitting in the spare bedroom that was Infosys's India office. He was staring at the wall in a way that worried her.

'What's wrong?' she asked.

'Donn didn't send the money,' he told her. 'He says he's having huge financial problems. He can't send anything until next month.'

'That's what he said last month, too,' Sudha responded angrily. Donn had not paid them since August, and it was now the end of September. Somehow, Murthy had managed to scrape together enough money to pay their employees in August, but it had severely depleted their funds.

'What will you do?' she asked him.

'Luckily, we had a bit of credit left over at the RBI,' Murthy said. 'So I managed to send maintenance allowances to Nandan for the team in the US. But there isn't enough money in the Infosys account to pay their Indian salaries or of those working in India. Also, I need to set up our new office in Bangalore.'

Worry lines creased Sudha's forehead. 'Maybe you can postpone the salary payments for a week or so?' she asked. But even before Murthy shook his head vehemently, she knew he would not agree. Paying employees on time was one of his highest priorities.

She thought hard for a while. Did they have any friends from whom they could borrow such a large sum? They did not. In any case, all their friends had advised Murthy against getting into 'a high-risk business', and when problems arose, even though they were sympathetic, there was an underlying sense of 'I told you so'. Sudha was not going to humiliate herself by going to them. Nor could she ask her ageing parents to help out. They were already doing so much for her. But finally, inspiration struck her. She went into the other room. In a while, she returned with her large purse and told Murthy, who was still sitting at his desk, 'Let's go to the bank tomorrow morning and ask if they can tide us over by giving us a loan until the money from Donn gets here. I'll give them my wedding jewellery as collateral.' She opened her purse. 'See, I've already put it in here.'

However, this did not make Murthy feel better. He had been brought up to believe that the pawning of a wife's wedding gold was a shameful last resort. Additionally, he had scarring memories of his mother being forced to sell her own jewellery at the time of his sister's marriage. His worst nightmare was coming to life, and nothing Sudha said could allay the sense that he was letting her down.

Sudha took his hand with her signature sunshine smile. 'Let's have dinner. Tomorrow morning I'll make an appointment with the bank.'

At the bank the next day, things went far better than Murthy had expected. The manager invited him and Sudha to his office and told them he was confident they would soon pay back the money he was loaning them.

'Ma'am,' he said respectfully to Sudha, 'I've known you both for quite a while now. I trust you fully and don't need your jewellery as collateral.'

But Sudha, who did not believe in receiving special favours, would not hear of it. She took off the bangles she was wearing and handed them to the manager. 'I want the bank to hold these, at least, until Donn's cheque comes through,' she said.

Tears rose to Murthy's eyes as he stared at his wife's bare arms. Sudha, however, was calm as they completed the transaction and deposited the necessary amount in the Infosys account.

On the way back, Murthy was silent and depressed, but Sudha, having solved the problem at hand, was in high spirits. When Murthy tried to apologize, she shrugged it away. 'It's not a big deal,' she said. 'You know I don't care about jewellery. For me, gold is just a good investment, to be used on a rainy day. As far as I'm concerned, my bangles have served their purpose. Anyway, I have full faith you'll get them back for me!'

The employees were paid on time. Once again, Sudha had turned out to be an 'angel' for Infosys.

The episode had a happy ending. Within a few days, a cheque from the US arrived and was cashed, and Sudha got her jewellery back.

It was November 1982 – time to put into action the decision that Murthy had made earlier: Infosys needed to formally relocate to Bangalore.

While they both realized it was necessary, it was hard for Sudha and Murthy to leave Pune, the city where they had met and fallen in love. Sudha was particularly attached to their apartment. It was the first house they had owned, the flat she had overseen personally as it was being built. It was also the first home they had lived in as a family with Akshata. She asked Murthy to put off his departure for Bangalore for a few days so they could go around Pune and revisit some of their favourite haunts – the restaurants and movie theatres that had given them so many happy memories during their carefree courtship days. He did as she said, though she could sense a certain impatience.

Passing by Mahila Niwas in an autorickshaw, they smiled, remembering how Sudha would slip in after curfew while her friends distracted the nightwatchman. But inwardly Sudha wondered if they would ever be that carefree again. The playful man who had come up with the plan to trick the watchman, the man who would watch movie after romantic movie with her just because she loved them, the man with whom she had fallen in love, was so different from this person sitting next to her, nursing the intense, single-pointed entrepreneurial dream that had taken over his (and her) life. Even in the midst of their laughter, his brow was creased, as though in the back of his mind, he was worrying about Infosys. When was the last time they had discussed a book just for fun, or gone to see a movie? She couldn't remember. *If I had known he would change so much*, she wondered, *would I have married him?*

At the end of the evening, Sudha said with a sigh, 'Leaving Pune feels like I'm leaving a dear old friend behind.' Murthy agreed, though she suspected he did not feel the loss as deeply as she did. After all, he had his company.

Moving to Bangalore also meant that Sudha would be resigning from her job in Pune. It would be the second time she would have to quit a job, putting her career on hold for Infosys. This time, though, it was not a psychological wrench, the way it had been when she left TELCO. Still, she felt unmoored and uncomfortable. Since graduating from college, she had always worked and earned a solid salary. Now she did not have a clear plan for her future, or a good sense of where her career was headed.

Perhaps, Sudha thought to herself, this would be a good time to have a second child. She was, after all, thirty-three years old. 'It's not good for Akshata to grow up as an only child, getting too much attention and not learning how to share things,' she said to Murthy. 'Besides, a relationship with a sibling is a very special bond. I want Akshata to experience that, too.' Murthy, who came from a large family himself and had a close relationship with his older half-sister Kumuda, agreed.

Sudha had to stay back for a few months to finish up her responsibilities at work, so Murthy said his goodbyes and moved to Bangalore along with Raghavan. In December 1982, the two men found a bungalow in Jayanagar where they set up the new Infosys office. They were delighted at how affordable Bangalore was. The rent for the two-floor space was reasonable, and there were restaurants close by where a lunch thali was just Rs 5. They recruited support staff – a clerk and a typist. They even found a caretaker, though he greatly offended Murthy's sense of responsibility as he rarely turned up at the office before ten in the morning.

The new office was a fifteen-minute autorickshaw ride from the MICO campus, so initially Murthy and Raghavan relied on rickshaws. But these were hard to find, and they would sometimes be late for meetings, or even miss them, for the lack of a ride. This would cause great tension for Murthy.

After a few such ulcer-inducing experiences, Murthy and Sudha talked to Sudha's father in Hubli. Dr Kulkarni had recently bought a car, so he was willing to assist them by lending Murthy his Bajaj scooter. This was very helpful. Even if Murthy had placed an order for a new scooter it would not have arrived for thirty months, which was the normal waiting period in India at that time.

Raghavan and Murthy started taking the scooter to work, Raghavan manoeuvring it while Murthy sat pillion. This worked well until the day Vikram Bhat, MICO's commercial director, spotted them puttering over to the gate. Aghast, he told Venkatarajan that a vendor arriving on a scooter for a large, five-year contract discussion did not inspire confidence.

Murthy was forced to start looking for a monthly car rental. It went against his thrifty nature. From day one of Infosys, he had been extremely careful with money and made sure the company was profitable. This meant he and his colleagues took very little money from the company for expenses. But he also understood the importance of optics in business. Finally, he found a well-priced second-hand Ambassador on a monthly rent which was reliable enough for their purposes. The only drawback: it was a garish peacock-blue. But as Murthy quipped to Sudha, 'You can't look a gift car in the mouth!'

Even as he was handling all the hassles of moving an office, Murthy had to continue to deal with Donn's demands, which were often difficult and sometimes downright unreasonable.

'You have to personally keep in regular touch with major Data Basics clients in the US,' Donn insisted, though, having worked in India, he knew exactly how tough it was to coordinate timings with the US. Making an international call, which entrepreneurs take for granted today, was a major enterprise. Calls in the US had to be routed through AT&T operators, and the Indian lines were usually busy.

Indian phones were rarely reliable, and sometimes it took Murthy several hours of trying before he got a working connection – and even then it was mostly fuzzy. Infosys did not have an office phone, so he had to call from the post office on the other side of the street. The post office closed at 5 p.m., and he had to pay them extra so that they would stay open a little longer. 'It's a wonder that I manage to get any of the US-related work accomplished,' he sometimes told Sudha.

Sudha pursed her lips, though she said nothing. She saw that Donn was a bit temperamental. He knew Murthy's team in the US was quite capable of handling all his issues, but he liked having Murthy at his beck and call. In addition to insisting that Murthy call him from India any time Donn needed him, he also insisted that Murthy travel to the US whenever a big meeting with a customer came up.

Murthy could not say no because, at this point, Donn was Infosys's only customer. But it made him even more determined to get Infosys out from under Donn's thumb as quickly as possible.

―――

The phone in the Pune apartment rang, and Sudha hurried to pick it up. She was hoping it was Murthy. She had some important news for him. But Murthy's voice on the other end sounded outraged, so she decided to wait until he calmed down. She guessed something was bothering him deeply. Otherwise, he wouldn't be making an expensive long-distance call.

'You won't believe what happened! Remember the vendor we'd hired to make some tables and chairs for the office after he showed us those wonderful designs? Remember how we gave him a 50 per cent advance?'

'Yes.' Sudha did not have a good feeling about this.

'Well, he's gone – no one knows where. Absconded with our money. Without the basic furniture, how can we work in there? And I don't have the money to order anything else.'

Sudha bit her lip, deep in thought. Then she said, 'Don't you have a nephew in Bangalore? Didn't you mention that he is involved in the furniture business? Maybe he can help you out.'

'You're right. My nephew Ravi Cavale recently started his furniture business.' He paused, and Sudha knew he was hesitating because he had not wanted his relatives involved with Infosys in any way. Finally, he gave a sigh and said, 'I'll call him right now.'

'Wait, wait,' Sudha said. 'Don't hang up. I have some news of my own. This morning when I woke up, I was terribly nauseous. I could barely manage to hold it in until I got to the bathroom.' With a smile in her voice, she added, 'Just like last time.'

Murthy's voice was filled with wonder. 'Does this mean–?'

'Yes!' Sudha replied, laughing now. 'We're going to be parents again!'

Murthy contacted Ravi and told him, up front, what had happened. 'We've got to get some office furniture within three weeks. It would be wonderful if you could supply it. But I must be really clear with you. Because the other vendor stole our money, I'll only be able to pay you after several months.'

An agreeable, kind young man, Ravi was willing to do this for his uncle, even though his own cash flow was somewhat precarious. He delivered the furniture in a timely manner, thus becoming the first official supplier for Infosys. He later told people it was one of the best decisions he had ever made.

As soon as he could leave Bangalore, Murthy came to Pune and helped Sudha pack up the house. Originally, she had planned to join him in Bangalore, but now she decided to go to Hubli instead, so she could stay with Akshata and her parents until the new baby arrived.

'It'll be a great opportunity to spend some one-on-one time with our daughter,' she said. 'I've really missed her! In any case, you're so busy right now.'

Murthy's heart wanted her to be with him. *I need you*, he almost told her. But he knew that what she planned was the best thing for the family, so he agreed.

Murthy accompanied Sudha to Hubli and had a much-needed break of two days in the quiet town. The phone lines in Hubli were rudimentary and connecting with the US was almost impossible. As a result, Murthy was forced to relax and put aside work pressures. He was so exhausted from all the running around he had been doing that he slept most of the time he was there. Dr Kulkarni, never one to miss an opportunity to tease his son-in-law, declared that sleeping seemed to be Murthy's real vocation!

While Murthy was visiting Hubli, Sudha's mother made her a generous offer. 'If you want to go back to work after the new baby is born,' she said, 'you can do so. I'll take care of him or her.'

When Sudha demurred, she said, 'It's not such a big deal for me. Anyway, I'm already looking after Akshata. This way, you can take up another job – maybe in Bangalore. I know how hard you studied and worked to reach this level in your profession.'

Her mother's generosity brought tears to Sudha's eyes. She was sorely tempted. She had always loved working. She felt good about having an income and helping with the family expenses as well as with any of Infosys's sudden needs. She particularly enjoyed the satisfaction of challenging her intellect and solving problems. But would it be right for her to weigh down her ageing mother with the daily care of a second child – and that, too, for an indefinite period?

Sudha thought about the issue for an entire day and night. It was not easy, making a choice. She had always been a working woman, proud to earn her own money and contribute to the family. Finally she came to her mother and said, 'I really appreciate your offer. And I know you would do a better job with the children than I can. But it wouldn't be right for me to push this major responsibility on to you. Also, I don't want the children growing up away from me, knowing me only as an occasional visitor. Already I regret missing so much of Akshata's childhood. Why, she doesn't even really feel I'm her mother.'

Her mother nodded. 'I think you're making the correct decision,' she said.

That night, when they were alone, Sudha told Murthy about her decision, and he agreed it was both ethical and intelligent. 'Children need their parents. Because of Infosys, I can only give them a small amount of time. So they'll need you twice as much.'

'But that means it's now your turn to put bread on the table,' Sudha said.

'It is, indeed,' Murthy responded. 'You can depend upon me to do that.'

⁓

Sudha had always been the gregarious one in the Murthy household. Since she was staying in Hubli, Murthy rarely socialized or invited people over to his home in Bangalore. His entire attention was focused on Infosys. The US projects with DBC were going well, and when Donn suggested an additional project that Infosys could do from India – developing a new software package for the apparel industry on an IBM machine for US clients – Murthy was very keen to follow up.

'If you're doing it from India, I can give you a second-hand Magnuson computer on loan,' Donn said. This gave Murthy an added incentive. A second computer could really expand the kind of work Infosys was doing in India.

But there was a catch. Donn had a condition. 'You'll have to get a permanent phone connection first. Without that coordination between the US and India teams will be impossible. Otherwise, the deal is off.'

Murthy agreed to do so, but his heart sank. It was a reasonable request in most countries – but not in India. Currently, he knew, the waiting list for a telephone connection in India had about 20 million people on it. The Indian communications minister at the time, C.M. Stephen, had stated openly in Parliament that a telephone was 'a luxury, not a right'.

Getting a phone line out of turn was almost impossible unless one was prepared to resort to bribery, and that was something

Murthy and Sudha refused to do. At the same time, he realized that unless Infosys could procure a phone connection, the project Donn offered them would not materialize. Murthy gritted his teeth and made an appointment to speak with the GM of Bangalore Telephones. He was a distant relative, though Murthy doubted this would help him – and indeed, he was right.

At the office, Murthy was made to wait a suitably long time to indicate the power and importance of the man he had come to see. When they finally met, Murthy explained to him the importance of the potential software development project for which he required the phone. 'It will create many jobs in Bangalore, and India would earn a significant amount of foreign exchange.' He ended with an enthusiastic prophecy: 'Bangalore is not a valley, but we can be the Silicon Plateau of India.'

The GM listened with increasing scepticism and impatience. Then he said, 'Do you realize that even government officials who are selflessly serving India's people and doing far more important work than you can't get phone lines? Try to be a little patriotic about this. You should convince the US firm to give you the project without this phone requirement. What's wrong with using the post office's public phone, as you are now doing?'

Murthy couldn't believe his ears. But he held on to his temper and persisted, saying that international customers had choices of many other vendors. 'The US client won't wait for us to answer his call at the post office. And the post office closes at five in the evening, before working hours even start in the US.'

Murthy tried to use logic to get the GM to see his point. 'Imagine a scenario,' he said, 'where your wife goes shopping for a refrigerator. She has the choice between a Godrej showroom with brand-new refrigerators and, next to it, a small store where some people are assembling a refrigerator. This storeowner might tell her that her duty is to encourage the small company and to wait for the refrigerator to be ready in a few months. But what would you advise her to choose: the patriotic option of buying from the small entrepreneur, or the Godrej fridge?'

'What impertinence!' the GM exclaimed furiously. 'This interview is over. Now.'

The next person waiting, Murthy noted while dawdling outside, came out quickly, grinning. He had been promised a line. Murthy had a good idea as to the reason for his success.

When he informed Sudha of the entire episode – from the post office phone, of course – she was quiet. 'It isn't easy being married to an idealist,' she told her sister Sunanda after she hung up. 'I admire Murthy, but he's quite impractical. He already gave away so much equity to freshers, and now he is arguing with the telephone general manager about patriotism! I don't know how the company is going to survive, and how we'll meet family expenses.'

A dejected Murthy was forced to inform Donn that he could not get a permanent phone connection. Donn had had his own experiences with Indian bureaucracy, so he did not blame Murthy for the failure. However, Infosys did not get the $500,000 India project, the free machine, or the jobs for Indian engineers. Fortunately, Donn listened to Murthy's suggestion that the Infosys team could execute the IBM project in the US and said he would try to work something out. But the entire episode illustrated to Murthy, once again, how difficult it was for an Indian company to compete with the freewheeling, business-friendly environment in the US. He extended his stopgap method, of paying the post office the required overtime money for a clerk to keep the facility open till 9 p.m., but he knew this was not sustainable.

Several months later, Murthy and Raghavan encountered the son of a senior Karnataka government official at a Chamber of Commerce function. The official's son listened to their woes and offered them a phone rental at an exorbitant price.

'Is this legal?' Murthy asked. Despite all his troubles, he was still unwilling to do anything shady. The man assured him it was.

That was how, almost two years after moving to Bangalore, Infosys got its first telephone connection.

14

Murthy's tussles with government regulations, however, were only beginning.

Early in the process of establishing Infosys, when Murthy applied for a licence to import a computer, he had specified Chennai as the city where the computer would be installed. He had chosen Chennai because, like Bangalore, the city had a low cost of living, and he wanted his employees to find decent, affordable places to live. But after getting the MICO contract, he had relocated the Infosys office to Bangalore and hired several employees there.

At that time, this did not worry Murthy. He was sure it would be easy to obtain a location change from Chennai to Bangalore from the DoE. But when he attempted to do this, he was in for a shock. No one, it turned out, had heard of a scenario where the government had agreed to a location change. Suddenly, the entire MICO contract, upon which the future of Infosys rested, was at risk.

For the first time, Murthy hid the direness of the situation from Sudha because he did not want to stress her during her pregnancy. She was having a hard enough time already. As with her first pregnancy, she was throwing up several times every day and had lost a dangerous amount of weight. Murthy could tell that Sudha's sister Sunanda, who kept Murthy up to date about Sudha's health, was concerned.

Without saying anything to Sudha, Murthy made a trip to Delhi to meet with Dr Seshagiri in September 1982. By now Seshagiri had risen through the ranks and was an additional secretary at the DoE and in charge of computer licensing. Murthy soon found out that this was the worst time to meet with him. Planning for the approaching Asian Games, which were to be held in Delhi, was in full swing, led by the prime minister's son, Rajiv Gandhi. Seshagiri was under a great deal of pressure as he was in charge of installing a large, real-time system for handling the events, where computers would be used to track schedules, event records, event results and all the other clerical chores connected with the games.

Murthy checked into the Lodhi Hotel, located near the DoE office. It was the ideal place for those unfortunates waiting for appointments with the officials, since one could dash over to the DoE whenever these exalted beings made an appearance. Murthy waited the whole day at Seshagiri's office, trying to set up an appointment, but he was busy handling problems at the site. A secretary finally took pity on Murthy and told him that Seshagiri might come by the office at 10.30 p.m. to catch up on some work.

Murthy waited through the day, wondering whether it was a bad move to phone the official so late, when Seshagiri would likely be exhausted and in no mood to listen to requests. But his situation was desperate, so finally at 10.30 p.m., he went ahead. The phone rang and rang. Finally, Seshagiri answered, sounding tired and irritable. Murthy introduced himself and told Seshagiri about the location problem regarding his computer

An Uncommon Love

licence approval. 'I would be most grateful if you could find a few minutes to meet with me,' he ended.

Seshagiri yelled, 'Do you realize I'm installing an operating system with 200 terminals? I have no time to meet you – or anyone else. All you people in the private sector are crooks, anyway, always asking for unreasonable favours.'

Murthy drew in a deep breath. He had everything to lose, but he felt he must take a stand. 'That's not a fair remark, Dr Seshagiri,' he said quietly but firmly. 'Not everyone in the private sector is a crook. There are plenty of us honest people here.'

There was a startled silence at the other end.

'Sir,' Murthy continued, 'I have immense respect for your work for the Asian Games. I know how challenging it must be. I was a member of the team that built a real-time operating system with 400 terminals for handling air cargo at the Charles de Gaulle airport many years ago. I also know it isn't fair of me to ask you for a meeting at the end of such a long day. But you are the only one who can help me.'

After a brief pause, Seshagiri agreed to meet him at 11 p.m. 'I'll see you for fifteen minutes,' he said.

Murthy ran all the way to the DoE office.

Seshagiri had calmed down by then. 'You're the first businessman to talk back to me like that,' he told Murthy with an amused smile. He heard Murthy out as he described the licence issue and why the computer location had to be shifted from Chennai to Bangalore. Then he asked him to submit an application for the change of location.

'I'll consider it on its merits,' he told Murthy.

A grateful Murthy submitted the application the very next day and returned to Bangalore. His discussion with Seshagiri had led him to hope that the matter would be resolved soon, but for weeks he heard nothing from the DoE. At the other end, MICO was putting pressure on him to get things moving fast. In desperation, Murthy travelled to Delhi several times. Not wanting to disturb Seshagiri, who was increasingly busy because of the Games, he met with other DoE officials to try and find out the status of his application. No one was helpful. Singh, whom Murthy knew from the time of his original application, was particularly unpleasant. He was suspicious and openly opposed to the change of location. 'Looks unlikely to happen,' he would say, with an uncooperative shrug, whenever Murthy spoke to him.

One day, luckily, Seshagiri happened to be around, and Murthy managed to meet with him.

'You still haven't received the approval?' Seshagiri asked, surprised.

Murthy shook his head. 'I've been meeting with your officers regularly,' he said.

Seshagiri was taken aback. 'You should have received the approval by now. I recommended the Infosys case to the secretary, Dr P.P. Gupta, myself and instructed Singh to follow through with the documentation.' He was so upset at this lapse that he said he would take the file personally over to the secretary at Lok Nayak Bhavan that afternoon.

'Meet me there at two in the afternoon,' he told Murthy.

Murthy was at the reception desk of Lok Nayak Bhavan long before 2 p.m. Seshagiri arrived soon after that and went to the conference room to meet with the secretary and Singh. When Singh started dodging Seshagiri's questions, he got upset, his voice got louder, and Murthy could hear the conversation from where he waited. Singh also raised his voice. Seshagiri defended Infosys, saying that he found Murthy to be an honest entrepreneur keen on exporting software. Singh insisted that

Murthy, like other entrepreneurs, was 'just a crook', looking only to earn 'huge profits' from his data centre operations.

Seshagiri came out after an hour and told Murthy that the change of location would be granted. He had won this battle on Murthy's behalf. Murthy was most grateful for his championship.

As Rajiv Gandhi's adviser, Seshagiri later became instrumental in simplifying regulation in the software industry, including the import of computers into India. Thanks to him, software entrepreneurs no longer had to jump through complicated regulatory hoops.

Murthy had been summoned to the US by Donn, so he asked Raghavan to collect the letter from the DoE in Delhi. For ten days in a row, Raghavan sat at the reception for eight hours every day before he was granted a meeting. When Raghavan eventually met the official and asked for the letter, he was told it would be mailed to Bangalore.

It took another twenty days for the letter to arrive. By this time, Murthy was back from the US. When he opened the letter, he received a shock. Murthy had mentioned to Singh, during one of his many DoE visits, that Infosys had a data centre contract with MICO, and the client wanted the computer to be installed in their premises. Now Singh had exacted his revenge. He granted the change in location for the computer from Chennai to Bangalore but made it contingent on the computer being located inside the Infosys premises.

Murthy was devastated. Despite all his efforts – the Delhi trips (he estimated he had made at least fifty), the pitch to MICO, the struggle to get a loan to import the computer and the long work hours spent to get the project up and running – the project now faced a whole new obstacle.

When MICO's head of information systems, Venkatarajan, heard what had happened to the change of location request, he grew sceptical. He told Murthy that perhaps he should withdraw from the deal so that MICO could go ahead and find another vendor. Murthy asked him for a month's time to figure something out.

He tried to stay optimistic, but it was difficult. He did not want to stress Sudha in the middle of a difficult pregnancy, so he said nothing to her. He did inform his colleagues, but the ones in the US left the matter to his discretion since they were in another country. Besides, they felt that he was their senior and definitely the savviest member of the team. Raghavan, who was in Bangalore, was extremely nervous and of no help at all. He wondered aloud if this would be the death of Infosys. He kept asking Murthy if he would have to pull out his children from the Kodaikanal residential school where he had placed them and leave Bangalore in search of a new job.

Raghavan's attitude was an additional stress for Murthy. But he preserved a calm demeanour and told Raghavan, 'We need to stay positive. It's especially important to remain upbeat and work hard when the chips are down.'

But privately, his anxiety grew. He had trouble sleeping at night. His ulcers started acting up. He would lie awake in his bed, which stretched vast and empty, listening to the ticking clock, hoping for a brainwave. Without Sudha to laugh him out of his dejection, he felt dreadfully alone. Finally, he turned to Raghavendra Swamy. He got into the habit of picturing the Mantralayam temple in his mind and imagined himself sitting there in front of Swamy's image. A deep calm would settle over him at such times.

Later he told Sudha, 'Faith gave me the energy I needed. It helped me overcome problems for which I had no solutions.'

Each day Murthy focused on the only thing in his control. He conducted a thorough search for a rental office located near MICO where he could install the Infosys computer, fulfilling both the government's and MICO's requirements. Unfortunately, the space on the front side of MICO was taken up by a military school and a mill. Behind MICO was a slum and several marble factories. Murthy and Raghavan checked the area and finally found an empty two-floor building in the middle of the slum behind MICO. But when they showed the place to the facilities team of MICO, they dismissed the idea as ludicrous. 'The directors will never approve a data centre located in the middle of a slum,' Venkatarajan said. 'The data centre will have to be either inside the MICO administrative block or within a stone's throw, in a clean, safe location.'

For the next few days, Murthy racked his brain, trying to come up with a solution. He avoided visiting Hubli, knowing that Sudha would pick up on his unhappiness at once. If she asked, he knew he would not be able to stop himself from blurting out what was going on. And the last thing he wanted was to cause her additional stress at a time when she was experiencing health problems: severe nausea and extreme, constant tiredness. He talked instead to Nandan in the US and to Raghavan in Bangalore, but neither of them could think of a way out of this dilemma. The MICO folks were getting increasingly nervous.

Venkatarajan told Murthy, 'You must find a solution quickly. Otherwise, we'll have to move to the next vendor on our list.'

One evening, while a dejected Murthy was sitting alone in his apartment with his eyes closed, meditating on Raghavendra Swamy, he was struck by a sudden idea. It was an unusual, out-of-the-box solution that he felt just might work. For the first night in several weeks, he slept well. The next day, in high spirits, he arranged a teleconference with Raghavan in the office and Nandan and Kris in the US.

'I suddenly remembered something I had read a while ago in a Sherlock Holmes book,' Murthy told them. 'It went like this, I believe: *When all possible options are eliminated, we must try the impossible.*'

The others were intrigued but unsure as to what he was getting at.

'MICO wants the data centre in their premises while DoE wants the computer installation in our premises,' Murthy said. 'Therefore, it is logical that the MICO premises must become our premises.'

The US team was taken aback, while Raghavan frowned. 'Is this a joke?' he asked. But Murthy was confident. 'It's the only way! We'll ask MICO to lease a part of their administrative block to us.'

Raghavan the pessimist spoke up. 'There's no chance that a German multinational will lease part of their prime campus to an upstart, financially weak company.' Even Nandan and Kris, who usually went along with Murthy's suggestions, were silent. But his team's lack of enthusiasm did not deter Murthy. It was as though a power from within was guiding him.

He met with the managers of information systems at MICO, Venkatarajan and Rajeev Lal, and after a few minutes of pleasant conversation, casually asked them whether MICO would lease Infosys enough space in the administrative block to install the new computer. The managers stared at him as if he had gone mad.

Finally, Venkatarajan said contemptuously, 'The discussion with Infosys on the data centre is now over. Thank you very much for a year-long association that wasted our time.'

Murthy was undeterred. 'I understand your frustration with these location problems,' he said. 'Both of you have been very patient, so I'll just ask for this one thing: can we please meet with the technical director and run this past him?'

Venkatarajan and Rajeev Lal were upset. They hinted that Infosys was making them look bad before their bosses. 'One of our German colleagues had warned us,' Venkatarajan said, 'that your lack of connections with the Delhi officers would be a significant problem for the data centre project.'

Murthy negotiated with them for the next hour, trying to reassure them and pushing for a meeting with the technical director. 'There's no harm in checking whether this is possible,' he told them.

Finally, they gave in.

A meeting with the technical director was fixed for the next day. It was a very short one. The director immediately dismissed Murthy's idea of a leased space in the administrative block as 'preposterous'.

'This kind of arrangement has never happened between Bosch and a vendor anywhere in the world, and it will not happen here either,' he told Murthy sternly.

So that, too, was a dead end. Now there was just one option left, a do-or-die manoeuvre. The commercial director, Vikram Bhat, had not heard the suggestion yet – and Murthy was determined to reach him.

Bhat was away on vacation in Europe, and Murthy had heard that he would end his vacation with a visit to the Bosch headquarters. Murthy decided he would also go to Europe, explain everything and ask Bhat to get the approval for Infosys's request from his boss in Germany. This entire scenario ran through Murthy's head in less than a minute. But when he approached the staff at Bhat's office, they told Murthy that MICO had a strict security policy of not disclosing the travel programmes of their senior officers.

Murthy had no idea where in Europe Bhat was. He had hit a wall, but he refused to let that stop him. He contacted Passage, MICO's travel agent, to get the details of Bhat's itinerary. He spoke to multiple people in the Passage hierarchy until he reached the managing director of Passage. There, too, he met a dead end. The managing director told Murthy he couldn't disclose Bhat's travel plans.

Anyone else would have given up by now, but amazingly, something gave Murthy the strength to persist. The Sherlock Holmes quotation that had risen in his mind a few days ago seemed prophetic to him. By chance, that evening, he had planned to meet an IAS officer in the Karnataka government whom he knew well. The officer had started his career under Murthy's uncle, who had been Karnataka's finance secretary in 1952.

It turned out this officer was a good friend of Bhat's, so much so that he had the phone number of the hotel in Stuttgart where Bhat was staying. He gave Murthy the number. Murthy guarded the precious slip of paper carefully and called the hotel at the first opportunity. When he got Bhat on the line, he explained his idea about the computer location.

The director heard him out. 'Let me think about this,' he told Murthy. 'I'll be back in Bangalore soon. Meet me on Monday at 9 a.m. at the MICO office.'

Bhat had not dismissed Murthy's idea out of hand, which gave Murthy some hope. Now, with a small chance of things going his way, Murthy called Sudha. Speaking over the crackle and whine of the phone line to Hubli, he shared with her the whole saga, from the DoE letter to the recent phone call with Bhat.

Sudha was amazed at the plan Murthy had come up with. 'How did you even think of such an unusual solution?' she asked.

Murthy said, 'I think it was sent to me! I know, that doesn't sound logical. But where the realm of logic ends, the realm of faith begins.'

'It makes perfect sense to me,' Sudha said. Her maternal grandmother had often said similar things when Sudha had accompanied her to the local temple.

Just hearing her beloved voice felt to Murthy like a drink of cool water on a blistering summer day. He realized only then just how much he had been missing her. He was not ready to hang up. Though he was really busy, he stayed on the phone, asking her to describe all the new things that Akshata had learnt. Sudha was happy to oblige him.

But in the middle of the call, Raghavan came to the office and asked Murthy again if he should withdraw his sons from the Kodaikanal school. Murthy sighed inwardly at the difference between Sudha, the eternal optimist, and Raghavan, the total pessimist. He told Raghavan to hold off on the decision until the end of next week. 'I see a ray of hope,' he said.

On Monday, Venkatarajan and Murthy met Bhat in his office. Bhat asked Murthy to go over the entire problem again. After hearing him out, he asked him for a note on why this computer was essential for MICO's growth. He also needed to see, in writing, how Infosys would comply with MICO's safety and security requirements. Bhat also wanted Murthy to emphasize the inflexibility of the Indian government in this matter, and to point to the fact that similar problems with the DoE would likely arise with another data centre vendor, too.

Murthy prepared the note the very same day and sent it across. Bhat asked him to wait for a few weeks. But on Friday itself, Murthy got a call from Bhat's office asking him to come by next Monday. It was an exciting but tense weekend for Murthy. He called Sudha to get her opinion on the matter. She felt optimistic. 'If Bhat wasn't considering the proposal seriously, he would surely have informed you of that on the phone. Why would he go through all the trouble of meeting with you?'

When Murthy entered Bhat's office on Monday, the MICO director was in a cheerful mood. He told Murthy right away he had convinced Bosch to lease the administrative block area to Infosys for its computer centre. 'It's nothing short of a miracle!' Bhat added. 'Bosch never leases their office space to a vendor.'

Overcome, Murthy closed his eyes in a prayer of thanks. It was unthinkable to have an MNC in India of the 1980s collaborating with a small start-up in this fashion. Even years later, when Infosys had risen to the greatest heights, he would say, 'Mr Bhat came into my life like a divine intervention and transformed it! I offer him thanks almost every week. Infosys would go on to gain greater victories and larger contracts, but this was my finest entrepreneurial moment.'

Could he get away with a little more? Murthy wondered. He took a deep breath and asked Bhat if Infosys could have a signboard at the MICO main gate to satisfy the DoE. Bhat considered the request for a moment that seemed, to Murthy, to stretch forever. Then he said yes.

Infosys had triumphed, meeting every tough condition set by the DoE! For the first time in his professional life, Murthy could not hold back tears of relief and gratitude. He wept openly in front of Bhat, who patted Murthy's shoulder and stepped out to allow him to recover.

Raghavan was waiting anxiously outside Bhat's office. Murthy, wiping his eyes, told him that he wouldn't, after all, be forced to take his kids out of the Kodaikanal school! After that, he made the most important call – to Sudha. She had been waiting nervously near the phone and was overcome with joy. She told him something which, knowing the tension he was under, she hadn't articulated all this while. 'Now we can afford a home in Bangalore! I've been longing to be together again, as a family, with the children.' Murthy could hear the pain, along with the excitement, in her voice.

The hard-won MICO contract was a turning point for the company. Without that steady domestic revenue stream, it would not have been possible for Infosys to invest in scaling up the export market. The days after Infosys's major victory were filled with a fresh exuberance: a win against all odds can be better for the spirit than an easy win.

Even years later, Murthy would often recall Bhat's kindness. He would tell Sudha, 'Bhat demonstrated to me that true courtesy is the kind that is shown when you are at the top.'

15

Soon after the MICO victory, Murthy received another piece of good news. His sister-in-law Sunanda called him to let him know that once again he was a proud father – this time, of a son. The baby had been born at Hubli's Medical College Hospital after a very short labour – so short that Sunanda had barely managed to get Sudha into a delivery room! Sunanda had taken charge of the delivery this time, too, sharing the tender first moment of viewing a newborn with her sister. Both mother and child were doing very well. In fact, Dr Kulkarni felt that his daughter had recovered enough to leave the hospital, and he had already driven mother and child home.

As soon as he could manage, Murthy took a bus to Hubli. He could only spend a day there before he had to fly to New York, but he was eager to see his family. Holding the new baby close to his chest, he was overcome by feelings of protectiveness. He could already tell that this baby was different from Akshata. He cried more and was an active, restless child, unlike his older sister who had, with her quiet, observant nature, taken after Murthy from the start. When the baby fussed a lot, Murthy told Sudha that this child had clearly taken after her!

A spirited discussion was already under way about the little boy's name. Sudha had been certain the second child, too, would be a girl, so she had not thought too hard about names for boys. Ever the history enthusiast, she announced, 'I want to name him Amoghavarsha, after the valiant Rashtrakuta king.'

Shrinivas, who was visiting at the time, had already warned Murthy that Sudha was considering some distinctly odd names for the baby, so Murthy was not too surprised. This time he put up a fight. 'That name is far too complicated. The child will have problems in school. And if he goes abroad to continue his studies, it will make his life miserable!' Shrinivas backed him up.

Sudha was not happy about her wonderful and original choice being vetoed, but finally she saw Murthy's point. 'Well,' she conceded, 'if simple and easy is what you want, I guess we could go with Ashoka. He was a great king, too.'

This time, too, Murthy disagreed. 'That's going to the other extreme! There are already too many people named Ashoka. I myself know several. A name like that will not stand out at all.'

Before Sudha could dive back into her large historical repertoire in search of another strange name, Murthy chose one himself, with the help of Shrinivas. Their son was named Rohan.

All through the flight to the US, Murthy kept seeing his two children in his mind's eye. When it was time for him to leave Hubli, Akshata had held on to him tightly and cried. 'Why can't you stay longer?' she had asked. 'Why do you always go away?' Sudha had had to pull her away from her father, and Murthy had felt a wrench in his heart. Now he pictured his son smiling in his arms. He had been told by Sunanda that newborns did not smile so soon, but he was sure Rohan was more advanced than regular babies.

This was going to be a lengthy trip. He would be in the US

for four months and unable to see Sudha for all that time. It struck him that they had never been separated from each other for so long in the last five years. He was sorry that he would miss Rohan's naming ceremony. Would Akshata forget him by the time he returned? Tossing and turning in his narrow economy class seat, trying vainly to get some rest before he had to rush to meet with Donn, he hoped that someone would take photos of his children so that he could enjoy some of the key moments of their growing up. But he wasn't sure if anyone in the Hubli household had a camera.

In New York, there was one final hurdle left for Murthy to cross – an extremely difficult one. He needed to get an export licence approved by the US Commerce Department so that he could ship the DG MV/8000 computer to India.

There was a reason why this was so difficult. Sometime back, an Indian national based in Delhi had created a minor scandal for the US and Indian governments when he diverted a powerful computer (similar to the DG MV/8000) meant for India to the USSR. This happened during the Cold War between the US and the Soviet Union, and was part of a broader conspiracy between USSR residents and multiple buyers. These unethical intermediaries would purchase high-tech components and machines from the US, purportedly for their home countries, such as Japan, Norway and India, and then illegally divert them to the USSR. Private smugglers in the USSR resold computers from the US in the black market, and even wrote and marketed their own programs. For example, the Russian hacker Maxim Khomyakov had helped create a popular local operating system called Chaos, which was meant for office file management.

Since the incident, the US government had suspended the export of computers above a certain grade to India. Eighteen months had passed since then, but they showed no sign of relenting. Murthy's challenge was to convince the American government that he was the genuine article and to get them to issue him an export certificate.

In order to keep Infosys's costs low, Murthy stayed in Dinesh and Ashok's tiny flat in New Jersey. Immersed in work, the three men barely noticed their surroundings. They did not mind having to share a living room, kitchen and bathroom, and they divided up the chores: grocery shopping, simple cooking and minimal cleaning. Most of their time was spent at work, anyway. When Shrinivas – who was by now a professor of physics at Caltech – visited Murthy, he was shocked at his brother-in-law's living conditions. The apartment was in a rundown building in a dangerous part of New Jersey. The neighbourhood was clearly unsafe, its alleys full of stray dogs and broken bottles. Vagrants, drunkards and drug addicts hung around street corners, and fights erupted regularly after it turned dark. Sometimes late at night, they heard gunfire.

Shrinivas tried to get Murthy to move to a better part of the city. 'Otherwise, you'll get mugged,' he warned.

But Murthy pointed out a basic fact: 'We can't afford it.' However, he did promise Shrinivas that he would take precautions. From that time on, he made sure that all three took extra care when they went to work. Fortune was kind to them, or perhaps it was the power of Sudha's prayers in Hubli. Though there were many violent incidents around them, the three men remained safe.

In addition to handling Infosys projects for Donn and developing a simulator for the DG MV/8000, Murthy would take the train to Washington, DC, every Thursday to meet with the officers of the Export Services Administration. Each visit would end with the officers asking him for more data. Murthy was no stranger to bureaucratic delays. After all, he had dealt with the DoE in India. Still, the stress – and being away from his family – took its toll on him. He found it increasingly difficult to digest the spicy Indian dishes his roommates loved to cook, even though it was the kind of food he had grown up eating. His ulcers grew worse. The antacids he picked up at the drugstore did not do the trick. Sometimes the burning pain in his stomach would wake him in the middle of the night, and he would drink a quart of milk straight out of the fridge, hoping for some relief. Illnesses he had been diagnosed with earlier – diabetes, hypertension and eye problems – started getting worse in this period of his life. At one point, his doctor warned him that, if he did not take better care of himself, his health problems might get very serious. Murthy refused to let this slow him down, though in later years he would have to pay the price for his stubbornness.

Eventually, his tenacity and sacrifices bore fruit. In February 1984, Infosys became the first Indian company to get an export licence from the US since the ban had come into effect.

―

By the time Murthy was able to return to India, four months had passed. He rushed to Hubli to see his family, taking the long seven-hour train ride from Bangalore, stopping only to buy some toys and books for the children. He was pleasantly surprised to find Sudha's younger sister, Jaishree, at the Kulkarni residence. He was fond of Jaishree, who now lived in Canada. She had first met him in Pune even before he was married to Sudha, and in her quiet way, she had supported Sudha's choice. He never forgot that and, when an opportunity arose, he would go out of his way for her.

Once when Murthy went to the US for work, Jaishree had asked him to bring her – of all things – a hammock she had seen in a magazine. Without question or complaint, Murthy had found a hammock, bought it with his slender funds and carried it back though it took up most of the space in his suitcase. On another occasion, he had adjusted his busy schedule to take Sudha and Jaishree on a trip to visit the scenic Jog Falls in the Western Ghats, because Jaishree wanted to see this famous tourist spot.

It was a trip Jaishree recalled fondly. Apart from the splendour of the falls, she remembered he had bought them soft drinks at the falls because Jaishree had mentioned she was thirsty. The drinks had been exorbitantly priced, and Jaishree had felt bad, but Murthy had shrugged and said, 'The sellers are poor people. It's important to buy things from them and help them and help the economy at the same time.'

Now Jaishree had come to spend some time in Hubli with her new baby, Pavan, who had been born just a couple of months before Rohan. When Murthy reached the Hubli home, the two sisters decided to play a trick on Murthy. They dressed their sons in identical, brightly coloured outfits and greeted Murthy, each holding a baby.

'Can you tell which one is your son?' Sudha asked.

Murthy examined each infant closely. He did not have much experience with babies, but he pointed confidently to the child Jaishree was holding because he seemed a little smaller. The entire family burst out laughing because he had guessed wrong. Sudha said accusingly, with mock anger, 'What kind of father are you? You can't even recognize your own son!' For the rest of his stay – and indeed, for months afterwards – the family teased Murthy mercilessly for his mistake; he submitted good-naturedly.

All that day Murthy carried baby Rohan around or played with Akshata. That night, when the children slept, he stood at their bedside for a long while, watching them. It was a precious time for him, but, as with all his family activities of that phase, far too short. He – and Sudha – knew that the very next morning he would have to leave because the long-awaited DG MV/8000 computer had arrived in Bangalore and was waiting at customs for clearance.

Sudha would have loved for him to stay longer so that his children – especially Akshata – could enjoy his presence. But she knew how crucial the arrival of the computer was for Infosys. She hid her disappointment and bid him goodbye and good luck with a smile on her face.

Though tired from the train journey back to Bangalore, Murthy did not stop to rest. He went straight to the Infosys office to pick up the necessary documentation for the computer. Then, Nandan and he hurried to the customs office. Murthy was light-headed with relief. This was the culmination of months and months of tireless striving. 'Finally!' he whispered to Nandan.

But when they went into the office where the customs officer on duty was seated and presented the documentation for clearance, the officer did not even look at the papers. Instead, he told Murthy, in a suggestive tone, 'If you look after us, we will look after you.'

Murthy, who with his hatred of bribery had made anti-corruption part of Infosys's corporate policy, was furious. But he kept a tight hold on his temper and spoke politely. 'Our papers are in order. So there's no need for anyone to "look after" us.'

Angered by this intransigence, the customs officer refused to accept the concessional duty certificate for the computer that had been issued to Infosys by the DoE. This certificate, issued because the company would be exporting software and bringing in valuable foreign currency, entitled Infosys to pay 25 per cent duty as opposed to the normal duty of 150 per cent that other importers would have to pay.

Murthy couldn't believe this was happening. He pointed out that the certificate was issued by a director from the DoE. 'Please call the DoE,' he said to the officer. 'You can check with them. They will verify it is genuine. I'll happily pay for the phone call.'

'I don't have time for such nonsense,' the officer snarled. 'I'm not going to release the machine until you pay the full amount you owe us.'

Worried about what might happen to such a delicate and expensive piece of equipment if it was left at the customs office under such hostile conditions, Murthy rushed to the bank and withdrew the money, though it created a substantial financial burden for Infosys. But he refused to give in to this kind of unjust and illegal behaviour. It would take Murthy seven years to get back the extra duty he paid – but he kept at it, complaining to the appropriate authorities, and finally he succeeded!

Over the next days, Murthy and his team in Bangalore worked day and night. Murthy and Nandan brought the machine to the Infosys data centre at MICO and contacted Murthy's close friend Harish Tandon. When he came over, they handed the computer to him with a sigh of relief. Tandon, who was head of hardware at PCS, personally installed the machine, which was a rare honour for Infosys. The next step was testing the simulator. Murthy did this himself, along with Shibu, working late into the night. Meanwhile, during the day, Raghavan and Nandan discussed their implementation of the new systems on the DG MV/8000 machine with the management. MICO was so impressed with Murthy's careful attention to detail and his twenty-four-hour work ethic that they decided to relax the company's strict scheduling policy and accept the computer for use forty days ahead of what was in the contract. The Infosys team's hard work and focus on quality brought them an extra revenue of more than Rs 5 lakh, which was a huge sum at that time for their fledgling company.

Murthy wanted to celebrate this milestone in a special way. The best thing he could think of was to take the weekend off and spend it with his family at Hubli. He particularly enjoyed being entertained by Akshata, who was very excited to see her father. She sang and danced and recited multiplication tables, showing off for him all she had learnt at school as well as from her aunt Sunanda. It was fun for Murthy to see how protectively she watched over her baby brother, though she was not averse to bossing over him from time to time.

In the evening, Sudha and Murthy relived their courtship days by going on a rare outing. They watched a Hindi movie and had dinner at a restaurant, where, in a quiet and private corner, they toasted each other with mango juice. Sudha was delighted to celebrate the fruition of the plans for which Murthy had been working so hard, but it was a bittersweet moment. She was keenly aware of the family time that she – and the children – had had to give up for it. They had been living away from Murthy for almost a year.

She reached across the table and grasped Murthy's hand. 'It's time to reunite the family,' she declared. 'Why, the children barely know who you are.'

'Let's do it soon,' Murthy said, tightening his fingers around hers. 'I can't tell you how much I've missed you. It'll be a real joy to come home to the two little ones at the end of the day.'

'I've missed you, too,' Sudha said. 'I'll join you in Bangalore as soon as Rohan gets his immunizations. Why don't you start looking for a flat for us?'

They sat at the table late into the night, the way they used to do in Pune, excitedly imagining this new phase of their lives. They had no idea that fate had orchestrated something quite different for them.

On Monday Murthy was back in Bangalore, planning the next crucial steps in Infosys's growth, looking ahead to the next challenge. It was not in his nature to rest on his laurels. He called the board together and persuaded them to accept a crucial resolution: in five years, they would grow enough in multiple areas (especially in the fields of software development) to be free of Dom's company, DBC. The board agreed unanimously.

Important developments were taking place in the US as well. As a result of the excellent presentations Murthy had made to American companies, Donn procured a major contract with H.H. Cutler and Co. Infosys became subcontractor to DBC for this project. Their responsibility was to develop the CAMP package to run on an IBM 4341 on the Cutler premises, where office space would be provided for up to thirty programmers for up to three years. As usual, Donn decided that Murthy's presence at this venue was essential for at least three months.

'I need you on the premises in order to get the project off the ground,' he insisted.

Though he longed to remain in India and establish a home for Sudha and his children in Bangalore, Murthy had to put together a team rapidly and go back to the US, while Sudha had to satisfy herself by imagining her dream flat where the family could finally be together. Murthy could not even be present for his son's rice-eating ceremony.

One morning as she awoke and went to change Rohan, Sudha was shocked to find his whole body covered in a rash. Worried, she rushed to fetch Sunanda and her father. After examining the baby carefully, both of them declared that it was infantile eczema that needed to be treated carefully. It was not particularly dangerous, but Rohan could not be vaccinated until it subsided, and that was risky.

'Rohan must be quarantined until then because he's totally unprotected from deadly diseases like polio and hepatitis,' Sudha's father said. 'You'll have to take over his care completely, and that means you, too, need to quarantine yourself.'

Sudha was worried. She asked how long this might take.

'Oh, maybe two or three months,' her father said.

That did not sound too bad to Sudha. Anyway, Murthy was away in the US. 'I guess I'll get to enjoy a couple of extra months of your cooking,' she joked to her mother.

None of them knew the condition would persist for the first sixteen months of Rohan's life, forcing both mother and child to remain housebound for that length of time. It was difficult for them both. As Rohan grew older, he was curious about the world outside, which he could see through the window. Being a very active child, he would often try to escape from the house. Sudha would have to keep a vigilant eye on him, and a couple of times when he did manage to get out, she had to chase after him and catch him. On his first birthday, while the adults were distracted with preparing for a birthday ceremony, he ran all the way to the bus stop, terrifying her. But just as she had been patient with her younger siblings, now too Sudha was patient with Rohan's naughtiness and did not shout at him or punish him. She realized how difficult it was for such an energetic child to be cooped up inside a room without a single playmate.

Sudha's prolonged stay at her parents' home was not an easy time for her, either. Because she lived there for so many months, people in Hubli began to question her situation. The gossips whispered that her husband must have abandoned her. She was amused, but the comments also stung, especially since she missed Murthy. They had not been apart for this long since they met each other. Additionally, the gregarious Sudha loved to get together with the many cousins and friends who lived in the area. But now, because of Rohan's condition, she was prevented from meeting up with any of them. Each day, the hours dragged on endlessly.

All her life, Sudha had kept herself busy, first by studying hard and then by working hard, constantly pushing herself to do better. Being busy, she believed, was a virtue; being idle was not. From the time Murthy began to follow his entrepreneurial dream, she had done the work of two people – all day in her office, and then, after coming back home, side by side with him. She had planned and advised; she had accompanied him on all those unpleasant visits to the RBI and the DoE, often with a baby on her hip. All of a sudden, it now seemed she had no office responsibilities and therefore no aim. That she was no longer a crucial part of

Murthy's endeavour. That she was not necessary. She felt cut off from the exciting events occurring in Bangalore, where Infosys was facing new challenges and achieving new victories each day. Inactivity made her fret and grow depressed.

Sudha's plan to grow closer to Akshata, which had been progressing nicely, had also hit a roadblock due to Rohan's condition. On the practical level, this was not a major problem as Sudha's mother and sister took over Akshata's entire care with efficiency. When Sunanda came home, for instance, Akshata spent much of her time with her, learning slokas and prayers and practising dance steps. They both loved arts and crafts – something that Sudha was not particularly good at.

One day, Akshata was colouring a picture of flowers and was wondering aloud as to what shade she should use for the petals. Peering out at the drawing from inside her room, Sudha suggested a colour. Akshata listened politely, then informed her mother that she preferred to wait and ask her aunt when she came home. Sudha appreciated the bond between Akshata and Sunanda – that was what she had hoped for when she sent her daughter to Hubli. But the incident also showed her that, even though she was physically in the same household, she was not an integral part of her daughter's life. It was a deflating realization, and added to her sense of frustration and loneliness.

There was something else that was bothering Sudha, though she could not put her finger on it until the day she needed to ask a servant to go to the post office and buy her a postcard so that she could send an update to Murthy. She suddenly realized she did not have the money even for this paltry purchase. Her father or her sister would have happily bought the card for her, and Murthy would have sent her the funds, had she asked for them, but that was not the issue.

Ever since she left college, Sudha had taken care of all her expenses – and often, Murthy's too – by herself, with her own salary. Her salary had allowed them to buy their flat in Pune. Her savings had enabled him to start Infosys. Now, without an income, she felt diminished. She felt she was housebound, a dependent with no means of her own. This was not how she had visualized her life when she fought to become the first woman engineering student in Hubli, or the first female engineer in TELCO.

It might have been easy, under these conditions, to spiral into depression. But Sudha's great gift of positivity stood her in good stead. Life, she understood, had taken away some things, but it had given her many others – including the gift of time. What would be the best way to utilize it? Finally, she came to a decision. She procured a notebook, and while Akshata was in nursery school and baby Rohan slept, she decided to use her time to write a novel.

Since childhood, Sudha had read widely and enthusiastically, and her mother had made her write every day when she came home from school. When they went on vacation – usually to stay with Sudha's grandparents, and once on a memorable trip to Goa – all the siblings had to write about their holiday experiences. Sudha was fond of these writing exercises. They helped develop her imagination and her writing skills. As a result, even at a young age, she had published several short pieces in Kannada magazines. After returning from her visit to the US, she had published a book about her adventures abroad. She had also written some books about computer programming, gearing them towards women. She had even penned the imagined life of a girl from Hubli who goes to Mumbai. But she had never taken up a long and serious fictional project like the one she had in mind right now.

Sudha did not know whether she had the talent for it. But she had always been game for a new adventure. *What do I have to lose?* she thought with a shrug. In the quiet of her room, behind closed doors, her thoughts grew loud. Away from Infosys and the pressures of job and housework, she found ideas coming quickly. A strange sense of lightness overtook her as the outline of a story took shape in her mind. At its centre was the shadowy form of a woman, at once like her but also very different. As Sudha focused on her, the words began to flow almost magically.

The novel Sudha wrote by hand, sitting on her bed through the hot afternoon while Rohan slept, was in her mother tongue, Kannada, and it was titled *Mahashweta*. Perhaps because she had been influenced at a young age by two strong and determined grandmothers who had faced many challenges, in this book she showcased a woman who undergoes numerous tragic situations through no fault of her own. Yet she remains strong. Married to a seemingly wonderful doctor, Dr Anand, who is infatuated with her because of her beauty, Anupama is happy despite her unfriendly mother-in-law and sister-in-law. But when she discovers that she has leucoderma, the family rejects her and sends her back to her parents' home. Treated harshly by her stepmother, Anu goes through much heartbreak before she is able to find her feet again. Ultimately, she chooses a career, makes new friends, and helps those around her. At the end of the novel, her husband realizes his error and wants her to come back to him, but she refuses. She also turns down a marriage proposal by Dr Vasanth, a man who knows her well and genuinely cares for her. She treasures her independence, is satisfied with her career as a college professor and takes satisfaction in the fact that she can mould many young minds positively.

Sudha was not sure how good her novel was, but she sent

it off to a new Kannada publisher. Deep down, she believed in herself and her subject matter. She felt this was an important book because she had highlighted some serious ideas in it about prejudices against women. She was delighted when the publisher accepted it right away. Her family and friends told her they liked the book, but she had no way of knowing how other readers were responding to it.

Ten years later, to Sudha's surprise, a young woman whom she did not know invited her to her wedding. The bride informed her that her arranged marriage had almost been broken off because her mother had leucoderma. But then, by chance, the bridegroom had read Sudha's book and changed his mind. The young man also came up to Sudha after the ceremony and told her that her book had helped him to think deeply, below the level of the skin. He had been inspired to do his part to banish unintelligent age-old prejudices.

Encouraged by her early success, Sudha went on to write her next novel, *Dollar Sose*, the dollar daughter-in-law. By now, she had recognized some things about her writing process. She did not write to please anybody, and she only began a book when the entire story was clear in my mind. But once it was clear, she wrote for days without stopping and with great joy.

Dollar Sose, also written in Kannada, was full of dramatic ups and downs; later it would be made into a popular TV serial titled *Dollar Bahu*. Women were the main protagonists of this book, too. In *Dollar Sose*, the mother-in-law Gouramma does not appreciate her hard-working daughter-in-law, Vinuta (another teacher) whom she treats badly. She is, however, enthralled by her 'dollar' daughter-in-law, Jamuna, who is married to her son Chandru and lives in the US. Gouramma loves all the things that their dollars can procure for her, including the admiration and envy of friends and neighbours. Vinuta, who is worn down by her mother-in-law's constant fault-finding, finally decides, with the support of her father-in-law, to live elsewhere. But when Gouramma visits her dollar bahu in the US she realizes she is nothing more to Jamuna than a provider of free childcare. Having learnt a difficult lesson, she returns to India with a new appreciation for Vinuta and tries her best to repair that relationship.

Both novels were not stories with simplistic or romantic happy endings. This was important to Sudha. She was interested in penning tales about difficult lessons and the independence that arises from them, tales of ordinary women making extraordinary decisions. She wanted her heroines, who faced many challenges, to inspire her readers. Interestingly, both heroines were teachers.

Perhaps this was a natural choice because Sudha had come from a family of teachers and thus knew the details of that kind of life very well. Perhaps it was a subconscious choice because somewhere deep down, Sudha was considering alternative careers which would allow her to be a more hands-on mother without giving up her professional life. Later, once her family circumstances allowed it, she would become a lecturer at Maharani Lakshmi Ammanni College, a women's college in Bangalore, where she would set up their computer science department in 1988, win many awards, and become an extremely popular teacher.

She may not have known it at the time, but through writing, Sudha was also negotiating her way into a unique future, figuring out how to build a life that integrated Infosys and her family more easily and yet allowed her to possess independence, creativity and an identity of her own. In that quiet bedroom in Hubli, as the words flowed through her into her notebook, she began to sense something important. The company was an immense and important presence in their lives, but it did not have to be the biggest factor in deciding Sudha's own choices.

A related realization came to Sudha at this time: writing made her happy in a unique way and gave her a great sense of purpose. It helped her figure out questions in her own life and arrive at decisions. She did not care whether she would be successful: she just knew she had to continue writing. However, once she moved to Bangalore, took up her teaching job, and had to handle child-rearing responsibilities as well as other household matters, she had almost no time for writing. For more than fifteen years, her talent would lie dormant. She only managed to write one Kannada novel, *Yashaswi*, during this period. In this novel, the protagonist, Uttara, has given up her career to become a housewife. Years later, when she meets her classmates at a reunion and learns about their many achievements, she regrets her choice deeply. The autobiographical elements are clear in this novel – although the positive-minded Sudha never felt less than her classmates, she too searched for purpose like her protagonist.

Murthy encouraged Sudha to write, and he listened when she told him what the books were about. But he told her frankly that he just did not have the time or energy to read for pleasure. This may have disappointed Sudha, but it also gave her the freedom to write whatever she was interested in without wondering what Murthy might think of it!

Sudha would not write again until 2000, when T.J.S. George, the editor of the *New Indian Express*, would invite her to write a column in his newspaper. Her simple and direct columns, filled with incidents and lessons the ordinary reader could relate to, would become wildly popular, and her first book in English, *Wise and Otherwise*, would be a collection of these columns. Brought out by East West Books, a Chennai publisher, it would become a bestseller and go into multiple reprints. *Wise and Otherwise* would be an early milestone in a remarkable writing career that would span several decades and produce upwards of forty books. Translated into all the Indian languages, plus Tibetan and Italian, her titles would number over 275.

Shut up in her bedroom in Hubli while the afternoon sun filtered through the shutters and made patterns on the floor, writing in a cheap lined notebook while she kept a careful eye on her son's little rash-covered body, Sudha would have laughed if someone had suggested that one day she would sell almost 6 million books, and become one of the most popular authors of children's books in India as well as the country's highest selling woman writer, receiving many literary awards.

Only later, looking back, would Sudha realize the enormous impact of writing on her life. 'Writing was a lifesaver for me at a difficult crossroads in my life,' she once told Rohan. 'Truly it was the blessing of Goddess Saraswati. It gave me confidence and joy. It made me who I am today. It's an expression of my deepest emotions and beliefs, my sensitivity. It's something that is totally mine. My heroines are like my own daughters. Writing has given me a unique identity and a unique joy. When I write, I feel light.'

But it did not matter that she had no inkling of any of this while she was writing her books in Hubli. She was building her own world, sentence by sentence. A world that was going to give herself back to her. Even as she helped her mother, took care of her children and provided Murthy with advice whenever he asked for her input, her heart was in the books she was creating.

16

In 1985, as soon as Rohan was vaccinated, Sudha moved to Bangalore with her children. She had been in Hubli for almost two years. The nuclear family, now finally – and joyfully – reunited, rented a house in Jayanagar. It was a home filled with laughter and activity. Because of Sudha's warmth and hospitality, it soon became the base for the Infosys co-founders and their wives whenever they were in the city. As in an extended family, people pitched in with cooking, cleaning and babysitting. It would not be unusual, for instance, to find Rohini balancing Rohan on her hip as she made him lunch while Sudha was running errands. Kris's wife, Sudha, also spent a significant amount of time with the Murthy family, and she and Akshata became very fond of each other.

Though she had two young children, Sudha continued to help out Infosys in many ways, doing whatever was needed, even though she was not an official part of the company. On occasions, she even drove Murthy to his meetings. And she kept a careful eye on the company finances.

'I'll look after your accounts,' she told Murthy. 'I'm a Kulkarni, after all!'

She was a very smart coder and took up that responsibility, too, when required. Most importantly, she would do things others did not want to do, such as visiting people who owed the company money and collecting payments from them. While Akshata was willing to stay with anyone, Rohan who was very attached to his mother, would throw a tantrum if he knew she was going to be away for a long time. 'I don't want you to go,' he would scream, throwing himself on the floor.

So Sudha would be forced to take him with her. If she had to travel in the evening, she wrapped him from head to toe in a sheet to protect him from mosquitoes because his skin was still very sensitive. It was a challenge, but she never complained. Murthy appreciated Sudha's positivity, recognizing how different her attitude was from his. Once he told her, 'You're a glass-half-full kind of person. I, on the other hand, always see the glass as half empty and have to set off looking for the jug.'

'That's why we make a good team!' Sudha replied.

However, Sudha also knew where to draw boundaries. As the children grew older, she told Murthy, 'Enough is enough. I can't spend all my energy helping you with Infosys. I will be there for you, always, as your emotional support, but now I need to focus on my career again.'

Murthy agreed this was important. But though he gave her his full moral support, Sudha knew she could not count on him for practical assistance. He was travelling too much, and even when he was in town, his workdays were too long. A scary incident had occurred soon after they had moved to Bangalore that was still fresh in her mind. Rohan was about two years old, and he became sick with a severe bout of diarrhoea and grew very weak. Murthy was out of town, and except for a young teenaged driver named Kannan, there was no one at home to help Sudha. Akshata was a little over four, and she was crying with hunger. Sudha asked Kannan to fix some food for Akshata because she could not leave the baby alone.

Kannan did not know how to cook, so Sudha had to give him instructions to make some Maggi noodles. The Murthys did not have a home phone at the time, and Sudha was at her wits' end. She finally had Kannan drive them to the post office so she could use the phone there to ask for help. She called extended family members who lived in Bangalore, but no one was available. Finally, not knowing what else to do, she called Sunanda.

She broke down on the phone and told her sister how dreadfully alone and helpless she felt. 'I can't keep on managing these family crises on my own,' she said. Sunanda calmed her down and told her what medicines to give Rohan. Then she took emergency leave from work, took the bus to Bangalore, nursed Rohan and stayed until he got better. Before leaving, she promised Sudha she would move to Bangalore so that Sudha would not have to handle such situations by herself. True to her word, by 1986, the committed elder sister had changed jobs and moved to be close to Sudha.

Sunanda's presence gave Sudha the confidence to start looking for a job. As a woman who had dedicated her life to her career, choosing to forgo marriage and children for the sake of healing the sick, Sunanda understood Sudha's urge to make a mark on the larger world outside the family. She gave Sudha the much-needed moral support she required at this time. Sudha's parents, too, encouraged her.

In 1988, once Rohan was settled in school and Sudha had started a serious job search, her father decided to take early retirement. He and Mrs Kulkarni could then move to Bangalore so they could be on hand for Sudha. She was immensely touched.

In Hubli, her father was well known and highly respected, and had many friends. He would willingly give up all of that and move to Bangalore, where no one knew him, just for her sake. But when she tried to thank him, he brushed her words aside. 'This is what family is about,' he said. 'You can go to work with a peaceful mind. Your mother and I will keep an eye on the children for you.'

Sudha was deeply grateful and often referred to India's joint family system as a great blessing to women who wanted to have a career.

Sudha did not want to abuse the help her parents were willing to provide. Though she could have taken up an engineering or programming job for a higher salary, she looked for a position where she could balance job responsibilities with parenting, a position with flexible hours and the option of doing some of her work at home. She realized that her best bet would be to go into teaching, even though it paid far less. The amount of money she made did not really matter to her.

For a while now, Sudha had been looking at building a place that the Murthys could call their permanent home. Her reasoning for this was very clear. 'It doesn't make sense to waste money every month on rent,' she told Murthy. Over the years, she had wisely invested in some stocks, including Pfizer and TELCO, which had appreciated significantly. She sold these stocks, along with her Pune apartment.

Sudha had been reluctant to part with the apartment in Pune – it was her favourite home, filled with sweet memories – but she had no choice. They needed the money. Murthy could not help out financially at this time because Infosys was still struggling.

When she pooled together all her money, she had just enough to buy a plot in Bangalore. She scouted around until she found something affordable. Then, sharing the cost of a modest 60-foot by 40-foot plot in Jayanagar with her brother, Shrinivas, she purchased it for Rs 4 lakh. She planned the two-storey home with care so that each floor was like a separate flat, with its own kitchen and bathroom. It was a simple home: Sudha's floor had only two bedrooms, a small drawing room and a sliver of a balcony. But she was delighted to once again have a home of her own.

Only in naming it was Sudha extravagant. She called the house Amoghavarsha, the grandiose name she had been prevented from bestowing on her son!

Once it was completed in 1988, she invited her parents and Sunanda to come and live with her. 'You can occupy the ground-floor apartment,' she told them, 'while Murthy, the children and I live upstairs. It will be wonderful for all of us, and most of all for the children.'

Sunanda, who was already in Bangalore, was the first to move in downstairs. Having her so close was a huge help. Especially when the children fell ill or injured themselves, Sunanda was like a second mother to them. She was known and respected at the local hospital, which was useful. She also provided Sudha with companionship.

Soon, Sudha's parents, too, shifted to Bangalore and moved in with Sunanda. Sudha's father would assist her by going to the market for groceries or dropping the children off at school, while her mother regularly cooked for them. The children moved freely between upstairs and downstairs and – even though their father was largely absent – never felt a lack of either attention or affection.

Murthy's hours at Infosys were very long through the early

years. Believing that he needed to model the behaviour he wanted his employees to emulate, he left for office at 6 a.m. after eating a quick breakfast prepared by Sudha, and rarely came home before 8.30 p.m., when the children were already in bed. What little time and energy he had, he spent sitting by their bedside, telling them a story or just watching as they slept. During times when the workload was particularly heavy, such as when the annual report was being put together, sometimes he would not return home until 4 a.m. He gladly left all household issues in the able hands of Sudha and her family.

Having the extended family around was a great blessing for Sudha. Later, she would credit them publicly for playing a crucial part in Murthy's and her success. Since they took care of many of the children's practical needs, she was able to give Akshata and Rohan other kinds of attention. Her pet activity with her children was to tell them stories, because she knew that stories were a fun and pleasant way to teach them life lessons. While she had completely stopped writing at this time, being too busy with home and teaching, perhaps this was when the idea of creating children's books took shape within her.

Because of her busy schedule, she made use of mealtimes, which was when they would all be together. As she ladled out sambar and rice, she would ask them, 'What kind of story would you like to hear today?' Her repertoire was huge, and she always managed to find something the children enjoyed. She told them stories that ranged from the Ramayana and Mahabharata to Aesop's Fables and the Puranas. She never talked down to her children. Instead, she challenged their intellect by telling them the story of Nachiketa from the Katha Upanishad, a text she loved.

One of Sudha's favourite stories was the tale of Bhamati, the wife of Vachaspati Mishra, who dedicates her life to her husband as he is writing, day and night, a commentary to the Brahma Sutras. He is so immersed in his work, from the very day of his marriage, that he forgets he has a wife. He does not even look up from his writing to see who brings him his food each day and takes care of his needs. Only after seven years, once his book is completed, does he look at Bhamati and ask her who she is! When she tells him, he is overcome by gratitude at her silent support and names his book *Bhamati* after her. Indeed, the entire school of Advaita Vedanta that grows out of his book is known as Bhamati. Perhaps Sudha liked this story so much because she felt a connection with Bhamati, who had sacrificed all the pleasures of married life for the sake of her husband's vision.

Sometimes she would tell them contemporary news stories that she felt were inspiring. She often ended these with a message. One of her favourites was, 'Run your marathon on your own legs.' She would have many creative activities ready for them when they returned from school, such as art projects for Akshata and colouring books for Rohan. As they grew older, she made sure there were plenty of books for them to read. In fact, for their birthdays, Sudha always gave them books as gifts, allowing them to choose whichever ones they liked. TV, on the other hand, was allowed only under supervision.

One day, Rohan got upset with Sudha and told her, 'This isn't fair. Why can't I watch TV? You watch it whenever you feel like it.'

'Very well,' she promised Rohan, 'I, too, will not watch TV.' And for many years, she did not.

Sudha bought a VCR and borrowed cassettes from friends and neighbours so that the family could watch them together. She chose quality movies, or sporting events such as tennis matches, or shows that would increase their vocabulary. One of her favourite things to do with the children on cold afternoons was to sit with Rohan on her lap and Akshata cuddled in a quilt next to her, eating steaming hot Maggi noodles and watching the British sitcom *Mind Your Language*.

They also watched the entire *Mahabharat* serial on cassettes once it became available. When Martina Navratilova played against Zina Garrison to win her ninth title at Wimbledon in 1990, Sudha relaxed her rule and the whole family watched the iconic match on the grandparents' TV downstairs. It was such an exciting event for the children that they were to remember it even as adults. Rohan and Sudha went on to see many Wimbledon matches together, into his adulthood.

An additional challenge for Sudha was the fact that Rohan continued to be a very active and curious child. Unless he was kept busy, he had a penchant for getting himself in to dangerous situations, climbing trees or cars, darting on to the road, or wandering off in the neighbourhood. Even with the extended family on alert, it was difficult to keep him entirely safe. Once he almost grabbed a live wire before someone pulled him away. Another time, he was about to stick his fingers into a power socket. Murthy, who was in the room, screamed at him at the top of his voice to move back.

'With Rohan around,' Sudha would quip to Murthy, 'you can be sure that you'll never get bored.'

Akshata, on the other hand, had settled well into her routine in Bangalore. Originally, she had been sad to leave her small school in Hubli, where she had been a minor celebrity due to her grandfather being a famous doctor and professor. When she was admitted to Baldwin Girls' High School in Bangalore, at the age of six, she was taken aback at being just one among the 120 students in her class. But soon, she made friends and grew comfortable with her new surroundings. She was a tidy girl, meticulous about homework. She also liked singing and dancing – she had learnt many songs and dances already from her aunt, Sunanda – and began to get selected for school plays.

Though Sudha was certain that she wanted to teach, she felt she did not have the experience to be a professor at a university. Also, she knew she would have many other administrative responsibilities at such an institution. Mindful of her commitment to her children, she applied for – and was chosen – to be a lecturer at Maharani Lakshmi Ammanni College, a small women's college. Here, she taught computer programming.

Going back to work after several years away from it was a big change for Sudha. She was now thirty-eight years old and had been away from the working world for a long stretch: over six years. Additionally, she was starting off in a whole new area. Emotionally, too, it was tougher than she had imagined. It was a wrench each morning to say goodbye to the children and head out to her job. She structured her work around their schedule: when Rohan's school timings were from 9 a.m. to 12 p.m., she dropped him at school, taught for three hours and then picked him back on her way home. As he got older, she matched her timings with his school hours between 9 a.m. and 4 p.m. It was as though the children didn't know she was working. Yet sometimes, as it happens, there were slips in this immaculate schedule.

But Sudha soon began to enjoy her new profession. Teaching was in her blood: both her maternal grandfather and her mother had been teachers. Her father, too, had taught in medical college. From the beginning, she thought outside the box and was not satisfied with merely lecturing about her subject to students. She pushed the administration to allow her to set up a computer lab in the college so that she could teach the students how to code. When she was told that such courses were not the focus at a women's college like this one, she insisted on the importance of hands-on experience. 'Being able to write programs is an essential skill for high-paying engineering work,' she declared. 'Don't you want our students to have that advantage?'

The administration capitulated, grumbling. But later they were very thankful because time proved Sudha to be right.

Sudha was an unconventional professor in many other ways. She devised college-level competitions ranging from games like Turncoat to garland making to debate contests. In addition to teaching from textbooks, she told them stories from the Sanskrit classic, *Vetala Panchavimshati*, which contains fascinating examples of superior decision-making and critical thinking skills, and the life stories of famous and inspiring historical women.

She opened her home to them, something none of the other teachers did. Young women – both Hindu and Muslim – would often come over to her house to study in groups or just for the camaraderie. Sudha taught them to be open-minded about other religions, modelling for them the behaviours she wanted them to cultivate. She casually mentioned how, if Rohan needed a babysitter after school, their Muslim neighbour often took care of him. And how, once when the staff of Infosys wanted a puja to be done in a new office space, Murthy said he would only allow it if they also called a Christian priest and a mullah to perform prayer services.

Though many of her students came from traditional households that were strict with their daughters, their parents would not object if they said they were going over to Sudha ma'am's house. It gave these girls the simple freedoms they craved – freedom to cook well-loved dishes, organize mehendi parties, have sleepovers – and overall enjoy a wonderful time that they would remember late into their lives. Sudha also took them on out-of-town trips to broaden their horizons.

Her children, who felt she paid too much attention to her students, did not like this but made their own accommodations. Akshata, the quiet one, spent most of her time with her grandparents, whom she was very close to, while Rohan often hung out with Sudha's students.

Once Sudha announced to her class, 'I feel like going to the Kateel Durga Parameswari temple. It is one of our oldest temples and worth visiting. Who wants to come with me?' Seventy-five enthusiastic students clamoured to accompany her. She organized the trip with meticulous care, making sure to keep the costs low so that everyone could afford it. At the last moment, Rohan threw a huge tantrum and refused to be left behind, so Sudha had to take him along. The journey went without a hitch, and the class returned with beautiful memories, a few simple but treasured souvenirs, and the goddess's blessings.

It was no wonder that Sudha was the most popular teacher on campus and won the best teacher award multiple times. In 1995, she also won the Rotary Best Teacher award. Nearly thirty years on, she continues to get cards on Teacher's Day, and if she comes across former students at a gathering, they make it a point to touch her feet with fond respect.

Throughout their childhood, Infosys loomed as a dominant and irksome presence in the lives of Akshata and Rohan. It seemed to the children that it was the third sibling, the baby who never grew up and required constant attention! Even when they were little, before they understood exactly what the word really meant, Sudha would often tell the children that they had to make sacrifices 'for the sake of Infosys'. She added, 'Please understand that it needs help right now – more help than both of you. It needs all of us to sacrifice for it, or else it might not survive.' Such statements put a lot of pressure on the children. They felt guilty making any demands, especially where their father was concerned. They also understood that Infosys was the reason why they rarely saw their father, why he was at work for such long hours, and why he had to travel for business so often – and they felt a deep though unarticulated resentment.

Understandably, they were jealous, particularly when it was Infosys's 'birthday'. The anniversary of the founding of Infosys was always celebrated as grandly as Murthy could afford it. There would be a cake, and festive food for the employees and vendors, and they would even get gifts such as crockery or, on landmark occasions, watches. The children's own birthdays, however, were quiet affairs, celebrated with homemade foods and with only the family in attendance. The gifts they received were mostly books; when they wanted something expensive, Sudha would tell them they couldn't afford it, but it was more than that. It was because Murthy had seen too many businessmen drawing money from their ailing companies so that they could flaunt their wealth at social events. He was determined to do exactly the opposite. But as with many people of deep convictions, he sometimes went to the other extreme, and as a result, the children had a spartan childhood. It is true that Sudha and Murthy applied the same principles to themselves, never celebrating anniversaries or their own birthdays except in the simplest way, but that did not console the children.

One day the children overheard a conversation between their mother and a board member at Infosys. He was telling Sudha, 'In Murthy's life, Infosys is Number 1.'

Sudha asked, 'Who would you say is Number 2? The children? Myself?'

The man paused. Then he said, 'Infosys is also Number 2. And Number 3 as well.'

The children waited for Sudha to disagree, but to their surprise, she only nodded silently and a bit sadly.

Soon after this, Rohan decided to confront Murthy. 'Who do you love more – me and Akshata, or Infosys?' he asked him bluntly. Akshata, too, waited with interest to hear his answer.

Murthy, taken aback, looked at the two young faces turned up towards him. 'Of course I love you both the most,' he assured them. But with a sinking heart, he saw that neither Rohan nor Akshata was convinced. He was, after all, gone most of the day, dedicating virtually every waking moment to the company. In fact, he was never able to attend any of the children's school activities and only made it to their final graduation ceremonies. Though the rest of the family – especially the grandparents – made up for it by attending these events, the children were very aware that their father was never there. The quiet Akshata, who missed Murthy silently, once said that her grandfather was her 'real dad' while her father was a 'bonus dad', someone who appeared at infrequent moments and tried to make up for his absence with fun activities. But it was not enough.

Murthy had to often travel outside India to meet clients, and when that happened, his absence was felt more deeply by the children. Akshata would help him pack his bags for these foreign trips. She knew it was useless to tell her father not to leave her, as she used to do when she was a toddler. But sometimes, after they finished packing, she would have tears in her eyes.

When Murthy travelled overseas, he and Sudha agreed not to call each other unless it was an emergency because they did not have a home phone. Every call required a trip to the post office, or later, an STD booth, and the time difference made it even more difficult. Calling Murthy in the US was prohibitively costly, at Rs 32 a minute. As a result, the children did not get to hear their father's voice for weeks at a time. This added to their heartache, and caused an emotional rift to open up between them and Murthy. Unlike most of their friends who could relax and share mundane details of their lives with their dads, the children were always hungry for the few moments they could grab with their father.

Sudha, too, missed being able to talk to Murthy, to discuss family issues, or to chat – just for fun – about movies and books, the way they used to do during their courtship days in Pune, a time that seemed to belong in another world. Yes, her parents and sister were there for her, and her children showered her with affection, but it was not the same thing. Especially late at night, when she lay down alone in their bed, she felt an icy desolation.

On those lonely, soul-searching nights, Sudha sometimes asked herself a question: *Would I have been happy with a man who was satisfied with a nine-to-five salaried job, even if that meant he was home with me every evening?* The answer was always a resounding no.

Sudha knew she had made the right choice – in deciding to marry Murthy, and later, in supporting him in every possible way so that he could stretch his wings and follow his dream. Early in his entrepreneurial life, Murthy had warned her that she would have to be 'the sole parent for our children', and she had agreed. Still, all the logic in the world could not assuage her heartache.

Entrepreneurship has a human cost, and it is the entrepreneur's family that pays it. The absence of his father – and the longing for more attention from him – may have caused Rohan to behave more naughtily. Perhaps it made Akshata quieter and more withdrawn until she entered her teenage years, when she underwent a period of rebellion like most young people of her age. As for Sudha, she withdrew into her teaching career and extended family, and later took refuge in her work with the Infosys Foundation and began to write more frequently, drawing satisfaction from her significant achievements in these fields.

And what about the price Murthy had to pay? His journey at Infosys had been not just hard but lonely – surrounded by much younger and inexperienced colleagues for whom he also felt a great burden of responsibility. His recurring dream of floating in space was most likely a subconscious expression of that feeling of intense isolation. But the isolation also made him lonely and withdrawn in his own life and marriage.

Things would have been far worse for the Murthys had it not been for Sudha's close relationship with her family. Sudha's parents and especially Sunanda realized the gap that was created by Murthy's absence. They made it a point to spend a lot of time with the children, showering them with care and affection. Rohan and his grandfather were great buddies. They were both connoisseurs of good food and liked eating out. Akshata, on the other hand, was particularly close to Sunanda, whom she called Tachi. Sunanda continued to teach her more advanced prayers and songs, which, years later, Akshata would pass on to her own daughters. They continued with their art projects; over the years they made some very creative things with leftover medical supplies such as tubes and bottle caps. Additionally, Sunanda oversaw Akshata's dance classes. Many nights, Akshata would run downstairs to sleep with her aunt or her grandmother. And at their weddings many years later, both siblings made sure that they had two equally fine saris – one to present to her mother, and the other to Tachi.

Sudha, too, was of course a grateful beneficiary of the extended family's presence, not just in practical matters but emotionally as well, and she has often advised young entrepreneurs to create a similar support system for themselves. Her parents went with her to all of the children's school programmes, while Sunanda accompanied her to social functions and extended family celebrations and thus saved her from having to answer embarrassing questions from nosy relatives about why she was alone. Her father remained her adviser all his life, and she gives him credit for helping her with her first major Infosys Foundation project with sex workers. And her mother Vimala inspired her by sharing with her – in more detail than ever before – stories of her own past difficulties.

When Sudha had been just a baby, Dr Kulkarni had taken an unpaid leave of absence, deposited the family at Sudha's maternal grandfather's house for three years and gone off to get his MBBS degree. He did this again for a two-year stretch (again unpaid) when Sudha was ten years old, so that he could get an MS in obstetrics and gynaecology, leaving Vimala to manage things on her own.

Vimala did not want to disrupt the children's schooling by moving from Hubli, where schools were better and education in English was available. So she remained alone in the Hubli home with four children. Sudha's mother described how tough things had been for her. Money had been tight, so that even scraping together Rs 50 for the monthly rent of the house had been a challenge, and she had been forced to ask the children to pitch in to do the housework. But somehow, she had managed.

I am her daughter, Sudha told herself after hearing these stories. *I, too, can bear my burdens.*

'Akshata! Rohan!' Murthy called as he hurried up the stairs to the first floor of the house. 'What are you up to?' The children came running, their faces alight. It was a special treat for them to have their father home, even on a Sunday like this, because Murthy often worked all seven days of the week. Sudha, too, emerged from the kitchen where she had been cooking bisi bele bath, smiling widely as she wiped her hands on a turmeric-streaked dishcloth.

'Are your preparations for tomorrow's meeting all done?' she asked her husband.

'Yes. I'm pretty sure the client will be pleased with the solutions we're going to propose. But enough of work talk! It's time for a celebration now.' Murthy turned to the children. 'How about going out for lunch? We can eat the lunch Amma has cooked at dinnertime.'

Rohan jumped up and down in excitement while Akshata moved close to her father in her gentle way and, with shining eyes, clasped his hand.

Sudha said, 'Aren't you tired? You hardly slept last night.'

Rohan and Akshata looked crestfallen. But today Murthy said, 'No! Things will get busier at work soon, especially if we win a big contract. I don't know when I'll get to spend another full afternoon with all of you. I want to remember this family outing. It'll give me something to think about when I'm far from you.'

Sudha could not argue with that. She was quite happy to put away the meal she had prepared. She was not a fancy cook and, in any case, she, too, loved eating out. It reminded her of the carefree time she had spent with Murthy in Pune. An afternoon spent with him, the children by their side, was precious indeed.

'Can we go to Mac Fast?' Rohan said excitedly. Mac Fast Food on Brigade Road, which served vegetarian burgers, pizzas and French fries, was a favourite of the children. Sudha tried briefly to persuade him to go to Shalini, where they could have a healthy thali meal, but as usual Rohan persisted until he got his way. And as usual Akshata was quite happy to go along with her brother's choice. Rohan ran to his room and changed into a looser pair of pants, holding them up with a belt. His parents smiled and shook their heads when they saw that, but they were not surprised. Rohan loved eating out. Often, when he finished what was on his plate, he would order a second dinner, loosening his belt as he demolished his new meal.

When they got to the bottom of the stairs, Rohan cried, 'Stop! We must take Ajja along with us. He also loves Mac.' Before his parents could say anything, he had rushed into the house. They could hear his high voice calling for his grandfather, telling him to hurry. Very soon, Dr Kulkarni joined them, inclining his head silently at Murthy. Even now, years into the marriage, he was protective of Sudha and suspicious of Murthy's priorities. But the children were very fond of their grandfather – and he of them – so he was happy to join their outing.

Dr Kulkarni and Rohan were particularly close, so once they got to the restaurant, they sat at their own separate table, consulted the menu together, and shared each other's choices with gusto. At the end of the hefty meal, Ajja, too, loosened his belt!

On the way home, the family passed by the Sapphire toy store, where Rohan spotted an action figure he had wanted for a long time – He-Man!

'I want it, Appa!' he cried, pointing.

Sudha said, 'No. It's an unnecessary expense. You have a lot of action figures already. You can have one later on, maybe for your birthday.'

Rohan could be stubborn. He grabbed the door of the store and refused to move. Sudha could see he was getting ready to throw a tantrum. She steeled herself for a scene.

But Murthy intervened. 'Let the boy have his action figure! I'm going to buy a doll for Akshata as well. And I'm going to get them a set of Legos because they help children develop puzzle-solving skills and spatial awareness.'

Sudha was not pleased at what she considered unnecessary and wasteful expenses. 'You're too indulgent,' she said. 'You do this all the time. You're teaching them to be wasteful.'

Murthy repeated something he had told her before. 'Without consumer purchases like these, how will our economy grow?'

He had a point, but then, so did she. She drew in a deep breath to argue, but the look in her husband's eyes stopped her. There was such a deep hunger in them. They made Sudha see the real reason why he was buying the toys, why he took them all to lunch as often as he could. And why, when he returned from business trips from America, he would bring armloads of gifts for the children: backpacks, pencil cases, scented pencils – and boxes of Jell-O. (The children both loved Jell-O, and Rohan would eat it up even before it set.)

An occasional indulgence like today's made Murthy feel better – and perhaps less guilty. His children's smiling faces, and the way they flung their arms around him as they thanked him, would be precious memories for him to safeguard as he travelled yet again to the other end of the world to deal with Donn's never-ending demands.

And so, after a long and challenging separation, the family were together now. Rohan and Akshata enjoyed the embrace of the extended family even as they clamoured for more of their father's attention; Murthy devoted most of his time to getting Infosys off the ground; and Sudha found a new satisfaction in a different career.

Soon there would be new waves of upheaval engulfing the family. Which of us are exempt from such challenges? Murthy would have fresh troubles with intransigent employees and spiteful government officers as he pushed to grow Infosys, Sudha's working life would encounter road bumps as the administration grew increasingly jealous of her popularity, and the children, precocious as they were, would develop minds of their own and rebel against what they considered unfair parental stringency. But the early uncertainties, and the great trial of separation the family had had to face, were over. Sudha, thirty-eight, and Murthy, forty-two, were finally together under a single roof, and here they would remain through good and bad times.

Part 3

Service and Joy

17

Soon after MICO became Infosys's main client in India, things began to move at a rapid clip for the company. Murthy's task was to grow Infosys in line with the values he had always envisioned for his company: a meritocratic, transparent and uncorrupt organization. The big challenge he faced in the coming years was to manage the growth with the organization's value building. This would be especially hard because his values of honesty and compassionate capitalism were not in sync with how the majority of businesses were run in India at the time.

By 1985, Murthy realized that Infosys's original home had become too small for the growing company, which had hired several young employees. He leased a larger bungalow in Jayanagar. This building, which would become known as Infosys House, was still a relatively modest space: Murthy was not one to waste his company's resources unnecessarily. The house had six rooms and two big halls, and could accommodate about twenty-five to thirty people. Additionally, in 1985, Murthy started Infosys Digital System (IDS), a separate entity, focused on providing telecom solutions. He appointed Kris as the managing director of IDS. In 1987, they also opened their first international office in Boston.

As the company grew, Murthy often needed to move his executives around, placing them where their talents would be of maximum use at the time. What further complicated the process was that he also considered their personal preferences, whether they wished to work in India or abroad, and emergencies in their families. For instance, when Dinesh's father had a stroke, Murthy dropped everything and travelled to the US at just a couple of days' notice to take over Dinesh's responsibilities so that he could return to India to take care of his father. Often, Murthy placed the needs of his co-workers ahead of his own family's needs.

In April 1987, Murthy sent Kris to Atlanta to become the technical vice president of KSA/Infosys, their joint venture with Kurt Salmon Associates, the best-known consulting company for the apparel industry in the US. This was an important step in their plan to be free of DBC and Donn. As part of this manoeuvre, Nandan returned to India with his wife, Rohini, in November 1986 and took over as the managing director of IDS.

Murthy put Nandan, along with Ashok Arora, in the front room of Infosys House. When Nandan protested, saying Murthy should be sitting in the larger front room, Murthy said he was happy with an inside room.

Sudha invited Nandan and Rohini to stay with them until they found a suitable home. The couple lived with Murthy and Sudha for an entire month. Though their home was a small one, Murthy and Sudha welcomed the Nilekanis warmly and made space for them. Personal touches like this, where the Murthys opened their homes and hearts to their colleagues, were an important part of the early success of Infosys. Murthy could not have made such decisions, which led to a genuine closeness with his colleagues, without Sudha's cooperation and warm generosity. This closeness is what made the founders and directors so loyal to Murthy.

Without this bond, they could not have continued making the sacrifices that Infosys demanded of them.

Murthy and Sudha would remember the time the Nilekanis spent with them with fondness. Nandan and Rohini were wonderful company: pleasant, courteous and fun. Rohini learnt Kannada quickly and had enormous respect for the local culture, which endeared her to both the Murthys, who were staunch Kannadigas. She helped around the house and spent a lot of time playing with Rohan, and the two of them formed a close and affectionate bond.

Each time Murthy went abroad, he would authorize one of his younger colleagues to handle the finances of the company, and when he came back, he would check the books to see what had occurred in his absence. This time, since Nandan was away, Kris had been in charge. Upon his return, Murthy noticed that Rs 70,000 had been inexplicably withdrawn from the company account.

Astonished, he asked Kris, 'How could such a thing happen?'

A reluctant Kris told him that one of the seniors had wanted to buy a plot of land. He took the money from the company coffers as a loan, promising to return it as soon as he could. The normally mild-mannered Murthy was livid at this breach of protocol. Honesty, to him, was the highest value, one he lived his life by. He strongly chastised the borrower for violating the unwritten rule that no one, no matter how high up in the company, would use Infosys money for any personal purpose. This was exactly the problem he had noticed – and detested – in family-owned companies, and he had always been extra careful in making sure he never transgressed this way.

The idea that senior managers could dip into the company's coffers for their personal expenses was the norm in those days. This was exactly the mould he wanted Infosys to break away from. It was what it meant for him to build a truly professional institution.

In fact, once when he was out of the country and Rohan was very sick, a worried Sudha had come to the office and made a brief phone call to ask him for advice. At the end of the phone call, before he hung up, Murthy had instructed Sudha to make sure to deposit Rs 100 into the office funds because it was a personal call. He himself would go over the office phone bill every weekend, marking any personal calls he had made during the day and paying for each one of them. Even his children were not exempt from this. If they ever came to the Infosys campus and ate at the canteen, Murthy would make sure he personally paid for their meal chits.

Now Murthy insisted that the money had to be replaced within forty-eight hours. To his credit, the senior manager was extremely contrite and returned the full amount within that time. Murthy then called a meeting of all the senior colleagues, told them about this lapse, and re-emphasized the rule of never using corporate resources for personal issues. He made such an impression upon them that this problem never recurred. However, the incident made Murthy realize something that in his stringent way he had not considered: even the best and most responsible of employees might have sudden financial emergencies. To deal with such situations, he soon set up an Employee Fund at Infosys.

The year 1989 was a very busy one for Murthy. He was travelling a great deal, especially to the US, with the twin targets of starting an Infosys branch office and bringing the contract with Donn Liles to a satisfactory close. The latter was difficult as Donn had not found a suitable Indian company to replace Infosys, and he was reluctant to let them go.

In June, Murthy returned to Bangalore after a long and arduous trip. When he reached home, his father-in-law was standing at the door of the ground-floor flat where he lived. Murthy greeted him courteously. Dr Kulkarni, however, turned away coldly and refused to speak to him.

An astonished Murthy went upstairs and asked Sudha, 'What's wrong with your father?'

Sudha silently handed him a recent copy of the *Deccan Herald*. There was a huge half-page advertisement created by Donn Liles and his new partner, Mafatlal Software Services, calling Infosys a thief and warning prospective customers that they should not buy any apparel packages from them. Murthy was astonished and furious. It stated that two senior officers of Infosys had claimed that the CAMP package, which belonged to DBC, was owned by Infosys. This half-page advertisement had appeared in all prominent national English dailies and was bound to be seen by most urban Indians and corporations. It could easily destroy the reputation of the fledgling Infosys as well as the personal reputation of the founders and even their relatives. Several relatives had contacted Sudha and her father upon reading this, with questions and harsh comments. Sudha, who was taken aback herself and deeply concerned, had no answers for them.

Now Murthy understood his father-in-law's reaction. He himself was filled with consternation and anger. Sudha did her best to calm him, but he spent a restless night.

Waking early next morning, Murthy hurried to the office to get to the bottom of this mystery. There, Nandan and Dinesh

– both very contrite – informed him that the popular and influential weekly *Computers Today* had wanted to do a big story on Infosys. Because it was difficult to get hold of Murthy, who was travelling, Nandan did not contact him to brief him on this opportunity and to include him in the interview. Dinesh and he spoke to *Computers Today* about the state-of-the-art features of the CAMP package that was built on an IBM mainframe under Infosys leadership for Data Basics. Nandan talked about how this package was likely to become a mission-critical application for several well-known apparel manufacturers in the US. When the article was published, the paragraph referring to CAMP introduced a sentence that could be misinterpreted regarding its ownership.

Nandan and Dinesh apologized profusely to Murthy for the problems that their interview, which they had been very proud of procuring, had caused. Murthy was angry and worried, but he controlled his temper. 'Intelligent men know what to say and when. But wise men know whether to say it at all,' was a favourite adage of his and it was his habit to remain silent until he cooled down. He did not want thoughtless words to damage, in a minute, the close relationships he had built in Infosys with so much effort over the years. Most importantly, he did not believe in holding grudges or berating people who were truly sorry.

He understood right away what was going on with Donn. Under normal circumstances, Donn would have understood the spirit and context of the statement in *Computers Today*. He might have asked for a letter from Murthy to the effect that the ownership of CAMP rested solely with DBC. He might even have demanded a clarification and public apology for any confusion the interview may have caused – and that would have ended the matter. But Donn felt as though he was teetering on the edge of a cliff. He had scouted several other Indian software companies and found none equal to Infosys in terms of competence, quality, productivity, commitment and customer focus. Though Infosys had helped train his new partner, Mafatlal, by holding classes on CAMP and had agreed to a three-year non-compete clause with DBC, Donn's sales were coming down. Upset about these losses, he had lashed out at Infosys.

His attack erased whatever sympathy Murthy had had for him and closed the door on any possible rapprochement with him. Sudha, who had lost all respect for Donn after he made Murthy sleep in his storeroom, urged him to fight back.

'But we mustn't lower ourselves to his level,' she said. 'I know you'll take a professional approach.'

Murthy put his emotions aside and, with a cool head, focused on how to repair the damage caused by Data Basics. After consulting an experienced journalist, Murthy, Nandan and Dinesh published a joint response as an advertisement in *Computers Today*. In it, they addressed and demolished the false allegations made by DBC point by point, each one supported with facts. Next, Murthy met with the president and vice president of the National Association of Software and Service Companies (NASSCOM) in Mumbai and updated them on the unfairness of the accusation, explaining their history with Donn. He also shared with them Infosys's point-by-point refutation of Donn's accusations. Convinced of Infosys's integrity, they invited Murthy to follow up with a presentation to their executive council. Murthy did so. He impressed them so deeply that not only were their doubts about Infosys removed, but they also elected him vice president of NASSCOM two years later, in 1990.

Through this painful and time-consuming episode, Murthy learnt some crucial lessons that would help Infosys in the long run. The founders and directors became very careful of what they said in interviews, often going over the ideas first with Murthy. When they gave talks, they read their speeches from a written text. Finally, every interview was recorded, both by the correspondent and by Infosys.

When Infosys was formed, Murthy had kept just 30 per cent of the equity, an extremely unusual act given both his seniority and the business norms of that period. He had given the three directors of the founding team – Nandan, Raghavan and Kris – large amounts of equity, ranging from 15 per cent to 19 per cent each (approximately equivalent to Rs 24,000–30,000 crore today); the three senior project managers – Ashok, Dinesh and Shibulal – were given 7 per cent each. This was crucial to his philosophy of sharing wealth with his partners and creating a company where they felt the deep satisfaction of ownership and respect (unlike the situation in the family-owned set-ups common in India). But towards the end of the 1980s, Murthy could see that the younger three were handling projects as big – or, in some cases, bigger – than some of the others.

Always concerned with fairness, Murthy suggested a major change. He wanted the three older directors and himself to give 3 per cent each of their equity to the younger ones. But when he called a meeting and explained his thought process, things did not go the way he had hoped. Only one of them, Raghavan, saw the fairness of the request and agreed with Murthy. The other directors were firm and vocal in their refusal to give up any portion of their equity, which they felt they deserved. Murthy persisted for a while, holding conversations with each of them separately, but finally he saw it was not helping. His colleagues had made up their mind and were only growing upset. It was a deeply disappointing result for a principled man.

A crestfallen Murthy came home and told Sudha: 'I'm truly saddened that I can't convince these essentially decent people to uphold the principles of fairness and equity that had led me to make the sacrifices from which they are now benefiting.'

Sudha listened in sympathetic silence. When he had finished, she said, 'That's just life. Even close friends we love and admire view wealth differently from us. You've got to accept this fact.'

After a few agitated days, Murthy solved the problem by giving up 6 per cent more of his own equity. With the contribution of Raghavan who had agreed to give up 3 per cent of his equity, he was then able to increase the equity owned by the junior colleagues to 10 per cent each. He slept well that night, his conscience clear.

At the same time he decided another colleague called Sharad Hegde deserved equity. So instead of convincing the others, he gave away another 1 per cent of his stake to him. Later, when news of his decision travelled, as news tends to do, outraged friends and relatives came to Sudha and demanded, 'How could you let him do something so foolish?'

Sudha smiled and shrugged. She knew they wouldn't understand if she told them that, just as with Murthy, a large amount of money was not high on her list of life priorities. So she only said, 'Murthy makes his own decisions about Infosys. I don't interfere. And about the equity – why, that's just the kind of idealist he is. I knew it when I chose to marry him. Should I now expect apples from a mango tree?'

One final Infosys-related event in 1989 caused both Murthy and Sudha a great deal of heartache.

Murthy had always felt that one of the founding members, Ashok Arora, was the best software designer and architect Infosys had. He mentored him, promoted him and put him in charge of the Infosys banking projects. Murthy grew to be genuinely fond of him. At first it seemed as though all was going well. A loner by nature, Ashok spent most of his time by himself, improving his designs. He rarely spoke to others though he seemed satisfied with his job. He had connected with Sudha, and when he came over to the Murthys' house for dinner, she was always able to draw him out of his shell and make him laugh. She appreciated his intelligence and told him that he reminded her of her brother.

Murthy, too, was impressed. He once told Sudha, 'Ashok has amazing concentration. He'll work silently at his table for days, then go to a computer terminal and type out a 4000-line COBOL program, compiling it error-free and running it successfully the very first time. I've never seen any designer or programmer at Infosys achieve this miracle!'

'You had better hang on to him, then,' Sudha replied jokingly. Neither of them thought this would be a problem. Because they were treated so well, and because their jobs were satisfying and often groundbreaking, employees rarely left Infosys, especially the ones like Ashok, who was a founding member of the team with 10 per cent shareholding.

But after a few months, Murthy received a call from the chairman of Saraswat Co-operative Bank. The bank was extremely upset because, despite sending several reminders about the significant problems they were having to Ashok, they had received no response from him. If things did not improve rapidly, the chairman told him, the bank would be forced to sue Infosys.

An Uncommon Love

Murthy was shocked to learn this, as customer satisfaction was very high on his list. He was additionally confused because, during his weekly meetings with Ashok, the young man had told him that customers were quite happy with Infosys.

Murthy put a stopgap solution in place by having someone else from Infosys take over the responsibility of handling Saraswat Bank. After that, he held a discussion with Ashok, who sullenly dismissed the bank's allegations without offering explanations. Murthy realized that it was futile to talk any further on this issue. He told Ashok to focus instead on the technical aspects of the product, such as architecture, design and project management, which were his primary interests.

In a few months, Murthy asked Nandan to head the banking project, relieving Ashok of all responsibilities except design and programming for the banking group. But soon Nandan told Murthy that Ashok was being a disruptive force in the banking group, wasting the time of other designers with endless arguments. He needed to be pulled out of the banking project if Infosys was to make the expected progress. Though Murthy would have liked Nandan to handle the issue since it was in his department, he agreed to find a solution. But he was disturbed as he could not think of any easy answers.

After a week, Murthy invited Ashok to have lunch with him at Shalini, a nearby restaurant that was nicknamed the 'second home for Infosys' because almost everyone from Infosys went there for lunch, while unmarried employees went there for dinner as well. Murthy began the conversation on a positive note, recalling some of the extraordinary designs Ashok had produced for CAMP. Murthy told him he would love to see such innovative work from him in another export-oriented package, this time owned by Infosys. He brainstormed with him for a while, then asked him to keep thinking about possibilities on his own.

Ashok did not disagree outright, but over the next month, he kept finding excuses to avoid talking to Murthy about the new project. Sudha in her friendly way tried to improve the situation by inviting Ashok home for a private dinner. He accepted and even had a pleasant time chatting and laughing with her. But he remained cold towards Murthy and refused to discuss work.

The next development shocked Murthy. Ashok met secretly with an official from DSP Financials, who contacted the auditor of Infosys, stating that Ashok wanted to leave Infosys and sell his shares. Murthy tried hard to dissuade Ashok from this ill-advised step, as did his other colleagues. They all pointed out that Infosys was doing very well, and that Ashok had 10 per cent equity in the company. Where else could he get a deal like that?

Ashok did not agree and threatened to go to court, so Bhatkal computed the amount due to Ashok based on the book value of the shares. He said he would be willing to accept an offer from any value-based investor who was ready to buy Ashok's shares at a price acceptable to Ashok.

But Ashok could not find an investor to buy his shares even at book value, as not many people knew enough about Infosys at that time to guess its bright future. Impatient to move on, he sold the shares back to Infosys at the price based on the book value, which was Rs 24 lakh for Ashok's 10 per cent ownership. At today's prices, what he got rid of for Rs 24 lakh in 1990 would translate to over Rs 16,000 crore! In time, Ashok would probably have realized his terrible mistake, but it would have been too late.

Ethically, when Ashok left, Murthy should have got back the 3 per cent equity he had given to Ashok. However, as a person who had consistently not focused on money, not only did he not ask for it, but he split the share with the other five of the founding team.

For several nights after the settlement, Murthy was so depressed that he could not eat or sleep properly. He wondered if he should have done something differently to have retained this talented young man. Sudha would wake up at night to the sound of him pacing the bedroom. After a while, even her parents grew worried. Sudha also felt bad personally because she, too, had grown attached to Ashok. But as often, for Murthy's sake, she hid her own sorrow. Instead, she pointed out that he had done everything he could to help Ashok.

'Things happen in life differently from what we plan,' she said. 'Life is the rangoli of God: only He is in control of the pattern.'

Still, Murthy took Ashok's leaving as a sign of the failure of his leadership. It left an indelible scar on his mind, and for many years following this event, when he spoke of this time, he would call it annus horribilis, the horrible year.

Early in 1990, Murthy received offers from two large companies that wanted to buy Infosys for the equivalent of $1 million. Murthy's heart was not in selling, but being a democratic person, he did not want to make this decision on his own. He gathered all his co-founders for a meeting and included those who were in the US via telephone. Several of them felt that a million dollars was a generous amount and that they should take it. Murthy listened politely and thoughtfully to them all. At the end, he gave an impassioned speech as to why they should not sell Infosys. He expressed his heartfelt belief that entrepreneurship was the best instrument for the betterment of India, and that through Infosys they were conducting a unique national experiment.

He added, 'For nine years we've lived a life of austerity and become masters of our habits rather than slaves of our greed. We've brought some of the finest technology ideas to the US apparel world. We've recruited some of the brightest talent in India and given them hope and opportunity. We owe it to the industry, our society, our families, the youngsters in the company, and finally, to our own dreams and aspirations, to run this marathon in its entirety. Therefore, I'm against selling the company. If you wish, I will buy out your shares.'

Murthy's positivism and deep belief swayed his colleagues. They decided, unanimously, not to sell the company. They celebrated their decision with a convivial thali lunch at Shalini. None of them realized exactly what an important step they had taken. None of them realized exactly how financially beneficial this decision would turn out to be. By 2023, the market cap of Infosys had grown to approximately $75 billion!

This was also the year Murthy was chosen to become the vice president of NASSCOM. He helped the young software organization a great deal by holding discussions with the Indian government to frame policies conducive to the growth of the industry. He held a training programme on the in-house IBM AS/400 for smaller companies, and this was enthusiastically attended by analysts and programmers from various member companies. During the 1990 annual conference of NASSCOM, N. Vittal, the secretary of the government's DoE, offered the Indian software industry an attractive bait. He said he would recommend income tax exemption for their export revenue if the industry – which was hardly $100 million at the time – promised to reach $400 million in five years.

There was complete silence in the hall after his announcement. People looked at each other, too nervous to say anything. Then

Murthy went to the podium and declared, 'We will do everything that is necessary to reach the target.'

Vittal was satisfied with this promise, the Indian software industry got its tax exemption, and – thanks to Murthy's confidence – NASSCOM 1990 was a huge success.

It was an eventful year for Infosys in other ways as well. Reebok (France) wanted to install an automated software system to handle all their day-to-day business activities, and Infosys submitted a proposal for this. They would develop all the functionalities required to fulfil orders and invoice customers for what was technically called 'order through remittance'. This proposal also included warehouse management and production interface with shoe factories in the Far East. It was called the Distribution Management Application Package – DMAP. Having learnt a hard lesson with Donn, Murthy insisted that the intellectual property would remain with Infosys. But they would install the first copy at Reebok (France) at a discounted price. Dinesh and Murthy made a presentation to the company in Paris. They did such a good job that they were awarded the project on the same day, without further financial negotiations, which was very unusual for Reebok.

The project started promptly on 1 July 1989 in Paris. Murthy joined the team there as he was negotiating the details of the contract with Reebok (France) and was also trying to sell the licence for the package to Reebok (UK). In whatever little spare time he had, he rolled up his sleeves and worked with the team as a designer, staying with them in their tiny apartment (with only one bathroom!). He shared in all the chores, including cooking and cleaning. He never thought of himself as the 'head honcho'. He would even wake up at 4 a.m. to take his bath first so that his younger colleagues could sleep a little longer.

The software was successfully installed at Reebok (France) in May 1991. Now Murthy focused on selling a copy to Reebok (UK). But Reebok (UK) wanted to evaluate Infosys's employees, systems, processes and technology before allowing them to bid for this project. Murthy, who felt he had nothing to hide, invited them to Bangalore to see for themselves. So Nigel Fenwick, the director of Reebok (UK), set off for India with a team of four. Since they were not familiar with the country, Murthy travelled to Mumbai to receive them at the airport.

The UK team's flight arrived at 12.30 a.m. Other passengers disembarked and left the airport, but there was no sign of Nigel and his team. There were no cell phones in India at the time, so Murthy had no way of contacting them to find out what had happened. He waited anxiously outside the airport for several hours. Finally, around 3.30 a.m., the team emerged from the airport, looking harried and exhausted. Murthy asked Nigel the reason for the delay. Nigel drew him aside and said that one of his team members who had never visited any emerging country was appalled at the jostling crowds and the dirty condition of Mumbai airport. He refused to pass through immigration and wanted to take a return flight to London! It took three hours and all of Nigel's persuasive powers to get him to change his mind.

Murthy realized that the Infosys team would have to be extra vigilant in taking care of these foreign visitors. So, in addition to demonstrating their technical prowess, the Infosys team made special efforts to keep the Reebok folks healthy and comfortable, arranging for food and lodging at the best and cleanest venues.

All went well for the first couple of days. On 21 May, Murthy had just returned home from hosting a successful dinner for the Reebok team at the Country Club in Bangalore when the phone rang. He was surprised because it was late at night, almost 11 p.m. Who would call him at this hour?

When he picked up the phone, he was even more startled because it was Sudha, who was in the US, paying a rare visit to her brother Shri and sister Jaishree. At present, she was calling from Jaishree's home in Boston. When he heard her voice, Murthy grew concerned because he knew it was not her habit to make expensive long-distance calls unless it was a serious matter.

And indeed, something was very wrong.

'Quick,' Sudha said to him, her voice agitated. 'Switch on the TV.'

Murthy did so and was shocked to learn that a few hours before, on the outskirts of Chennai, in Sriperumbudur, a suicide bomber had approached the former prime minister Rajiv Gandhi, who had been campaigning for the upcoming elections, detonating a bomb and killing him, herself and fourteen others. Murthy wept, overcome with emotion at the untimely and violent death of this forward-thinking leader who, more than any other prime minister before him, had tried to liberalize the country's economy. Rajiv Gandhi had made import quotas less stringent and reduced taxes and tariffs on technology-based industries, especially computers, and this had helped companies like Infosys greatly. With him gone, and in such a violent manner, it was unclear as to what would happen in India now. Murthy still remembered with horror the riots that had swept many parts of the country when Rajiv's mother, Indira Gandhi, had been assassinated, and he was very concerned about the safety of his visitors.

Murthy had to put his grief and worries aside and make plans to handle the Reebok team. He knew that any official activity the next day would probably be disrupted by hooligans, and that it might not be safe to travel long distances in the city. Conferring with Nandan, he acted quickly. He called Nigel, though it was late at night, informing him of what had happened and warning him to make sure his team members stayed in their rooms. He then told them they would be transported early in the morning – much earlier than planned, before any demonstrations began in the city – to Infosys House instead of to the larger office in Koramangala where the presentations were originally scheduled. The Reebok team, too, had been shocked by the assassination and nervous about what might happen to them. They agreed right away to the change of plans.

The next day, Murthy and his colleagues arranged for their visitors to be driven over quietly to the much smaller Infosys House. It was a residential home converted into an office, and Murthy's hope was that it would therefore escape scrutiny. They closed the main doors, made the presentations, and brought in lunch and snacks. They transported the visitors safely back to their hotel only after making sure everything was peaceful in the city. The Reebok team went back to their home country satisfied by the professional quality of the presentation and appreciative of the extra care taken to ensure their safety. Soon after this, Infosys won the bid for the UK project.

Murthy called Sudha and said, 'Even while you're half a world away, you're still Infosys's guardian angel.'

Despite Infosys's triumph, Murthy remained worried about the larger picture. India was now in the middle of elections, and he was afraid the country would lapse into anarchy.

Luckily for India, Narasimha Rao, the new prime minister, would continue Rajiv Gandhi's work and accelerate it in a manner that would transform the future of technological growth for India and for Infosys. Once Narasimha Rao realized that the country was on the brink of foreign exchange collapse, he gave carte blanche to Manmohan Singh, the finance minister; P. Chidambaram, the commerce minister; and Montek Singh Ahluwalia, the commerce secretary. These three set in motion a regime of liberalization, and unbelievably, in less than a week, India was transformed from a command-and-control economy to an almost free economy! Murthy was incredulous – and incredibly excited – about the new possibilities liberalization opened up for the country and for Infosys. He had personally experienced and suffered from the highly controlled economy that had stifled India's growth until then.

He told Sudha, 'I can't tell you how happy I am to finally see India waking up, showing confidence and swinging into action in this manner.'

Sudha, who remembered the fruitless, frustrating occasions she and Murthy had wasted going back and forth from the RBI, with baby Akshata in her arms, said, 'It's about time!'

In this new era, the import of computers would not need to be licensed; hard currency was available to enable a company to send its staff overseas and open offices there; and, finally, the government realized the futility of mandating the initial public offering (IPO) prices and allowed Indian companies to set the IPO price in consultation with their investment bankers.

In the post-reform era of the 1990s, Murthy was quick to realize that, for Infosys to stand out, the company would have to embrace globalization. He called a meeting of the Infosys board and told them, 'We need to set into motion a global delivery model to source talent from where it's best available, produce where it's most efficient, find capital where it's cheapest and easiest, and sell where the markets are. This means that the work involving heavy customer interaction will be delivered at or near customer premises. However, activities such as detailed technical design, programming, testing and documentation, which require low customer interaction, will be delivered from our scalable, talent-rich, cost-competitive development centres in India.'

Everyone agreed this was the way to go.

There remained, however, one other major issue: India was ahead of the US by nine and a half hours to twelve and a half hours. Murthy insisted they could come up with a solution for this as well. He brought the board together for a Saturday meeting. 'We'll keep at it all day if we need to,' he declared.

In the end, they did not need all day. In six hours, the Infosys 'brains trust', as Murthy affectionately called his board, came up with an elegant solution, which they named the 24-hour workday concept. It was brilliant in its simplicity. The Infosys staff at the customer site abroad would document the problems unsolved for the day by 5 p.m. their time and fax them to India. The Indian staff would work on them all day. By 6 p.m. India time, the Infosys staff in India would have solved most of these problems. They would send the results to their staff abroad. When the Infosys staff in the US returned to their office around 8 a.m. (India time 8.30 p.m.), they could immediately start using the solutions developed in India. By leveraging the time zone differences, Infosys combined the customer's prime time with the prime time of the India staff to create a seamlessly productive twenty-four-hour workday. This became hugely popular with customers abroad and helped propel Infosys's rapid growth. Later, this strategy would be adopted by many other tech companies, and people would forget that Infosys is where it began.

In 1992, after the government decided to allow 100 per cent ownership in technology areas to foreign corporations to attract foreign investment, companies such as IBM, Digital Equipment Corporation, Coca Cola and Citibank rushed back to India (which they had left in 1977) to set up operations in Bangalore. Several of Murthy's friends warned him it would be very difficult for smaller companies like Infosys to attract and retain talent in such a competitive environment.

NASSCOM wanted to deal with this problem by lobbying with the government to rescind the order allowing 100 per cent equity for multinationals. But Murthy, now president of NASSCOM, did not agree with this approach. He felt it was not the honourable way. 'India would suffer hugely if the foreign companies withdrew again,' he said. 'Instead, our strategy should be to learn what these world-class technology companies do to attract and retain talent, and to do the same.'

Upon investigation, Murthy realized that multinationals did four things to attract talent. They created a clear career growth path for their professionals and communicated it to their employees from day one. They also created an attractive physical infrastructure, with canteens, gymnasia, company stores, etc., and provided a world-class working environment for their employees. Third, they provided their employees with up-to-date technology. Fourth, they paid their employees handsomely.

While the first requirement could be easily satisfied by Infosys, the second and the third required capital outlay. Murthy knew he would have to wait on that. The fourth was perhaps the most difficult, since Infosys did not have the same kind of funds as the foreign companies. In addition, Infosys operated as a profit centre for software development, responsible for both its revenues and costs, whereas IBM operated in India as a cost centre and was only responsible for its costs.

Once again, Murthy and his think tank went outside the box to solve the problem. They decided to use employee stock option plans (ESOPs) as a method to attract and retain the best talent. In 1994, Mohan Pai, Infosys's CFO, would implement India's first large-scale ESOP scheme. This method, unseen in India at the time, would end up making Infosys a very popular employer. It was a huge step in the history of Indian business. Many start-ups would follow in Murthy's footsteps in this. But, as is true of many innovations, at first this system created a challenge for Infosys. When the plan was getting started, a frustrated Raghavan came to Murthy and told him that employees did not understand what ESOP was, and what the value of stock meant. Therefore, it was hard to convince them to go for it.

Murthy and Mohan called a meeting and explained the value of ESOPs to Infosys employees, patiently answering questions and giving examples. Even after that, there were many non-believers. One young man came to Murthy's office and asked him to take the stock back and give him a few hundred rupees instead as part of his salary because he needed it at home. Murthy had to use all his persuasive powers to convince him to keep his stock and believe in the long-term future of the company. This person later on became worth Rs 300+ crore.

How Mohan joined Infosys is an interesting story. He was a chartered accountant who was the CFO of a company in Bangalore and would come to the Infosys annual general meeting to ask tough questions regarding the company's growth plan and profitability projections. Murthy realized Mohan had a razor-sharp mind, and that he would be the perfect person to get Infosys to the next level. He asked Mohan if he'd like to join the company as its head of finance.

Mohan was enthusiastic. But, being a straightforward person, he told Murthy, 'There's just one problem. My father is in the hospital with a serious illness. As long as he is hospitalized, my first priority is to spend some time with him every day. Will this work for you?'

Murthy promised him, 'You can be one of our consultants for as long as your father is in the hospital. Spend as much time with him as you need.'

Mohan was overcome with gratitude. He joined the company right away and soon mastered the inner workings of Infosys. He worked very hard but made some time every day to spend with his hospitalized father. Murthy developed a soft spot for this young man as he observed how sincerely he fulfilled his responsibilities, both professional and personal.

Now with this new project, Mohan had his work cut out for him. No company in India had ever created an ESOP scheme, so the task at hand was no easy matter. For one, the income tax department did not know how to process or tax ESOPs. Under Murthy's guidance, Mohan fought a case in the Supreme Court to make ESOPs legal in India. Once again, Murthy and his team had paved the way for other start-ups. Infosys gave 19 to 20 per cent of its overall equity as ESOPs to employees, which is between $18–20 billion today. Murthy felt deeply satisfied with the proceedings. His long-held values of democratizing wealth was transforming the lives of a multitude of his fellow citizens.

Infosys also began to hire a good number of women in

important positions. They would go on to make significant contributions to the company. One of them coined the creative term 'Infoscion' to refer to all Infosys employees. This built a deep sense of togetherness and belonging among the employees, even if they were on different rungs of the corporate ladder.

'I think we're now ready to do one more thing,' Murthy said to his board. 'Let's put a full-page recruitment advertisement in the *Times of India* all over the country and see how people respond to it. The ad can highlight some of Infosys's policies and the opportunities we provide to bright young talent. It should also mention our dedication to values. We'll invite people to participate in our dream to make India the software factory of the world and grow prosperous at the same time.' The board was taken aback as none of the major companies had ever used such a strategy for hiring, but finally they agreed.

This advertisement was startlingly popular, indicating that Infosys was far more famous than Murthy had surmised. It also showed Murthy that young people respected and identified with his philosophy of compassionate capitalism. Thousands applied for the open-house tests in Bangalore, Mumbai and other major cities. The rush to register for the interview was so huge at the Leela Kempinski Hotel in Mumbai that a glass door shattered! Murthy happily agreed to the hotel's demand that Infosys pay for the loss.

That year, Mohan's father's condition worsened, and he went into a coma. An emotional Mohan shared this sad news with Murthy. Then he added, 'I know I'm going to lose my father very soon. Can I please ask you to treat me like your son? You are the only person I know whom I respect as much as I respected him.'

Murthy was touched, and agreed. And indeed, their relationship did become like that of a father and son. Mohan repaid Murthy's affection with complete loyalty. For the next several years, he would work day and night until, in 1999, Infosys was listed on NASDAQ.

Sudha would have been within her rights to protest against Murthy's fatherly affection and care for a man he had not known until a few months ago, while she had to run around taking care of all the things their own children needed. But she did not.

Instead, she understood that ultimately actions such as these set Infosys apart, making the employees realize that, unlike in most companies, the people 'on top' here were truly concerned with their welfare. Murthy's example would inspire others and create a positive company culture. Finally, she realized that mentoring his younger colleagues gave Murthy a great deal of joy. If, inwardly, she wished for him to spend more of his time with Akshata and Rohan, she kept that wish to herself. Instead, she reminded herself of a formula she lived by, one she often repeated to the children. *Happiness equals Reality minus Expectations.*

A few years earlier, before the ESOP scheme, there had been one more milestone for Infosys to clear. Clients abroad had indicated to him that if Infosys truly wanted to be a major player and get larger projects, it needed to go public and become a listed company in India. So, in January 1992, Murthy invited the Infosys board, the CFO and the auditor to plan for this. He made it a point to include everyone; the people stationed abroad called in for the discussion, despite the prohibitive telephoning costs.

Murthy pointed out the benefits of listing Infosys. It would create liquidity and wealth for the founders and some of the employees; it would strengthen their use of stock options to attract and retain high-quality talent; and the enhanced brand equity would result in their ability to obtain larger projects from clients. After his presentation, the group unanimously agreed to list on the Bombay Stock Exchange, and G.R. Nayak, Infosys CFO at that time, was charged with readying all the required documents. Within a week, Murthy engaged ENAM, a financial advisory company, to assess the strengths and weaknesses of Infosys, and informed the board that they needed to get to a minimum equity of Rs 3 crore post the listing.

At that time, Infosys's equity was just Rs 1 crore. Arriving at this figure itself was a big deal for the founders, who had started out with just Rs 10,000. To achieve this, they had made huge sacrifices and followed the stringent rules set down by Murthy: spending less than what they earned; declaring dividends using a part of the profits every year; and putting back the after-tax amounts from those dividends as the founders' equity. Based on discussions with ENAM, the founders decided to offer 800,000 shares to relatives and friends at Rs 80 per share. Additionally, Murthy suggested that they offer 40 per cent of the company or 1.2 million shares to the public at Rs 95 per share. They needed to complete the private offer to relatives and friends by October 1992 and hold the IPO in December 1992. Murthy pledged to sell 65 per cent of the 800,000 shares earmarked for family, while Nandan took charge of the remaining 35 per cent.

The experience of selling 520,000 shares was a lesson in human psychology for Murthy. He saw that the better-educated and more sophisticated friends had lots of questions and lots of scepticism, while close relatives and not-so-well-to-do friends simply believed in him and gave him most of their savings. This touched his heart. He came home and told Sudha, 'I completed my quota of 65 per cent thanks to the affection, confidence and trust of these relatives and friends. Now I won't be able to sleep well until they get good returns on their investment.'

Due to the turmoil caused by the demolition of the Babri Masjid in December 1992, Infosys decided to postpone its IPO to February 1993. Working with the public relations firm Ogilvy and Mather, the founders placed a full-page advertisement in important newspapers and trade journals, titled '95 Reasons Why You Should Buy into Infosys'. Nandan, G.R. Nayak and Murthy, along with a couple of others from the office, prepared an IPO presentation. But at that time, there were very few technology IPOs and, sadly, no understanding at all of the extraordinary market opportunities for Indian tech companies, particularly in the software arena. Therefore, investors were sceptical and felt that the IPO price for Infosys (Rs 95 per share) was too high. Since they had pulled the trigger, there was nothing Murthy could do now. He was extremely nervous on the first day of the IPO when he was informed that the subscription was a very low 12 per cent. He knew this could be a disaster for the fledgling company.

'Please pray to Raghavendra Swamy,' he requested Sudha. She promised to do so. The children, too, hearing the worry in his voice, offered to pray for Infosys.

Murthy flew to Mumbai that evening, but he was too anxious to go to his hotel room and rest. Instead, he went to the street where ENAM's co-founder, Vallabh Bhansali, lived. He paced up and down outside his house, longing to talk to him about the current situation but reluctant to disturb him so late at night. The long years of sacrifices of his colleagues and his family, not to mention all the effort he had put into the company, squeezing out every drop of energy and calling on every ounce of willpower, seemed to be evaporating in front of his eyes. A sudden gust of wind made him shiver. Mumbai was colder than Bangalore that day, and in his distracted hurry he had forgotten to bring any warm clothes. Or perhaps it was a psychological chill he felt as he stood there, forlorn and alone.

Murthy had walked a solitary path ever since the birth of Infosys; on his entrepreneurial path, only fear and doubt were his recurring companions. His co-founders had always respected and admired him, and though that was wonderful in its way, at challenging times like this, it became a problem. Murthy chose never to share his sorrows or anxieties with his co-founders because he felt they were too young and inexperienced to bear that burden. So, at stressful moments – whether it was obtaining a licence to import a computer, or getting a loan, or finding an initial data centre client, or even getting MICO to lease their premises to Infosys – he had taken the entire burden on his own shoulders. Today, more than ever before, he felt the crushing weight of the loneliness of leadership.

The only person who had given Murthy solace at times of worry was Sudha, his anchor. Through the years, she had uncomplainingly suffered along with him. But on this night, he felt he did not have the right to weigh her down further. He knew that if he contacted her, she would not sleep the rest of the night. And she was already juggling so much: her job and difficult employers, the children with their many demands, her ageing parents. She would also soothe the wives of the Infosys board members when they were anxious. Her students were a big responsibility because she had become like a mother to them, and they increasingly turned to her when they had problems, both in their academic and personal lives.

So, instead, Murthy went to his hotel room and focused on the one friend at whose feet he could lay down all his burdens: Raghavendra Swamy. It took a while, but slowly his breathing calmed, and he fell into a half-sleep. By the time the sun rose, he felt better. He sensed he had been granted the strength to face whatever lay ahead of him.

Murthy met Vallabh in his office where they discussed that, based on the first day subscription, it was clear that many investors felt that the IPO was overpriced. Vallabh was kind and reassuring. After talking the matter over with his partner, Nimesh, he told Murthy not to worry. He would manage to get it underwritten since some of his close friends were confident about Infosys. Over the next few days, Vallabh and Nimesh made good on their promise, picking up the unsubscribed portions. The company was saved.

Murthy would never forget Nimesh and Vallabh's support in this dark hour, when so many others (including some at ENAM) were openly sceptical of Infosys's potential. He silently vowed he would include ENAM in every one of Infosys's listings, for Vallabh had been kind and respectful to him when he had nothing – and he lived up to that promise till he retired.

After the company's rocky IPO in February 1993, there was a three-month wait for formalities to be completed before Infosys was listed on the stock exchange on 6 June 1993. This would be a crucial moment for the company, indicating public opinion of its value. It was a time of agonizing impatience for the Infosys board as they tried to guess the price at which the scrip would open and would sustain. Many evenings were spent at Murthy's home or Nandan's, discussing the market capitalization and what the future might hold for the company. Rohini participated enthusiastically in these talks. But Sudha, though she joined them, was less involved. Money had never been a prime mover for her, and by now she was more concerned with home, the children and her own career, where she had many new responsibilities as the head of the department of computer science at her current workplace, Christ College. The only part of Infosys that truly mattered to her was that Murthy should be happy and that all his hard work in getting the company off the ground should not go to waste.

In those days, there was no opening bell by the CEO. Therefore, the senior management of Infosys did not go to Mumbai for the listing. Instead, on 6 June, Sudha and Murthy got up early in the morning, woke up Akshata and Rohan, had their baths, and prayed to Raghavendra Swamy that the day may bring good news. The children did not really understand the meaning of stocks and listing, but they knew that something important involving Infosys was about to happen on that day, and they complied willingly.

At the office, the founders waited impatiently in Murthy's room for the opening.

'At what price do you think the stock will open?' Kris asked, his voice nervous.

'Maybe at Rs 100,' Nandan ventured. Everyone looked towards Murthy for confirmation. But he only shrugged. 'It's out of our hands now. Be patient. We'll know everything in a little while. Let us go to our desks and focus on our current responsibilities.'

Just then, the phone rang. It was Vallabh, calling from Mumbai. In an excited voice he announced that the stock had opened at Rs 145. There was a moment of silence as the founders tried to digest this unexpected and positive development. Then the entire board burst into a cheer. Murthy immediately called Sudha, who had been waiting by the phone. His voice was choked with emotion as he gave his life partner, who had been with him from the first step, the good news. Then he celebrated by buying snacks for everyone who was in the office, from the board members to the janitor.

The stock ended the day at Rs 155, far better than Murthy had hoped, making a premium on the IPO price. By 1996, Infosys's revenues had begun to double. Its market value, which started at Rs 191 crore on 31 March 1994, would jump to Rs 731 crore in 1997, and to Rs 9,672 crore in 1999. In 1999, Infosys would become the first Indian company to be listed on NASDAQ, and in 2006, on Infosys's twentieth anniversary, Murthy, along with Nandan, would be asked to ring NASDAQ's opening bell from Mysore – a great honour.

―

The IPO, though, in February 1993 had not been as successful as Murthy wanted, raising less money than he would have wished. However, Infosys had managed to raise Rs 13 crore, and now Infosys could move ahead. True to his driven nature, without taking any time off, he immediately turned to the next task on his agenda: building the first and best software campus in India. 'I want to create the kind of environment where our Infoscions would be excited to come and work,' he told Sudha.

This was not just a wishful vision. With the rapid expansion of Infosys, it had become a necessity. In their current location at the Koramangala office, two people had to share a table and three shared a PC. There was no cafeteria and people were forced to have lunch at the nearby eateries that often served unhealthy, oily food, causing people to fall sick quite regularly. Since there were no parking spaces, employees spent valuable time searching for places to park on the street. This created traffic jams and general dissatisfaction in the neighbourhood. Murthy was determined to take care of these needs and much more.

Murthy spent many evenings sharing his vision for a dream campus with Sudha. 'It will not only have ample workspace,' he told her, 'but also gardens, libraries, conference rooms, car and scooter parking, food courts and gymnasia.'

'That sounds wonderful and innovative,' Sudha said. But, ever the pragmatist, she had some tough questions for her husband, the dreamer. 'How many square feet are you allocating per person?'

'Approximately 200 square feet.'

'And how many employees are you expecting to have in Phase 1?'

'One thousand.'

Sudha raised her eyebrows. 'That means you would need 200,000 square feet right away. You do realize Bangalore doesn't have such large buildings – not a single one? And even the best office buildings don't have the parking or the recreational spaces you've envisioned.'

'It's a problem,' Murthy agreed quite cheerfully. 'But not an insurmountable one. Haven't we overcome greater obstacles already?'

It seemed that his optimism was not misplaced, for in a few days he came back to Sudha with good news. 'I found out that the Karnataka government is providing some Bangalore-based companies land outside the city boundaries. I'm going to ask them to do the same for Infosys.'

As was his habit when he was enthusiastic about an idea, Murthy did not delay. Infosys filed an application with the single window agency of the KSIIDC. Murthy had great faith in this organization. It had shown exceptional speed and efficiency in sanctioning Infosys's loan to import its first computer, thanks to efficient and helpful officers such as K.S.N. Murthy, M.R.S.N. Rao, Rudra Dev and G.L. Jere. He had high hopes that this time, too, he would have a similarly positive experience.

In September 1993, just a few months later, Murthy received a call from the office of the chairman of KSIIDC. Impressed that the organization had got back to him so soon, he greeted the chairman with excitement and anticipation. To his astonishment, instead of discussing Infosys's application, the chairman said, 'I'm sending one of my relatives to Infosys for a software job – and I expect you to employ him.'

Murthy could not believe his ears. First, he was flabbergasted; then he was furious at the man's sense of entitlement. But he kept his temper and responded politely. 'Infosys has a standard procedure for all applicants – without exception. Every one of them must pass a written examination in analytical thinking and problem-solving before they can even be considered for an interview.'

The chairman interrupted him rudely. 'Don't give me that red-tape nonsense. I know you folks happily bend rules whenever it's necessary. Well, you'd better do it now!'

Murthy used all his self-control to speak professionally. He repeated that passing the written test was a must at Infosys, and even he could not – and did not wish to – break such an important rule. 'My own nephew,' he said, 'fell short by one mark on the written test and was not selected for an interview.'

The furious chairman slammed down the phone.

It was a most unpleasant experience. However, Murthy did not dwell on it. After a few days, he got involved with some other issues and forgot about the call.

A week later, Nayak asked Murthy if he would like to

accompany him to the interview that had been set up for them that afternoon at the offices of KSIIDC. Murthy agreed and took Nandan along, too. At the venue, they were the first company to be called in. Nandan, Nayak and Murthy sat on one side of a long table. On the other side there were several state government officers, with the chairman in the centre. The chairman was rude from the first sentence he uttered. He asked Murthy's group whether they wanted the land for speculation, and what commission they had paid to the architects to inflate requirements. Murthy was annoyed but remained courteous and business-like. When he started explaining the detailed cost breakdown of the project, the chairman interrupted him and said, in a derisive tone, 'I've seen many crooks like you!'

Murthy could not let such an insult pass. 'You may reject Infosys's application based on merit,' he said firmly. 'But you have no right to cast aspersions on me.'

'You think you can talk back to me like that? You think you're my boss?' the chairman shouted.

Murthy used all his willpower to remain in control of his temper. In an icy voice, he replied, 'I don't have to be your boss to fight for my integrity.' Then he walked out of the meeting, followed by Nandan and Nayak. He left a room full of stunned officials behind him.

Later he was informed by some of these officers that this was the first time an applicant who had come to ask for a favour from the government had walked out of a meeting. He was also told that the chairman wanted to reject Infosys's application outright, but his more honest colleagues managed to convince him to give at least 4 acres to them (instead of Murthy's request for 15 acres). Spitefully, the chairman allotted Infosys the most unsuitable 4 acres in the area that would grow to become Bangalore's bustling

Electronic City. Infosys's allotment had a huge ditch running through it and was close to the cremation grounds, which were considered inauspicious.

Murthy and his team accepted this begrudging gift with good grace. In that ungenerous allotment, they went on to create India's first software campus, the finest of that time, which became operational in June 1994. In line with Murthy's practice of frugality, the architect kept the costs for the entire facility (which included 160,000 square feet of office space) to only Rs 1200 per square foot. Even then, most of the money raised by the IPO went into building this campus. The final specification Murthy had was that his own office should not be ostentatious in any way. The only thing he asked for were walls lined with shelves so that he could have his beloved books within easy reach.

18

The children were growing up – Akshata was ten years old in 1990 and Rohan was seven – and Murthy was busier than ever. Sudha knew she would have to be the parent who had the responsibility of guiding and disciplining them.

In order to foster a closer relationship between them and Murthy, Sudha would let them stay up late. Because Murthy had such a long workday, 8.30 p.m. to 10 p.m. became the bonding time for father and children. Often, he would tell them stories about his growing-up years. They liked those well enough, but their favourites were tales of their adventures together as a family, perhaps because there had been very few of them. These storytelling sessions were a great way for Murthy to decompress from the day's stresses.

A story they asked to hear over and over was about a journey they had all taken by train to Hubli when Rohan was six years old. The parents were forced to lock the compartment from the inside because Rohan tried to jump down from the train and wander off whenever it stopped at a station. The children also clamoured for him to repeat the story of a journey they had taken to Ooty, and to have him describe the miniature 'toy' train they rode and the various animals, including the spotted deer, they glimpsed along the way.

Sudha also encouraged Murthy to participate in the children's schoolwork, but this did not always turn out well! Where Sudha was patient with the learning process and with the children's mistakes, Murthy was strict about studying and sometimes scolded them. Even though he had promised himself he would not become angry like his father, that template of paternal severity was lodged deep inside him. Because he held himself to such high standards, he did the same for his children.

Akshata usually went to her grandfather for homework help, but Murthy often told Rohan, who would bring his physics problems to him, 'If you don't study hard, the only job you'll get when you grow up will be that of a watchman.' He was a stickler for following the correct process, too, so he would get upset if Rohan did not do this. 'Rohan,' he would say, 'this is not how you solve a problem. Where are the steps that demonstrate your thought process? Where is the problem statement? Write them neatly!' Sometimes, in his frustration, he would just grab the notebook from Rohan and solve the problem himself! Some of his other favourite sayings were: 'Today, things are good, but tomorrow may be different. Use your time efficiently.' And, 'Don't think you are better than others. Many may be better than you. So be sure to treat everyone with respect.' Rohan confesses that, until he went off to college, he was quite afraid of his father.

One evening, Murthy came home a little early because a problem at work was bothering him and he wanted to talk it over with Sudha. They sat on the veranda, discussing the issue in low voices. Inside, Rohan and Akshata were playing Nintendo. They were supposed to take turns, but Rohan was being naughty. He refused to relinquish the controller. Usually Akshata would let him have his way, watching as he played, but today she wanted her turn. She grabbed for the controller, but Rohan snatched it away. Their voices got louder and louder as they argued and fought. Sudha, who knew Murthy was in a bad mood, called to them several times to quieten down, but the children ignored her.

All of a sudden, Murthy got up, strode into the room, and grabbed the console. 'If the two of you can't share something in a civilized manner,' he shouted furiously, 'then neither of you deserve to have it.' He threw the console across the room, where it hit the wall with a loud crack and broke into two pieces. The noise reverberated in the sudden silence as father and children stared at the damaged Nintendo in horror. The children were alarmed because they had never seen their father lose his temper in this way. And Murthy was mortified because he felt that by having this violent outburst, he was following in his father's footsteps – something he had promised himself never to do.

Rohan, who had an innate aptitude for mechanical things, was able to fix the broken Nintendo later by taping it together. But he was smart enough, from then on, to keep it out of his father's sight! Perhaps as a result of this incident, he began to spend more of his leisure time reading, an activity Murthy admired and enjoyed, even if he could only indulge in it occasionally. This gave them a common interest, and until Rohan went away to college, every mealtime his father and he would discuss the books they had read – many of which were technical and meant for adult students.

One day Akshata came home very excited.

'Amma, Amma!' she shouted. 'My class is going to perform Cinderella. And guess what, I've been selected to play Cinderella!'

Sudha gave her a pleased hug. 'That's wonderful! Performing in front of an audience will give you a lot of confidence.'

Akshata told her mother that the school expected students to get their own costumes. Cinderella would thus need some shabby dresses which her stepmother forced her to wear.

'Not a problem!' Sudha said. She always kept some of the children's old clothes on hand, in case she needed to give some to the servants' children.

'And you need to buy me a special Cinderella dress for the ball. It has to be long and white, with lots of lace and frills,' Akshata added.

When Sudha looked into the price of buying such a dress, or even getting it stitched, she could see it would be very expensive. She sat Akshata down and explained to her that they could not afford such a dress. 'In any case,' she added, 'even if we could manage it, it doesn't make sense to spend so much money on an outfit you'll wear only once. Instead, why don't I buy you a pretty but regular white dress that you can wear for many other occasions?' Akshata listened attentively and said she would tell this to the teacher.

But the teacher insisted that the proper kind of dress was mandatory for the play, and she gave the part of Cinderella to someone else. Akshata was heartbroken. She came home and went straight to bed, where she shed many tears.

Sudha, too, felt bad. She came and sat on the bed and rubbed Akshata's back, trying to console her daughter. When Akshata calmed down, Sudha spoke to her as one adult to another. She explained that she believed she had done the right thing. Parenthood was tough. 'It's my duty to teach you lessons which will help you later even if they make you angry with me now.' The first, she explained, was the importance of living within one's means and not trying to keep up with the 'neighbours'. The second was the importance of being practical in matters of spending, recognizing wasteful behaviour, and getting good value for your money.

No doubt what Sudha said was true, but it took a long time for Akshata to forgive her mother.

Rohan's perpetual naughtiness led to many headaches for Sudha. He was always wanting to watch movies, and he did not like to rewatch the same ones, so at times Sudha would borrow videos from her neighbours. One time she brought home a Superman movie. Rohan was fascinated by Superman. That was the one movie he watched over and over. For his birthday, he asked Sunanda for a Superman costume from Kids Kemp. He loved the suit and wore it everywhere and even wanted to sleep in it. Once, he tried to 'fly' from their first-floor balcony like Superman. Fortunately, Sudha caught him before he could do so. She scolded him roundly and made sure the balcony door stayed locked after that.

Undeterred, Rohan climbed on to the roof of the company car, shouted, 'I am Superman!', and jumped off. He promptly dislocated his arm and began screaming in pain. Sudha was at the college, teaching, and Murthy was in France, but luckily Sunanda was nearby. She rushed Rohan to the hospital and had his arm taken care of. When Sudha came home and found out what had happened, she was upset, partly because of the accident, and partly because she felt guilty she had not been there to take care of things. She sat Rohan down and scolded him roundly, telling him never to do such a stupid thing again. Rohan agreed, but three years later, he jumped off the car again and dislocated his arm a second time!

This time, Murthy was home, and he accompanied Rohan and Sunanda to the hospital. Murthy sat in the front seat, next to the driver, while Sunanda held Rohan and sat in the back. Murthy was very soft-hearted where his children were concerned. Perhaps this was because he was away from them for such long periods of time. He kept looking over his shoulder to check on Rohan. When he saw Rohan in pain, he could not stop his tears. This, of course, made Rohan cry more. Finally, Sunanda had to speak to Murthy sternly and tell him to pull himself together!

Later, she said to him, 'You put on a tough front for all the world, but in reality, you are a softie.'

The one household chore Murthy insisted on doing was cleaning the toilet. The toilet was the place where caste inequality played out most obviously in India, and Murthy being strongly anti-caste had always responded to issues around it – from Unilever's segregation policy to who cleaned it in his own home. He told the children it was not right to make servants perform this unpleasant task. Every Sunday morning, no matter how busy he was, he would go into the toilet area armed with a couple of brushes and a canister of Vim. The children would hear him singing Hindi movie songs at the top of his voice as he scrubbed vigorously, following this up with a long shower.

Once in a while, Murthy would find himself with a little more time on Sunday – perhaps because a project had progressed faster than expected, or because a meeting had been cancelled. He cherished these rare, precious moments and used them to read.

He read not for enjoyment but for instruction, going through many business books, teaching himself how to be an innovative CEO. He also read works by or about people like Einstein, Oppenheimer, Feynman and the Singaporean prime minister Lee Kuan Yew, who had transformed his nation from a third-world country to a first-world one in Murthy's lifetime.

But Murthy's most treasured leisure activity was listening to music. Music energized him in a unique way. His most-loved kind was Western classical: Beethoven, Mozart, Chopin. He had a decent stereo system – one of the only luxuries he allowed himself. He would invite Sudha and the children to join him as he sat on the sofa in their small living room, eyes closed, listening intently. There would be a joyful, meditative glow on his face.

Rohan was too active to remain still for long, and Sudha always had housework or tests to grade, but Akshata would stay in the room, sitting as close to her father as she could. It was not because she loved this strange music, so unlike the cheery Hindi songs that her mother sang along with the radio. But she knew this was one way for her to have her dad to herself, and that was something she hungered for. With the passing of time, however, she grew mesmerized – as much by Murthy's still, devout attention as by the exquisite music. She would run her fingers reverently over the images on the covers of the record albums, memorizing them, letting the sounds of this foreign music seep into her soul.

One day, Akshata asked her father, 'How did you become so fond of Western classical music? Was it a taste you developed during your time in Europe?'

Murthy said, 'Actually, I learnt to love it a long time before that, when I was only eight years old – and from an unusual source. At that time, my father was posted in Mandya, a mid-sized town near Mysore. We didn't have a radio at home, but a friend of my father who was a doctor had one. My father would go to his friend's house every Sunday morning to listen to Western classical music, which, in those days, All India Radio used to play for an hour. One day, he invited me to accompany him. This was a rare event. My father was usually a stern, strict man who spent much of his family time lecturing us. So I was very excited.

'That day, the radio played "Canon in D Major" by the German composer Johann Pachelbel. I was struck by the beauty of this very different kind of music. Later I asked my father how and why he was attracted to Western classical music. He said that when he became a high school teacher in Koppa, the British headmaster there had introduced it to him. My father had been struck by the way in which a group of highly accomplished musicians of instruments as different as the piano, cello, harpsichord, violin and viola came together under the direction of a conductor, played as a disciplined and well-coordinated team, and produced music that was divine. He told me that he did not see that kind of team play and ego suppression in either Carnatic or Hindustani classical music. I saw a different side of my father that day.

'My father's explanation instilled in me a value for teamwork that has stayed with me all my life. And because this incident was one of my few happy memories of my father, I still love to listen to Pachelbel's "Canon in D Major".'

Akshata would become a great lover of Western classical music, and whenever she listened to it, she, too, would bask in her own sunlit Sunday morning memories of time spent with her father.

'Rohan's school has called me for a parent–teacher meeting,' Sudha said to Sunanda with an exasperated sigh. 'Again! What do you think that child has done now?' She was concerned because Rohan had got into trouble several times already. And Murthy, as usual, was out of town, placing the burden of handling this unpleasant issue squarely on her shoulders.

'Would you like me to come with you?' Sunanda asked in her quiet way.

Sudha looked relieved. 'That would be a big help.'

When the two sisters met with a group of teachers at Bishop Cotton School, they all said the same thing. 'Rohan is really intelligent and very capable. But he just can't seem to pay attention in class. He's smart, but he needs to learn how to concentrate.'

One of them added, 'He's always talking to the students sitting around him, causing disturbances and distracting them.'

Another one shook his head with frustration. 'Several times, I've made him and the other offenders stand outside the classroom as punishment. The other children feel ashamed, but the punishment has no effect on him. He chats with his friends or passers-by quite cheerfully.'

The teachers fixed their eyes on Sudha as though it were all her fault. She felt guilty and promised to do something about Rohan's behaviour, but she was stumped.

'He listens when I scold him,' she told Murthy when he was finally back in town. 'But I think my words go in one ear and straight out the other. I don't know what to do!'

Murthy, too, had no solution. He had been brought up in a family of many children, few resources and very little attention and had always been self-motivated, pushing himself to study harder because he knew that was his only ticket to a better world. He did not understand, what he considered, his son's naughtiness.

A concerned Sudha started to spend more time one on one with Rohan, watching over his studies. Mother and son would sit together on the narrow upstairs balcony (the one from which Rohan had once tried to jump off), and while Sudha chopped vegetables for dinner, Rohan would work on his school assignments. She kept a careful eye on him, making sure he didn't fall behind. But the problems at school did not diminish.

After several more instances of the school complaining about his behaviour to Sudha, she grew frustrated and decided to send Rohan to boarding school so he would learn the discipline she had failed to inculcate in him. She did some research, found a suitable international school in the city of Gudibanda in Karnataka, and took Rohan there. They looked around the school – the dormitories with the bunk beds, the classrooms and dining hall, the playing fields where a cricket match was going on. At first Rohan seemed intrigued, but then the seriousness of the situation struck him. He realized he was not going to be with his family anymore!

He grabbed hold of Sudha's sari and started to cry. 'I promise I'll do everything you want,' he said. 'I won't cause any trouble at school.'

Sudha was a loving but tough mother. She took out a piece of paper from her purse and had Rohan write down his promise and sign it. Only then did she take him back home.

But after a few days, Rohan reverted to his old ways – it was as though he could not help it – and the teachers complained again to Sudha. Sudha was at the end of her rope. Exasperated beyond measure, she packed his bags and was ready to ship him off to the boarding school they had visited.

This time Rohan went to his father and begged not to be sent away. He wept so much that Murthy, who at the end of the day was the more soft-hearted parent of the two, could not bear it. 'Let him remain with us,' he told Sudha. 'He will grow out of his naughtiness soon. We have to find a way to keep him occupied.'

Against her will, Sudha capitulated, but she was not as sure as Murthy that the problem would get resolved on its own. She racked her brains to find something into which she could channel Rohan's intelligence and energy. 'He's bored, that's the real issue,' she told Murthy. 'What he needs is something at once interesting and challenging, something into which he can pour his full attention.' But they did not know what that might be.

Finally, when Rohan was around eight years old, Sudha went to Brilliant Tutorials, where students could get extra help with computer classes. Her plan was to have Rohan go to the tutorial centre after he finished his regular school day at Bishop Cotton. The original idea had been Murthy's. He didn't like the fact that Rohan had no hobbies and suggested to Sudha that their son learn programming. When she was filling out the forms, the administrators thought the registration was for Sudha. Once they realized it was for Rohan, they protested that he was too young.

'We don't have a single student anywhere near his age,' they told Sudha. Most of the students were about twenty-five years old. 'He'll be totally out of place. Plus, he'll never be able to make sense of the complicated material.'

Sudha, who knew how smart Rohan could be when he was focused, insisted they let him try. 'Let's see what he learns,' she said. 'He might surprise us all.'

For the first few weeks in the tutorial centre, Rohan struggled. He could not follow anything in class. The textbooks did not make sense either. Frustrated, he wanted to quit, but Sudha persuaded him to try it for a little longer.

She was supposed to pick Rohan up every evening, but one day the centre closed early, without notice. Rohan was dropped off at home by a man in his mid-thirties on a scooter.

Sudha was immediately apprehensive. 'Who was that stranger?' she asked her son.

'That's not a stranger,' Rohan said airily. 'That's my classmate.'

Six months into the programme, something clicked. Computer code began to make sense to Rohan. He started to enjoy coding and took several advanced courses. He began helping the man who had given him a lift as well as some of the other students. Though he was so young, his classmates showed him respect, admiring him for his intelligence and appreciating his willingness to assist them. He learnt BASIC programming first and then C programming. He designed his own courses to progress faster and became a deft programmer within a year. His final project was the most advanced in the class: he designed a checkout system for a grocery store, spending countless hours to make it perfect. It was as though someone had waved a magic wand! All his restlessness vanished almost overnight. At school, too, he quietened down. Sudha was delighted to see these changes in him. For the first time, he had discovered passion and focus, and she thanked God for that. 'Now I only have to make sure he eats and sleeps properly,' she told Murthy. 'Everything else he does on his own.'

The institute asked Sudha's permission to use Rohan to advertise their programme. He was, after all, a startling success. They called him 'the child prodigy'. At first Sudha, who was a private person, did not like the idea. But when the management pleaded with her, explaining that it would help them to get more students, which they needed, she relented. She insisted on one thing, though: she would not accept any money for this.

In a few months, Rohan's photo appeared in several print advertisements with a talk bubble from his mouth declaring, 'This Brilliant Tutorials course puts me on the fast track.' And, as the institute had hoped, their membership rose by leaps and bounds!

By 1993, Infosys had become more successful and money was not as tight as before. Three years on, the company began to grow at a rapid rate. Paradoxically, even as the family's finances eased, it became increasingly stressful for Sudha to raise her children in the way she wanted. She had been brought up to believe in 'simple living and high thinking', and tried to inculcate the same values in Rohan and Akshata.

However, what had been easy to inculcate in a village setting, or even in small-town Hubli, was not so easy in the more materialistic milieu of the rapidly expanding city of Bangalore. The children had by then hit adolescence and they began to question their mother's approach. At times, in desperation, Sudha wondered if she was being puritanical and unrealistic.

Both Rohan and Akshata went to excellent – and expensive – schools because Sudha and Murthy believed in giving them the best possible education. But this also meant that their classmates often came from rich families. This became an issue as Rohan and Akshata grew more aware of their surroundings. They knew that their peers at Bishop Cotton Boys and Baldwin Girls lived more lavishly and possessed many more 'fun' things than they were allowed to have. When they wanted the same things, Sudha would have to spend a great deal of energy explaining to her children why they could not have them. She could no longer tell them, in all truth, what she used to say earlier: 'We can't afford it.'

Akshata and Rohan had many 'why can't I' questions for Sudha and weren't always satisfied with her answers. Sudha had to face the truth: their problems were very different from hers as a child. She would have to find new solutions. The children, smart beyond their years, were hyper-aware of the rising value of the company. Finally, Sudha made them promise they would not read the financial pages in the newspapers about how the Infosys stock was doing!

Sudha felt that in order for the children to buy into her values, she first had to build a stronger relationship with them. She carved out quality time from her busy day for her children, each of whom needed a different kind of attention from her. Sudha knew that Akshata, because she was the quieter one, sometimes got overlooked. So, despite increasing responsibilities at her college, she made sure to have private mother–daughter moments. Sometimes, on these occasions, they would have meaningful conversations about principles.

But they also used the time for carefree outings to watch movies or to eat at Chinese restaurants, where their favourite dish was Gobi Manchurian. As Sudha began sharing her feelings and worries with her daughter, Akshata started to understand the lonely nature of her mother's life and the difficulties she faced as the wife of a highly driven entrepreneur. Later she would describe Sudha's role as 'being COO to a CEO who was never there'.

This, however, did not mean that Sudha and Akshata did not have serious differences of opinion. Akshata was growing into a free-thinking girl who – like the young Sudha – questioned many things. For instance, she argued about why Rohan should get a rakhi and a gift on the occasion of Raksha Bandhan, while she got nothing just because she was a girl. Akshata was also becoming more and more interested in fashion. On the one hand, she obeyed her mother and took care of chores such as keeping her school uniform ready each night, and her shoes polished. But she also wanted stylish clothes similar to what her classmates were wearing, especially since the family could afford them now. This caused some tussles between her and Sudha, who never cared about what was in vogue and could not fathom why such frivolous things were important to her daughter. Coming from a small town, she simply didn't understand why a teenager might like fashion or things that were trendy. Wearing simple clothes was more than enough for her. Once, exasperated, she told Akshata, 'If you spent half as much time on your studies as you do on fashion, by now you would be Einstein!' Akshata, on the other hand, felt that her mother was being unnecessarily tight-fisted.

While Rohan was not interested in clothes, he posed a different kind of challenge for his mother. Once, his classmate had a birthday party to which the entire class was invited. The party was held at a very fancy restaurant, and Rohan had a delightful time trying all the delicious items on the menu. When his own birthday came around, Rohan told Sudha he wanted her to host a similar party for him at the same restaurant. Sudha made enquiries and found out that it would cost her Rs 1,000 for each guest. To her frugal mind, this seemed like a criminal waste. But she did not want to merely impose her ideas on her son.

Instead, she told Rohan, 'There are fifty students in your class. If you take them all to the restaurant, it will cost us Rs 50,000. Whatever satisfaction you get by spending that Rs 50,000 will evaporate in a day. I feel it is wrong to spend so irresponsibly. On the other hand, our driver has two children, and their schooling costs him Rs 20,000. If you give that amount of money to them, it will help their family immensely and possibly change their lives. You can still have a celebration at the school. I can treat your friends to samosas and Frooti instead.' She told him to think about this for three days before deciding what he wanted to do with the money.

Rohan wasn't happy about this; he sulked around the house and would not talk to her.

But at the end of the three days, he came back to Sudha, having made up his mind. He was not thrilled about it, but he agreed to do what she asked. 'But you have to give me something in return,' he insisted. 'You must give my friends some extra treats. At the very least, along with samosas and Frootis, they should also get gulab jamuns.'

Sudha happily agreed to this menu, and on his birthday, she gave Rohan Rs 20,000 so that he could give it with his own hands to the driver.

As he grew older, Rohan created a new difficulty for his mother. He became very particular about the food he ate and about cooking it the right way. Sudha had never been interested in learning to cook anything beyond the everyday dishes. She did not see any point in it. If she had a few extra moments in her busy day, she preferred to spend it reading or listening to music. This had not been a problem for the easy-going Murthy or for her daughter. If Akshata wanted a change, she went downstairs and ate what her Ajji had prepared. And Murthy and Sudha would joke about how it was her cooking that helped him retain his slim, boyish figure!

Now, suddenly, Sudha discovered that her culinary skills did not meet her son's finicky standards! Nor was he satisfied with his grandmother's traditional Kannada repertoire. Rohan was keen to try new recipes – where he got them from was a mystery to Sudha

– and he wanted them followed meticulously. He even wanted to go shopping for the right kinds of pots and pans, claiming that the size and shape of the pot, as well as the material it was made of, played a crucial part in the taste of the final product. He was very particular about spices and was appalled by his mother's habit of throwing in a pinch of this and a pinch of that and substituting freely when she ran out of a particular ingredient. Mother and son got into heated arguments about this. Rohan insisted that cooking was an art, while Sudha was convinced it was merely a necessary evil.

Finally, after spending many frustrating hours trying to cook something to suit her picky son's palate, Sudha came up with a unique plan. The next time she was invited to a wedding, she took along a large embroidered bag. After everyone had eaten, she opened the bag and took out a tiffin carrier! She asked the hostess if she could take a few of the fancier items back to her son.

'At least this way,' she told her friend frankly, 'I'll get a break from listening to his complaints!'

The hostess was happy to oblige: the extra food would have been given away, in any case, at the end of the evening. When Sudha arrived home and opened the tiffin carrier, Rohan was so delighted by this unexpected bonanza that she decided she would do it again. So, whenever she was invited by a close friend who would not mind, she repeated her request.

Mother and son had found a happy solution.

Sudha believed that keeping children busy kept them out of trouble, so as part of her 'training programme' for the children, she involved them in doing regular pujas and prayers at home

– Hanuman and Lord Venkateshwar were two of the family's favourite deities. She taught them the meanings of the different forms of God, and whenever they visited a particular temple, she would share with them its history and any stories related to the deity. All of them were staunch followers of Raghavendra Swamy. Thus prayers to him were an important part of their religious life, especially whenever an important event came up.

The children especially loved their trips to Mantralayam because their father would make time to accompany them there. That made it special because, unlike his co-founders, Murthy never took regular vacations. They ate at roadside dhabas on the way, stayed in temple quarters for devotees, and wore traditional Indian clothes when they visited the deity. It was at once a pilgrimage, a vacation and an adventure!

Sudha also inculcated a love of volunteering in both her children early on. She took Akshata and Rohan on regular visits to the neighbourhood temples where she had them participate in cooking and donating food to the poor. She took them to organizations that helped the handicapped, and she got them involved in groups that cared for animals who were ill or homeless. Akshata grew interested in volunteering with one of the local schools for the disabled, which pleased Sudha greatly. Rohan, on the other hand, became fond of helping dogs that were abandoned or maimed. Sudha loved animals and encouraged Rohan to express his empathy in this manner. This would remain a passion for Rohan all the way into adulthood, when he and his wife Aparna, would adopt several homeless and handicapped dogs.

Murthy did not have the time to get involved in any of these child-rearing activities. But he tried to encourage them. He applauded Akshata for her work with the disabled. He believed in giving back to society and strengthening it in whatever way possible. In principle, he approved of the volunteer work his son was doing, too. But he was very uncomfortable around the numerous stray dogs Rohan loved to bring home with him. When Murthy was young, a friend of his had been bitten by a street dog and had had to go through a painful series of rabies shots. He had never forgotten that traumatic event. Even years later, it would take him a significant effort to get used to Gopi, the charming golden retriever puppy Rohan gifted to his parents.

Just as she did with her college students, Sudha loved to teach her children values indirectly, through reading. Together, they went over stories from the Puranas, the Ramayana and the Mahabharata, and then discussed important and controversial issues, especially those dealing with women's roles. From an early age, she made them both sensitive to challenges faced by women and girls, and how society often had different rules by which they were judged. She also shared with them whatever she had learnt by reading the scriptural commentaries written by Swami Chinmayananda, whom she had met at a young age when he visited Hubli. One of her favourite verses of the Gita which she often quoted to the children was: *uddhared atmanatmanam/ natmanam avasadayet/atmaiva hy atmano bandhur/atmaiva ripur atmanah* (Elevate yourself through the power of your mind, and do not degrade yourself, for the mind can be the friend and also the enemy of the self).

She also told them, 'As long as you are doing the right thing, don't worry about what others think of you. You know who you are!' Another of her favourite sayings was: 'In order to gain something, you have to be prepared to lose something. Nothing is free in life, except mother's love.'

Akshata took these activities and lessons to heart. Sudha was happy to see her daughter maturing and thinking about the lives of those who were less fortunate than her. Her special passion was helping blind children, reading to them, and assisting them at exam time.

But there were two sides to Akshata. On the one hand, she remained very interested in fashion and stylish clothes. On the other, she spent a good amount of her time getting involved in various altruistic programmes through her mother. She balanced these very different aspects of her personality adroitly. In this, she was very different from her parents, who were single-minded, driven individuals.

The family's increasing prosperity didn't just impact the children. It also created new dilemmas for everyone. When rumours of Infosys's success spread (and, as happens with rumours, were sometimes exaggerated), relatives – even the ones who had belittled Murthy before – became more ingratiating and demanding. Friends who had ignored them for years at functions would now hurry across the room at events or in restaurants to ask how they were doing and to pay them compliments. Murthy was large-hearted, courteous and quick to forgive them. His large-heartedness could be seen, especially, in his attitude to Donn. When Infosys's revenues hit a billion dollars, Murthy invited Donn to the celebration as a speaker. For Murthy, Donn had played a key role in the early days of Infosys, despite the challenges he had posed, and was thus someone to feel grateful to.

His family was not as forgiving. Once Rohan told him, 'Boss, you can be like Gandhi, but I can't.'

There were practical problems, too. Distant cousins who had never cared to visit them earlier would now routinely land – often unannounced – on their doorstep. They would constantly ask Sudha for things, and if the plainspoken Sudha said no (as she did when she thought their demands were frivolous), they had many uncomplimentary things to say about how tight-fisted she was. If she attended a wedding or a baby-naming ceremony, she was now expected to bring expensive gifts, preferably gold ornaments.

And when she chose not to meet those unfair and unrealistic expectations, people whispered that she was stingy. When she planned a small, private upanayanam for Rohan, the complaints grew louder. 'Her only son! And even for his holy-thread ceremony she refuses to pay for a grand celebration. What are they going to do with all that money!' The relatives to whom she had given money for their children's education and marriage were quick to forget Sudha's assistance and continued to criticize her.

With time, Sudha's tastes had matured. For formal occasions, she would wear a sari, but she preferred simple, elegant ones Though her hair was still short, she would tie it back. Around this time, she decided to no longer buy new saris because she felt she had more than enough. As a result, sometimes she wore the same clothes when she attended events. This gave rise to further gossip.

'Why doesn't her husband buy her better saris and jewellery?' mean-tongued people would whisper. 'Surely he's making enough money!'

'And have you noticed how he rarely accompanies her anywhere?' others would respond with relish. 'I think they're having marriage problems, don't you?'

Sudha was quite aware of these comments. She did not care to deal with this kind of pettiness. As a result, she reduced her outings to a great extent and only accepted invitations from close friends and family. Sometimes she had to be careful even when visiting cousins whom she had been close to when growing up. This was difficult for her as she was a social person, unlike Murthy, a loner by choice. She had grown up surrounded by a huge extended family. Now, suddenly, many of them were looking at her with critical eyes.

Sudha was also forced to change some lifestyle habits against her wishes. For several years, her children had gone to school in the school bus, or, if there was no bus, they shared an autorickshaw with other children. The same person picked them up every day, a man they got to know well and fondly called 'rickshaw uncle'. They loved piling into the crowded autorickshaw and chatting with the other kids all the way to school. But at a certain point in Infosys's growth, Sudha was told it was no longer safe for her children to use public transport. With a sigh, she capitulated and began to send them to school and to their extracurricular classes by car.

***

As Sudha learnt, sometimes leaping, sometimes stumbling, to deal with the changes in her family she also had to negotiate her own career. She was by now the most popular teacher at her college and continued to win awards every year. There was, however, a downside to this popularity. Sudha's colleagues, including the principal, grew jealous of her accolades and made life difficult for her in many petty ways. At times, the administration would even delay her paycheque. At other times, she would be refused money to buy basic classroom supplies and would pay for them out of her own pocket. Sometimes, by the end of the month, she had spent most of her salary on such things.

She also felt she was not getting a chance to teach the complex subjects that she knew in depth. At moments like these she would feel depressed, frustrated and alone. She would wonder aloud if she had squandered her talent and if she had made the wrong decision in quitting her engineering career, where she would have been applauded for her knowledge and vision, not punished for it. She would have also been compensated more generously and got the chance to work on more intellectually challenging problems. While Sudha did not care much about her salary, she realized that a higher salary led to higher respect.

Perhaps most painful was the fact that she knew – and Murthy knew this, too – that she was as capable as Murthy and his junior colleagues. She had demonstrated this many times. Yet they were all enjoying flourishing technical careers, and she was stuck in a place where she worked hard but received little recognition.

One day, after going through a tough time in a faculty meeting, Sudha came home, threw her book bag into a corner, covered her face with her hands, and wept. 'What have I achieved?' she said. 'I had so much potential, but I'm not making use of any of it. And when I try to make things better, I face obstacles on every side.' Rohan was distressed to see his mother in tears. Though he did not understand exactly why she was sad, he put his arms around her to console her.

Murthy had known that Sudha was unhappy at her job but, preoccupied with many problems at Infosys, he had not paid it much attention. On this day, he realized the depth of her despair and it wrenched at him. Perhaps, deep down, he felt guilty because he realized that, had he not been so adamant, she would have been a crucial part of the Infosys team. He paced the room helplessly and kept saying, 'Just quit that job! Just quit!' Later, he told her, 'They don't deserve you. I'm serious – send in your resignation letter. We'll manage without a second salary.'

Sudha appreciated his support, but she knew that quitting was never the answer, at least not for her. She gritted her teeth and stuck it out. To Murthy, she said, 'I'll leave on my own terms when I'm ready.'

That opportunity would come in a few years when Sudha would be offered a job at Christ College. Here she was assigned more advanced subjects such as database management, computer applications and computer science at the master's level. After many years, she felt that finally she was using her brain fully. She was well liked and was receiving promotions; at a certain point she was offered the position of head of the computer science department. She liked the place so much that she continued as a guest lecturer even when she became busy with the Infosys Foundation. But sometimes she felt as though everything was happening at once and she could barely keep her head above water. On other days, she thanked God – for making so many of hers and Murthy's dreams come true.

She remembered herself as a twenty-four-year-old, full of ideas and optimism. And the bespectacled, intense young man who had captured her heart, a man like no one she had ever met. They had been married now for nearly twenty years. Those years had been hard. There had been heartbreak and tears. And there had also been so much joy: the birth of two wonderful children; the nurturing of another child, Infosys, which had made its way into the world against all odds: long-lasting friendships; books she had sent into the world, where they had changed lives; the loving embrace of siblings and parents.

Above all, the man she had married had remained fundamentally unchanged. His values and beliefs hadn't been weathered by the years or lost to pragmatism or avarice. And she, too, luckily, had not lost her essential self, that young Sudha with all her passions and ideas and rebelliousness. Here they were: Mr and Mrs Murthy – or should it be Mrs and Mr Murty? It didn't matter which way you looked at it – they were still dreaming the same dreams.

Life had given her many riches – literally and metaphorically – but this was the greatest of them all.

Epilogue

It was just another busy day in 1996 – or so Sudha thought. She was in a rush and not in the best of moods. She scrabbled frantically through the piles of paper on her table, which was in a corner of her living room. She looked into her desk drawers and even checked the wastepaper basket. No luck. In a little while, she was supposed to be at an examination committee meeting for computer science at Christ College, and she needed to find a stack of old question papers that she had stashed carefully – too carefully – somewhere. As the head of the department, she took her responsibilities very seriously.

Just then Akshata walked in, looking stressed and sad. 'Amma, I need to talk to you,' she said.

Sudha located the elusive question papers at the bottom of a pile and grabbed them triumphantly. 'Ah, found them! Now, where did I put last year's syllabus? The other professors are sure to ask for it.'

'Amma!' Akshata said in an unusually insistent voice. 'I need to talk to you.'

Today was a stressful day for Sudha. She was running late and scrambling to keep up. 'Can't this wait?' she said to Akshata, a bit brusquely. 'If you're worried about your upcoming Class 10 exams, we'll talk about it when I get back. In any case, as I've told you time and again, you can only do your best. The results are in God's hands. *Karmanye vadhikaraste ma phaleshu kadachana.*'

'Yes, yes, I know.' Akshata's tone was irritable. 'We need to perform our duty. The results are not in our hands. But I'm not here to talk about my exams. Remember Anand Sharma from the Ramana Maharshi Academy for the Blind?'

Sudha did, indeed, remember him. Akshata volunteered at this school, and on many occasions, she had helped this blind young man with his studies.

'Anand is one of the smartest boys I've met,' Akshata said. 'He's about to take his second pre-university exams, and I'm positive he'll do really well. He wants to go to St Stephen's College in Delhi, but he doesn't have the money—'

Sudha had located the elusive syllabus and was impatient to be on her way.

'Maybe you can help sponsor him,' she said, 'by giving up your birthday money this year. Maybe some other students can pitch in, too.'

'That won't get him very far, and you know it,' Akshata said angrily. 'If an educated and well-read person like you isn't willing to help a deserving boy who is poor and disabled, then how can you expect others to do it? You have enough money now, and you don't really care for a lavish lifestyle. What are you going to do with all this wealth? Amma, what is your duty?' She stomped out of the room angrily, leaving a startled Sudha behind.

All day at the college, Sudha could not forget what Akshata had said. In between meetings and classes, she agonized over her daughter's words as they kept reverberating inside her head. What *was* her duty? She wondered. She had thought it was to help her students, but perhaps that was not enough. She thought of how, for years now, she had put aside the writing she had loved so much because of lack of time. Didn't she owe something to the creative part of herself?

Then an old, half-forgotten voice rose up from a corner of her mind. It was J.R.D. Tata, giving her his final advice: 'When you are successful, you must give back to society.'

Sudha knew what her first priority had to be. The writing would have to wait for now.

Never one to rush into an important decision arbitrarily, Sudha thought about her future path for an entire week. She was unusually silent during this time, often staring into space with a creased brow. Murthy could tell that something serious was on her mind, but he waited patiently for her to tell him what it was, in her own time.

At the end of the week, Sudha sent a letter to the college administrators, stating that she would like to resign as department head and go back to being a guest lecturer. The administration begged her to reconsider because she had been doing such a fine job. They also pointed out this would mean a significant pay cut. But she was adamant.

When she came home, Sudha told Murthy what she had done. She added, 'God has given us so much. He has made your Infosys dream come true. Isn't it time we make some dreams come true in the lives of the less fortunate?'

Murthy, ever the compassionate capitalist, asked, 'What do you have in mind?'

'Infosys needs to start a foundation,' Sudha said in a firm voice. 'And I want to be part of it.'

'You can be a founder-trustee,' Murthy said at once, 'and decide on the kinds of philanthropic projects we take on. Would you like that?'

Sudha hugged him. 'I would like that very much indeed.'

Infosys Foundation, established in 1996, would go on to support programmes in the areas of education, rural development, healthcare, arts and culture, and destitute care all over India, transforming the lives of millions of people. For twenty-five years, Sudha would be its chairperson and guiding light. By 2022 its endowment would be worth more than Rs 50 billion. In 2023, they would impact the lives of nearly 2 million people.

At one point, the *Economic Times* would give an award to Infosys Foundation, and it would be Sudha's job to accept this honour. By then Akshata was a student in the US, but Sudha would request her to attend the award ceremony in Mumbai, even if it was for just one day.

'If you hadn't woken me up at the right time,' she told her, 'I wouldn't have changed my life's course, and none of this would have happened.' At the ceremony, she would acknowledge her daughter as her guru.

In response, Akshata would say, 'You are my hero.'

It was late at night. At dinner, Murthy and Sudha had told the children of Sudha's big career move and their subsequent decision to start a foundation. It would be an organization that would help all who were in need, regardless of religion, caste or language. Its motto should be '*Bahujan hitaya, bahujan sukhaya*': For the welfare and happiness of multitudes. The children had been excited and full of questions. Akshata, particularly, had been pleased. Now everyone had gone to bed, but Murthy and Sudha were still awake. They lay side by side, their fingers intertwined, their heads brimming with exhilarating ideas.

Murthy was envisioning the future of his beloved company.

I need to figure out the right strategy to take Infosys to the next level, he thought. *If Infosys is to be a globally significant player, taken seriously by the mega corporations abroad, I'll have to get it listed on NASDAQ. Advisers have been pointing out to me that seeing the Infosys stock symbol on the ticker tape on CNBC (US) and in the* Wall Street Journal *every day would encourage CFOs abroad to sign off on big deals with Infosys. My personal discussions with several CFOs, too, have confirmed this view. Listing in the US will give us a sense of permanence to Infosys's presence in that country and, indeed, in other foreign countries as well.*

More importantly, I believe that a corporation should strive to get respect from every one of its stakeholders through its actions. Investors are important stakeholders. Operating as responsible trustees of shareholders means creating systems and processes that enhance fairness and transparency. As I always tell my board, honesty, accountability and transparency are not only important personal values. They also provide us with a competitive advantage. Such transparency – and the resulting respect from customers and shareholders – will become easy once we list our company on a global exchange like NASDAQ.

This is the perfect time to set this plan in motion! Infosys's revenues have almost doubled within this past year. I'm determined to make this my next major project. I'll ask Mohan Pai to help me. I know he'll come up with the right plan.

And the Infosys campus! The one we have now is beautiful, but it isn't going to be large enough, because we're going to have more employees – many thousands more. We'll need another campus, one that has enough space for India's first leadership institute. The new campus should hold 20,000 people. One part of the campus should be for professionals who are working on advanced software development for manufacturing clients from all over the world, but most of it will be for our trainees.

The training courses will last a whole year. I'm going to train all our Infoscions there and make it the world's largest corporate education centre. Here, trainees won't sit passively and listen to monologues by teachers but become curious, critical thinkers and proactive problem solvers. We will hire the best talent as faculty. Of them, 50 per cent will be girls. All our senior management – including me – should teach there each year for at least a few days each year.

Jawaharlal Nehru said: 'A university stands for humanism, for tolerance, for reason, for the adventure of ideas and for the search of truth.' And that is what our campus will stand for. It will truly be an institution worthy of the nation's respect.

The campus must be comfortable, well-lit and safe – especially for the women whom we will attract. Above all, Infoscions should feel it is their home away from home. Therefore, I want multiple food courts, serving South Indian, north Indian, Chinese, Mexican, Thai and Western dishes – and pizza because it's the favourite dish of youngsters!

I want our Infoscions to be healthy. So, there should be an Olympic-size swimming pool, a running track, tennis courts, a bowling alley, a gymnasium and a yoga centre. And because my dear Sudha loves movies, there should be a multiplex with four digital screens for movies in different languages shown every weekend. I want lakes, gardens and hundreds and thousands of trees. I'll have to look outside of Bangalore for such a large tract of land. Perhaps Mysore, famous for its history and its heritage, but less crowded, would be a good fit.

I think I know what I want the motto for this campus to be: Our company is our campus; our business is our curriculum; and our leaders are our teachers.

Murthy's heart expanded as he visualized the future of Infosys, which to him was embodied by this new campus he had imagined.

As the ocean of sleep pulled him into it, he thought, *I'll make it happen! With Swamy's blessings and Sudha's support, I'll make it happen!*

He had no idea of all the hurdles he would have to face because he could not imagine anyone not getting excited about such a unique idea. He did not realize that the 400-acre area he envisioned would be extremely challenging to locate. Nor that his colleagues in the education and research group would be unwilling to teach a course that lasted an entire year. Or that faculty would be unwilling to move to Mysore, or even commute there every week. Most importantly, his board would protest vociferously that the campus was costing Infosys too much. (The company's revenues in 2002, when the Infosys Mysore campus construction would begin, would be a hefty Rs 2603 crore; the campus would end up costing Rs 2250 crore.)

But even had he known all this, it would not have deterred Murthy. He would have repeated to himself his favourite saying by John F. Kennedy: 'Our problems are man-made – therefore, they can be solved by man. And man can be as big as he wants. No problem of human destiny is beyond human beings.'

Sudha, lying in bed, was busy with her own dreams. There were many ways, she thought, that the foundation they had committed to today could make a difference to India. Libraries, like she had promised her grandfather, were a must. And women's toilets – she knew from personal experience how crucial those were. Scholarships, access to healthcare, flood and famine relief – and much, much more. *We'll start in Karnataka*, she told herself, *then spread out to the rest of the country. But so many people are in need! Who should I help first?*

Suddenly, unexpectedly, an image came to her. Some years back, she had visited the Yellamma Gudda, or the Renuka temple, in Belgaum district of Karnataka and seen a group of devadasis living in difficult and depressing conditions there. Originally the devadasi tradition had been a beautiful one. Devadasis had been women who chose to dedicate themselves to their art – music or singing or dance – and performed in temples to please the gods. They were respected by society, and even kings sent them gifts.

Sudha had heard tales of famous devadasis like Vinapodi, who had been loved by the monarch of the Chalukya dynasty. But the practice had become corrupted over time, and now devadasis were no longer respected. They were often 'given away' as girls to temples by parents who were too poor to afford their marriage dowry. Without anyone to protect them, these women were forced to become sex workers, at which point society shunned them. Corrupt temple administrators often made use of this situation, exploiting the women however they wanted. Many times, the daughter of a devadasi received no education. Thus, she had no recourse other than following in her mother's footsteps. The women Sudha had seen in Belgaum, dressed in garish saris and cheap bangles, their faces harsh and defeated under turmeric smears, were clearly victims of the system.

I've found the perfect project! Sudha thought. She pictured herself walking up confidently to these women, finding out about their issues, and solving them efficiently, in the same way that she solved complex mathematical equations. She had no idea of the severe challenges she would have to face before she learnt that one can only truly help people by respecting them, understanding them, listening humbly to them, and allowing them to take the lead in reclaiming their lives. Nor did she know that, before she could move forward, she would have to give up her way of life. She would have laughed in disbelief if someone had told her that soon she would exchange her everyday wear of jeans and T-shirts for cotton saris, pin flowers to her hair, and don a mangalsutra so that the people she wanted to help would feel at home with her. She especially had no idea that, when she started on her project, she would be insulted and pelted with sandals!

Blissfully ignorant of the difficulties that lay ahead, Sudha moved closer to her husband, who was fast asleep by now. She laid her head on his arm and breathed in his dear, familiar smell. They had been companions on life's journey for twenty years now, enjoying its beautiful vistas and weathering its fierce storms. How amazing was that!

Just before she gave in to the current of sleep sweeping over her, a quotation swirled up through the dark, lines from Tagore that she had forgotten in the hustle and bustle of life: 'I slept and dreamt that life was joy. I awoke and saw that life was service. I acted, and behold, service was joy.'

I must share it with Murthy and the children tomorrow, she thought as her eyes closed.

The moon sailed slowly across the sky, pushing through clouds. A nightbird cried out its lonely song. Sudha and Murthy lay side by side, dreaming their separate, unique dreams.

A Note on Infosys

Today, Infosys is a global leader in digital services and consulting. It pioneered the global delivery model that Narayana Murthy designed and articulated, which laid the foundation for the success of the Indian IT industry and became the first company from India to be listed on NASDAQ. True to Murthy's philosophy, it established India's first and largest employee stock options programme, creating the largest group of billionaires and millionaires in the country. From a capital of US$250, it has grown to become a $18.38 billion company with a market capitalization of approximately US$ 70 billion. The company has been voted one the world's most innovative companies, best-managed companies, most respected companies, most ethical companies, green companies by *Time, Forbes, Fortune, Newsweek,* among others.

A Note on Narayana Murthy

Narayana Murthy founded Infosys in 1981, inviting six junior colleagues to join him in the venture. He led the company as the CEO and chairman from its start till 2002. He then became the chairman and chief mentor, serving until 2014, when he retired.

During his time at Infosys, the company pioneered financial performance in the annals of corporate Indian history, shareholder returns, global equity listing, corporate governance, transparency and disclosure norms. Under him, the company built over 50 million square feet of corporate campuses globally and spread to over sixty countries. He also set up the Infosys Foundation and the Infosys Science Foundation during his leadership.

Murthy was also India's first founder to democratize wealth creation, giving away 39 per cent equity worth more than $25 billion (Rs 200,000 crore) to his colleagues at Infosys. This included not just the first six adopters and senior members of the company, but also all Infosys employees through the creation of India's first employee stock option plan.

Described as the 'father of Indian IT' by *Time*, Murthy has also been listed among the ten most-admired global business leaders by the *Economist*, as one of the twelve greatest entrepreneurs of our time by *Fortune* and one of the global business leaders of the last twenty-five years by CNBC. He was awarded the Padma Vibhushan by the Government of India in 2008, the Légion d'honneur by the government of France in 2008 and the CBE by the British government in 2007.

A Note on Sudha Murty

Sudha Murty has broken many glass ceilings in her life. She began her professional career as the first woman engineer to be hired by TELCO, later becoming a successful college lecturer in computer science in Bangalore.

Today, Sudha is best known for her philanthropic work and her writing. She is a member of the NCERT's textbook panel for the NEP (National Education Policy) 2020. As the founder of the Infosys Foundation, she is responsible for establishing several orphanages, toilets, roads, schools, ponds, hospitals, dharmshalas, as well as vast relief work during natural disasters. Her endeavours have also helped provide Karnataka government schools with computer and library resources.

She is also India's top-selling children's writer and the highest-selling female writer, selling over 6 million copies of her books for both adults and children. Her bestsellers include *Gently Falls the Bakula, Grandma's Bag of Stories, Here There and Everywhere, Three Thousand Stitches* and many more. Her books have been translated into more than thirteen regional languages and three foreign languages.

In 2006 she was awarded the Padma Shri, and in 2023, the Padma Bhushan, the third-highest civilian award in India. She is currently the chairperson of the Murty Trust, a not-for-profit organization dedicated to the preservation and celebration of culture, science and knowledge systems born out of India.

A Note on the Infosys Foundation

Established in 1996, the Infosys Foundation is a not-for-profit initiative aimed at fulfilling the social responsibility of Infosys Ltd. It works with NGOs on the ground to fund programmes across some of the most remote regions of the country in the areas of education, rural development, healthcare, arts and culture and destitute care. The foundation today works in Karnataka, Andhra Pradesh, Arunachal Pradesh, Bihar, Delhi, Gujarat, Jammu & Kashmir, Kerala, Madhya Pradesh, Maharashtra, Odisha, Punjab, Rajasthan, Tamil Nadu, Uttarakhand and West Bengal.

Some of its work has included increasing computer literacy in schools among teachers and students in rural areas, creating a library for every school programme in Karnataka, financing the midday meal scheme by the charity Akshay Patra, and doing flood relief work in the aftermath of the 2004 tsunami. The foundation has built 15,000 toilets, donated to 70,000 libraries, built 500 houses, handled 13 natural disasters and a national pandemic, and has rehabilitated 3,000 sex workers to normal lives. In 2018 it started the Aarohan Social Innovation Awards to help scale up ideas that would enable social change. In 2023, the foundation committed over Rs 100 crore to launch a STEM scholarship programme for underprivileged girl students.

Author's Note

When Chiki Sarkar asked me to write a biography covering the early years of Sudha Murty's and Narayana Murthy's lives, I was honoured but hesitant. I was a fiction writer, after all, not a biographer.

But as I researched the subjects (I knew them a little already, from having gone to university with Sudha's brother Shrinivas) and conversed with them and their family, I realized their story possesses all the elements of good fiction: it is often astonishing, touching and funny. Sometimes it is complicated and tragic. And it is always relatable.

Most of all, I felt this challenging project, of capturing in words the lives of two extraordinary people from ordinary backgrounds, who have changed the face of entrepreneurship and of philanthropy, was at once important, worthwhile and timely as India moves rapidly to take on a leadership role in the world.

My great hope is that readers of all ages and backgrounds will be as moved by the book as I was when I wrote it. That it will inspire their own journeys, provide solace in their dark moments, give them a very human template for success, surprise them into smiling when they least expect it, and offer them the values and confidence they need to realize their own dreams.

At its heart, this is a love story, an uncommon one. It chronicles not only Sudha and Murthy's love for each other, but

Author's Note

also their love for their values and for their country – and their determination to use the former to transform the latter. It shows us that human love – no matter what the romantic movies profess – is fraught with failures as well as successes, sadness as well as joy.

Special thanks to Sudha Murty and Narayana Murthy, their children Akshata and Rohan, and Sudha's siblings – Sunanda, Jaishree and Shrinivas – for the frank, generous (and sometimes laugh-out-loud) conversations that helped to shape the book.

And to Chiki for trusting in me more than I trusted myself.